Boruto is already in its fifth year of serialization! It's entirely thanks to all of you readers that we've made it this far, especially considering the changes in publications, production team, etc.! Kawaki and the members of Kara will start appearing in the anime. It's about to heat up, so please support it too!

–Mikio Ikemoto, 2021

池本幹雄

BARREL ROLL

小太刀右京

My assistance comes to an end with this volume. I shall be handing the baton back to Kishimoto Sensei and Ikemoto Sensei, as was always intended.

Readers, thank you so much for your long years of support. I shall never forget the letters of encouragement you sent me from all across the world. Thank you from the bottom of my heart.

Boruto and his friends' journey will be continuing for a good while yet. Please cheer them on ever more fiercely than you have already!

–Ukyo Kodachi, 2021

VOLUME 13

SHONEN JUMP MANGA EDITION

Creator/Supervisor MASASHI KISHIMOTO
Art by MIKIO IKEMOTO
Script by UKYO KODACHI

Translation: Mari Morimoto
Touch-Up Art & Lettering: Snir Aharon
Design: Alice Lewis
Editor: Alexis Kirsch

BORUTO: NARUTO NEXT GENERATIONS © 2016
by Masashi Kishimoto, Mikio Ikemoto, Ukyo Kodachi
All rights reserved.
First published in Japan in 2016 by SHUEISHA Inc., Tokyo.
English translation rights arranged by SHUEISHA Inc.

Printed in Canada.

Published by VIZ Media, LLC
P.O. Box 77010
San Francisco, CA 94107

10 9 8 7 6 5 4 3 2 1
First printing, January 2022

viz.com

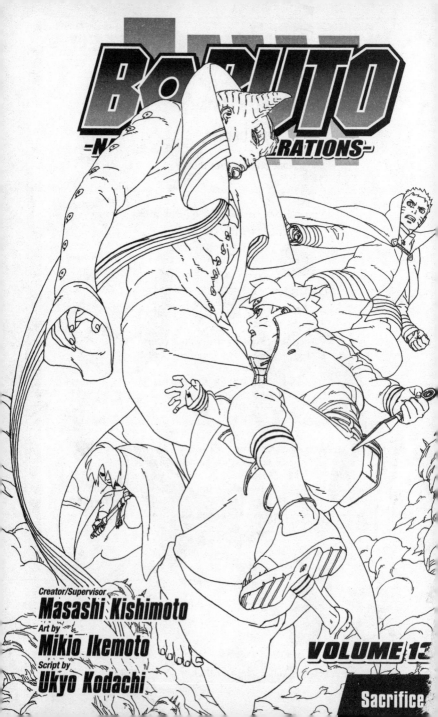

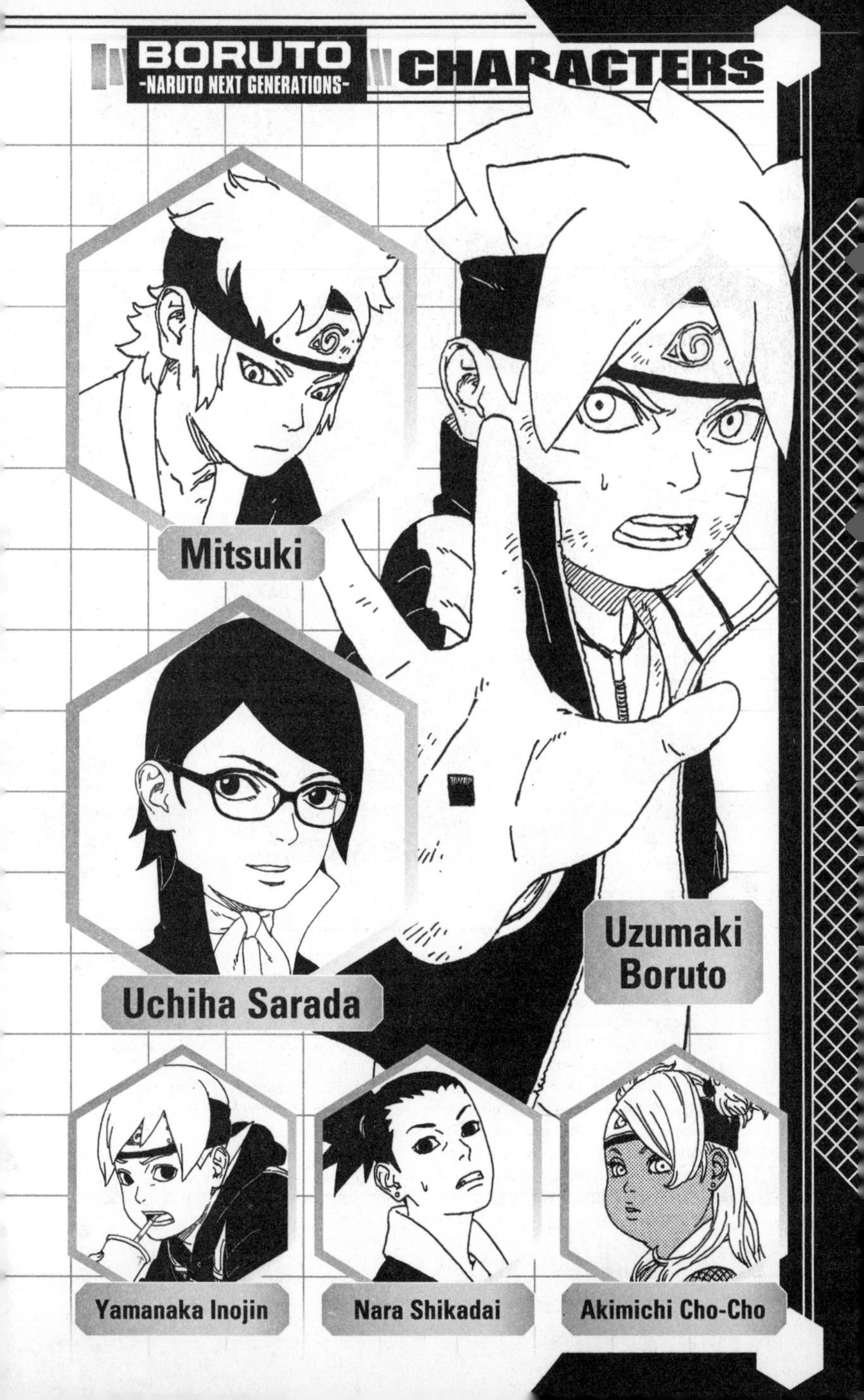
BORUTO
-NARUTO NEXT GENERATIONS-
CHARACTERS
Mitsuki
Uchiha Sarada
Uzumaki Boruto
Yamanaka Inojin
Nara Shikadai
Akimichi Cho-Cho

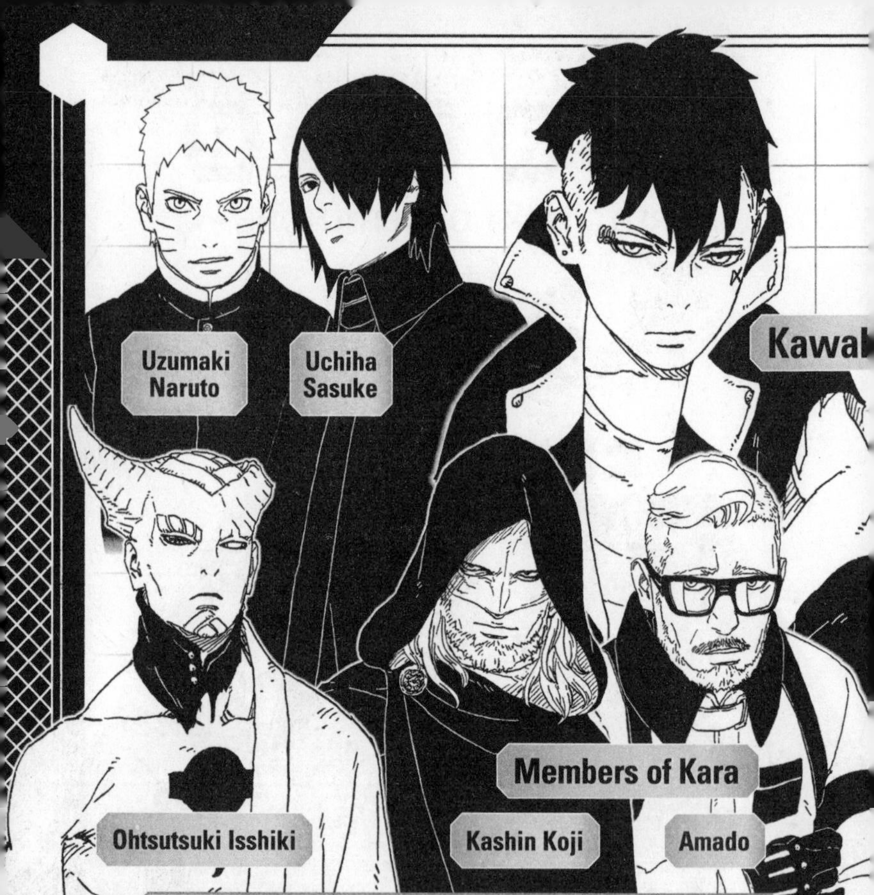
Uzumaki Naruto
Uchiha Sasuke
Kawa
Members of Kara
Ohtsutsuki Isshiki
Kashin Koji
Amado

STORY

The Great Ninja War that shook the world and shed much blood is now history. Naruto has become the Seventh Hokage, and the people of Konohagakure Village are enjoying peace. Yet Naruto's son Uzumaki Boruto has a glum life, perhaps due to his father's too-great influence.

Rebelling against Naruto while simultaneously craving his praise, Boruto decides to enter the Chunin Exam along with his teammates Sarada and Mitsuki. However, Boruto ends up secretly using a prohibited Scientific Ninja Tool and is stripped of his shinobi status by his father.

Just then, members of the Ohtsutsuki Clan attack the arena! Boruto faces off against them alongside Naruto, Sasuke, and others, and they achieve victory with a Rasengan that father and son weave together. However, a strange mark appears on Boruto's right palm...

Afterward, Boruto happens upon a young man named Kawaki who bears the same Karma as himself. And it is he who is proven to be what Kara has been calling the Vessel.

In order to place Kawaki under his protection, Naruto moves him into his own home. Boruto and Kawaki keep butting heads, but Kawaki starts acclimating to the Village...

However, Kara shows up to reclaim Kawaki and takes Naruto prisoner. Naruto is successfully rescued, but Boruto's Karma-caused transmutation progresses...

Later, Kara member Amado defects to Konoha! In addition, Kashin Koji betrays Kara and faces off against Jigen. During their battle, Jigen reveals his true form as Ohtsutsuki Isshiki!

BORUTO
-NARUTO NEXT GENERATIONS-

VOLUME 13
SACRIFICE

CONTENTS

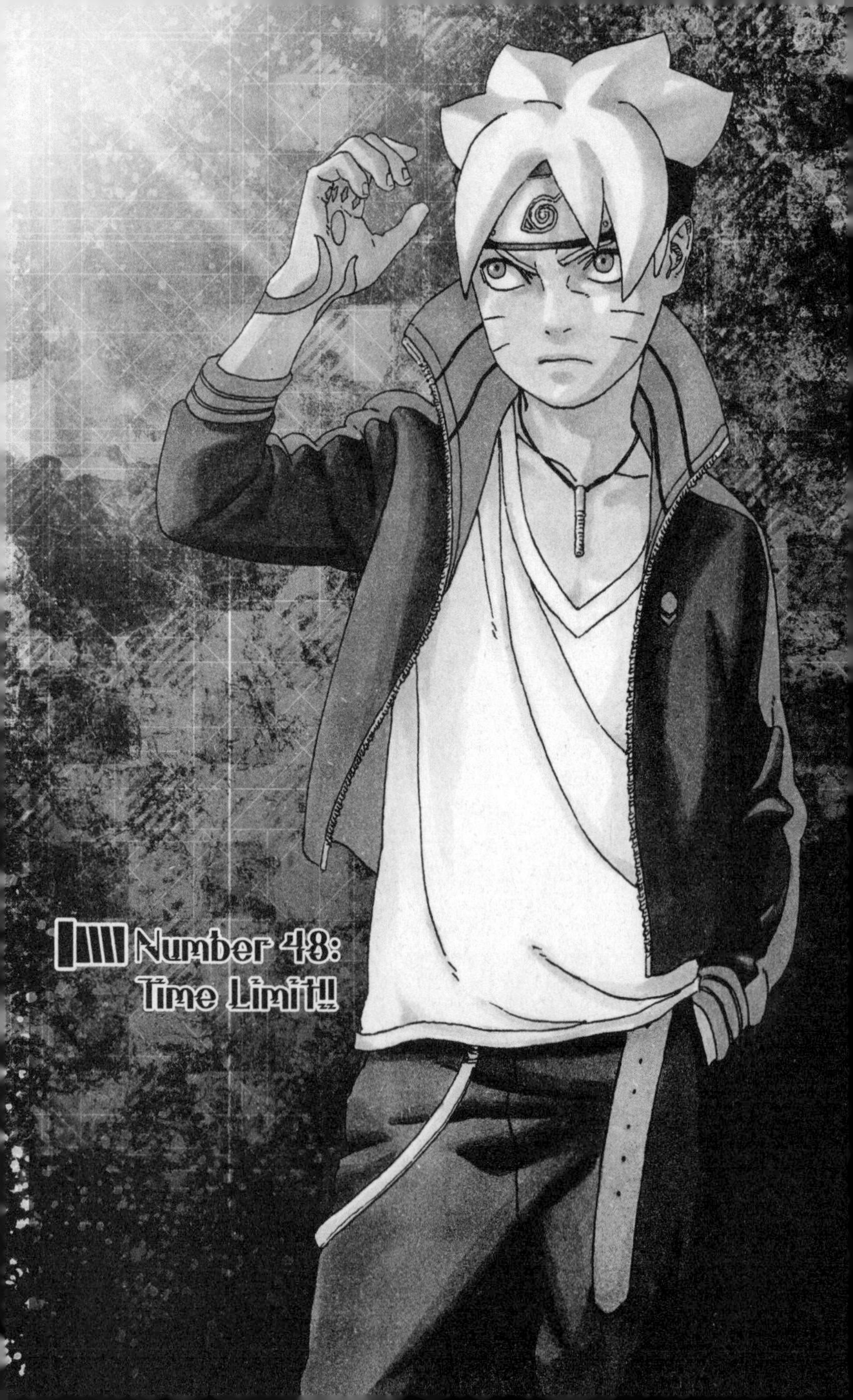
Number 48:
Time Limit!!

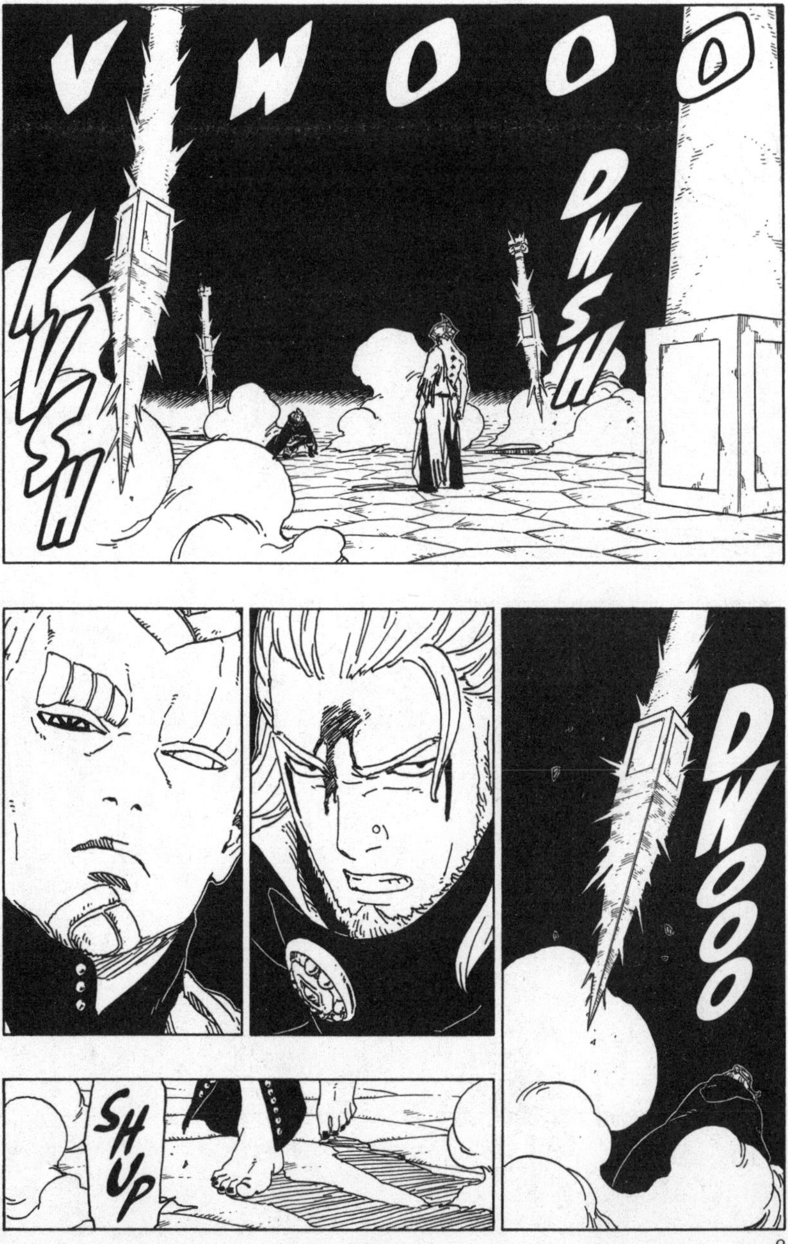
VWOOO
DWSH
KRSH
DWOOO
SHUP

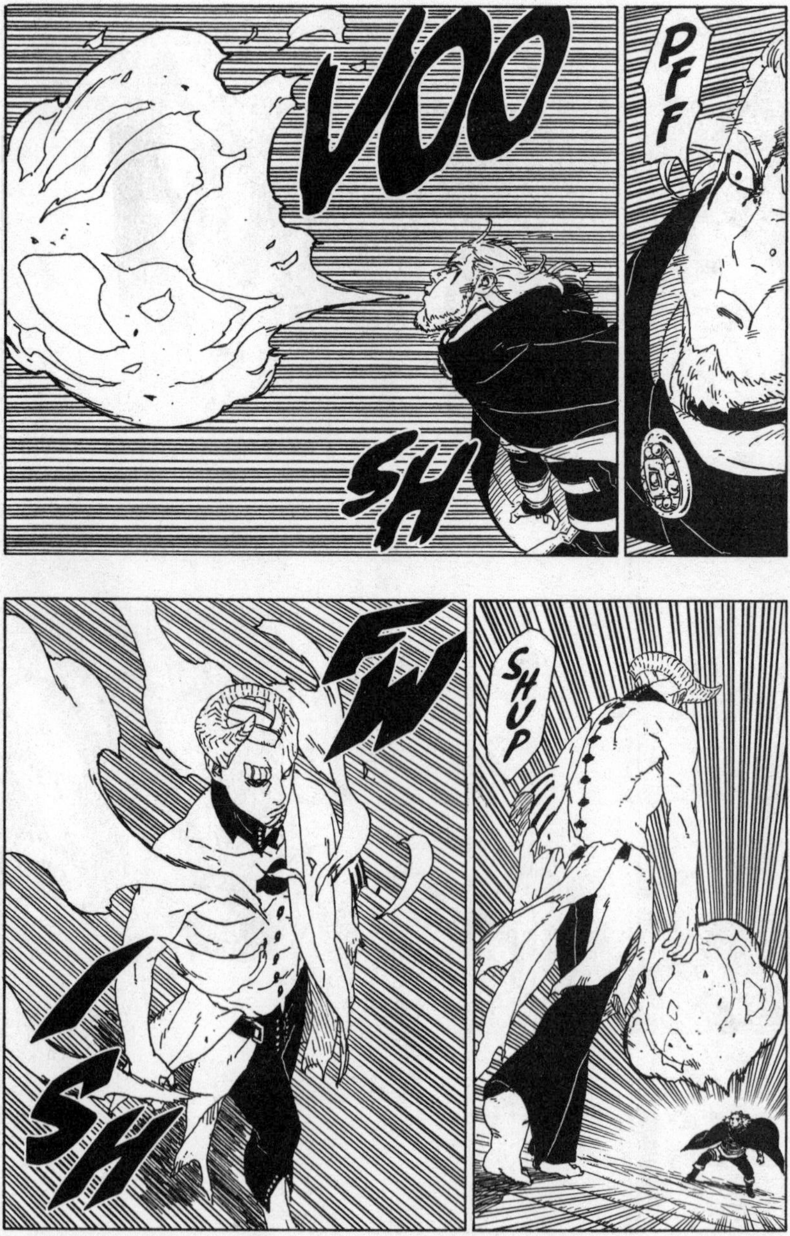
PFF
VOO
SH
SHUP
FW
SH

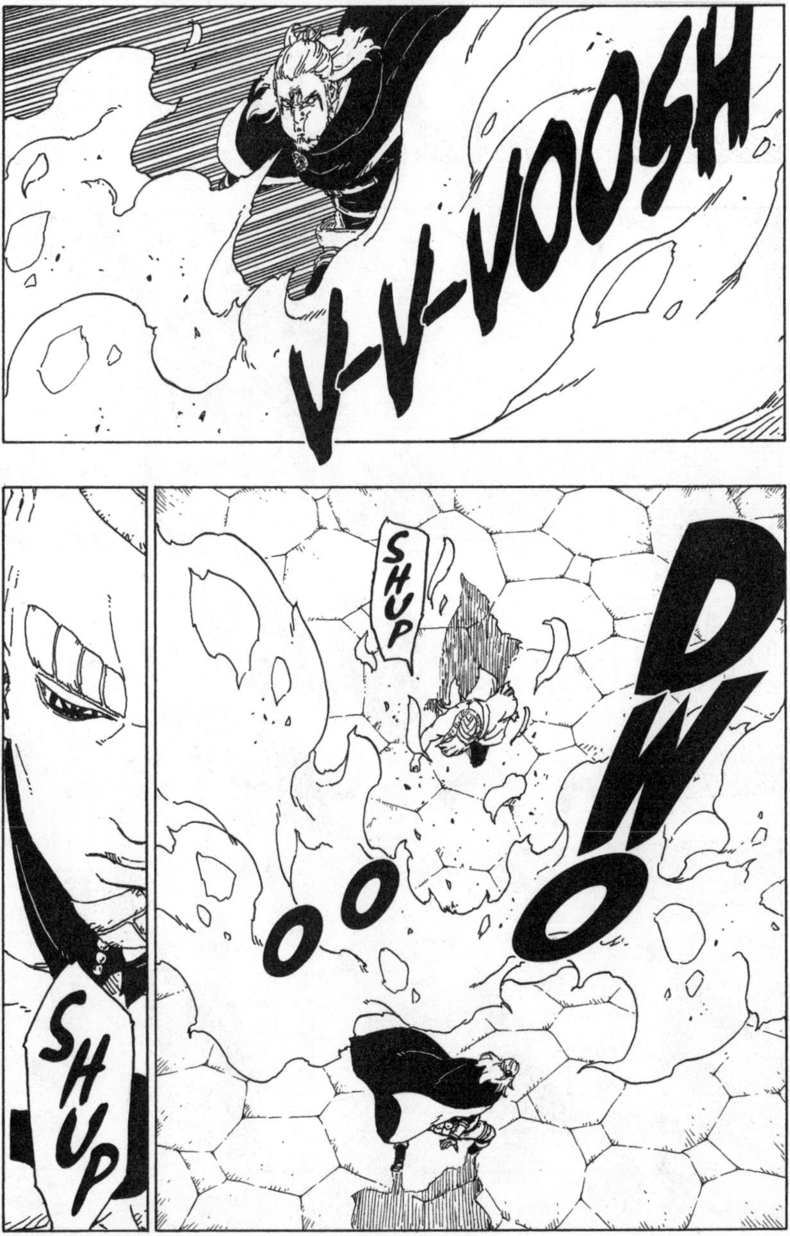
V-V-VOOSH
SHUP
DWOOOO
SHUP

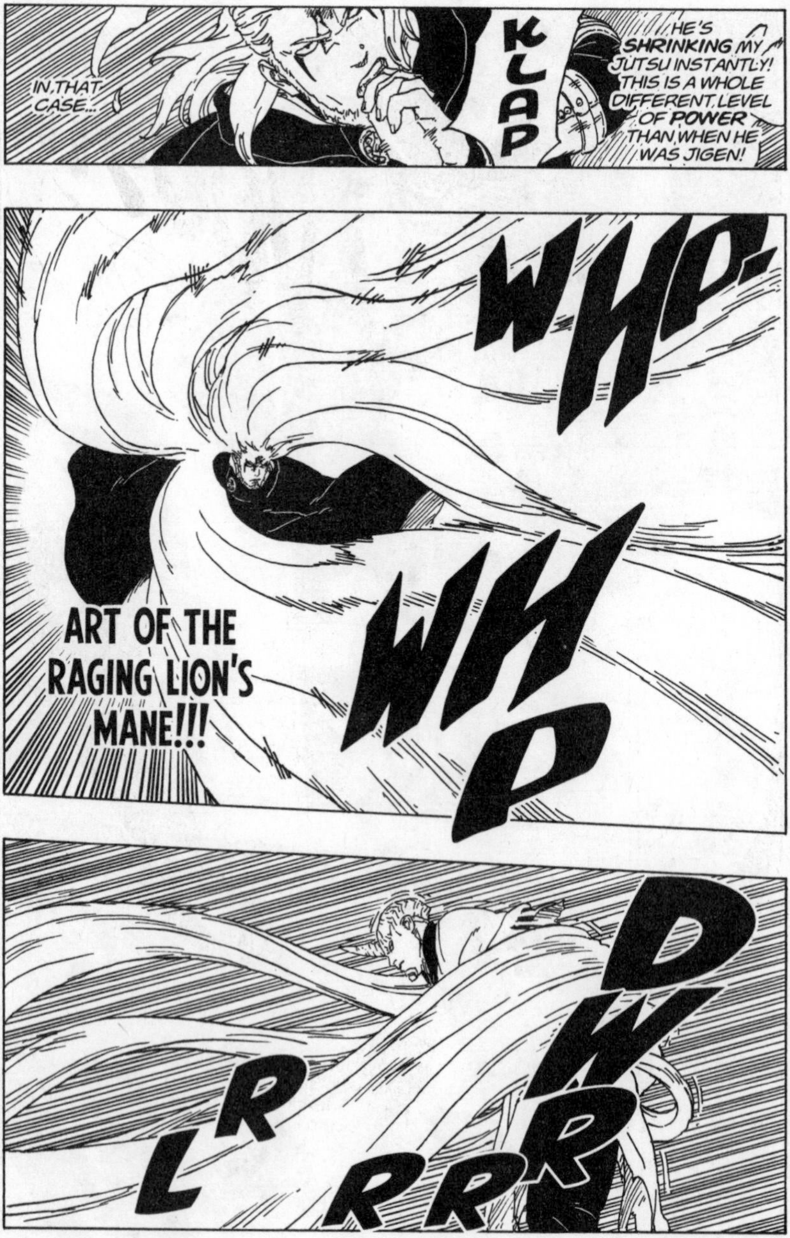
HE'S SHRINKING MY JUTSU INSTANTLY! THIS IS A WHOLE DIFFERENT LEVEL OF POWER THAN WHEN HE WAS JIGEN!
KLAP
IN THAT CASE...
WHP-
WHWP
ART OF THE RAGING LION'S MANE!!!
DWRRRRL

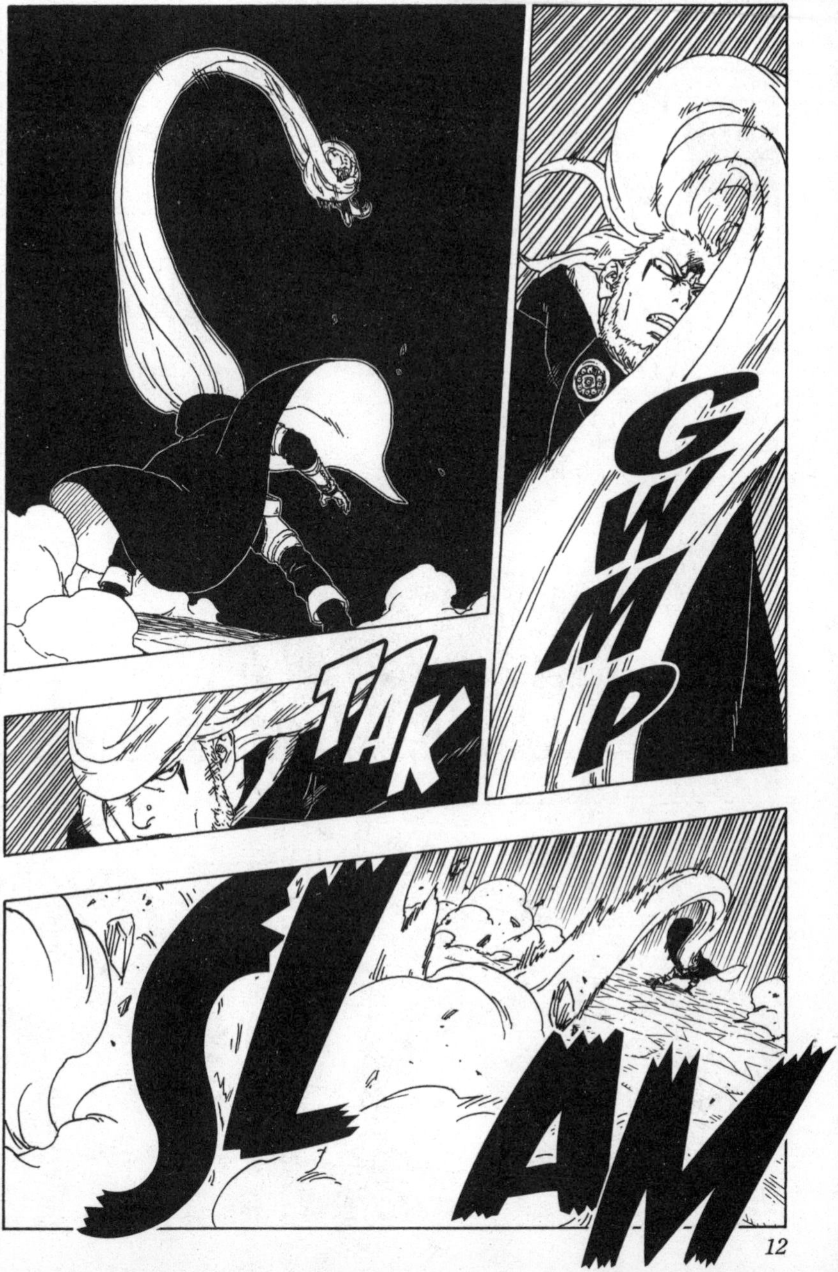
GWMP
TAK
SLAM

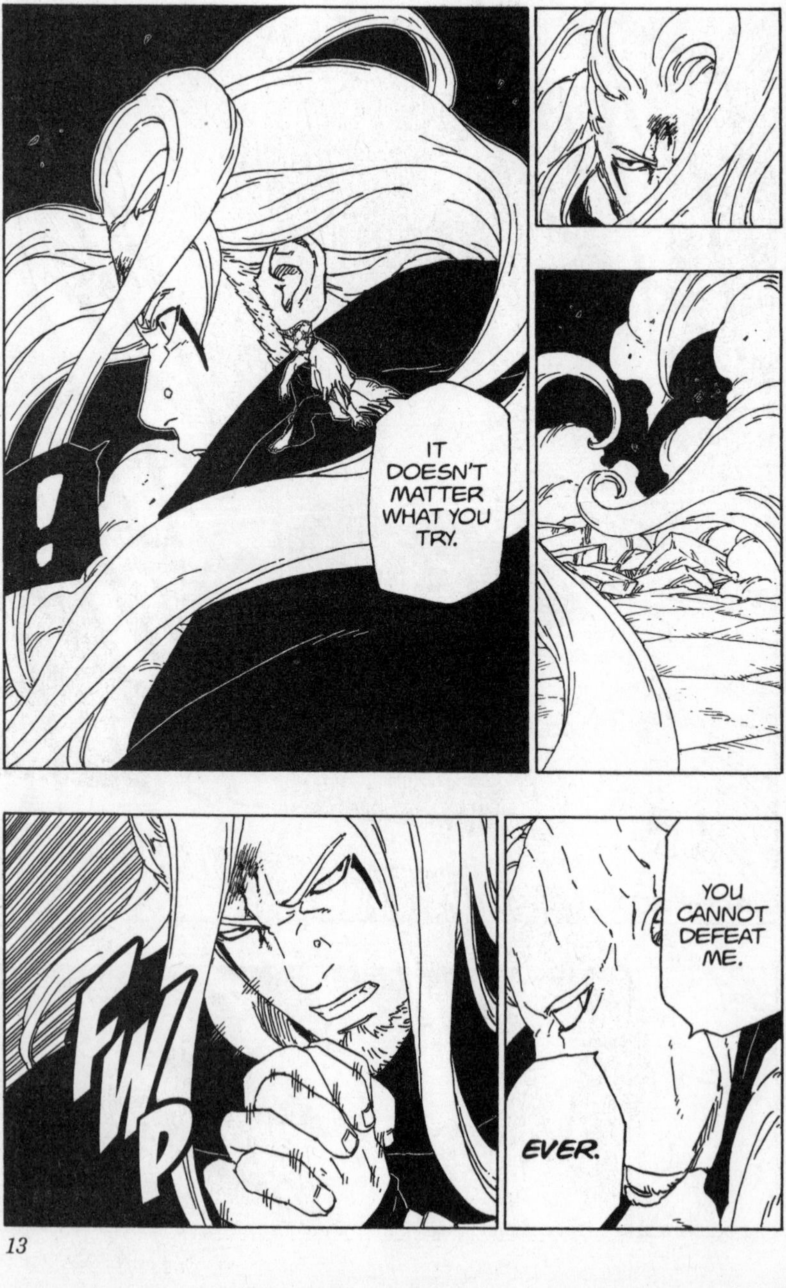
IT DOESN'T MATTER WHAT YOU TRY.
!
YOU CANNOT DEFEAT ME.
EVER.
FWP

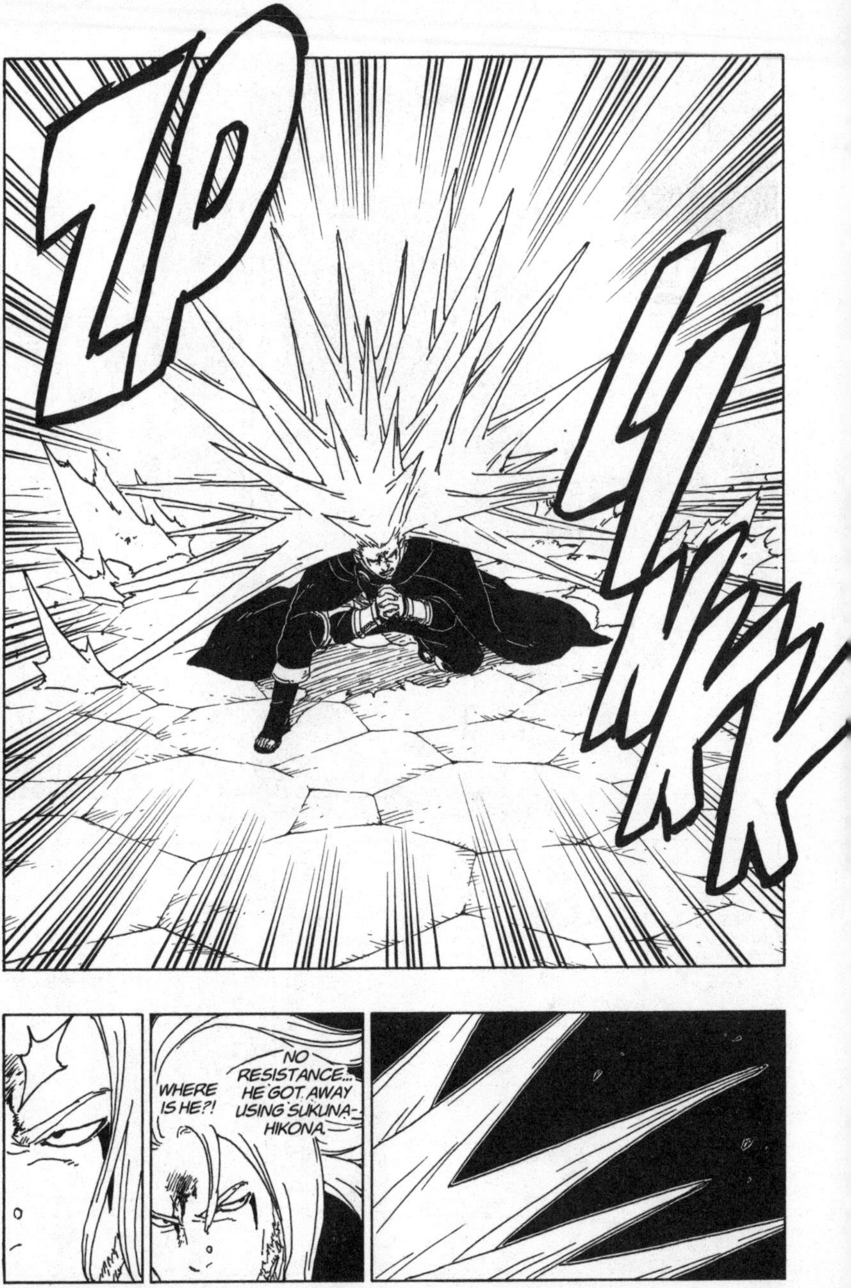
ZIP
NO RESISTANCE... HE GOT AWAY USING SUKUNA-HIKONA.
WHERE IS HE?!

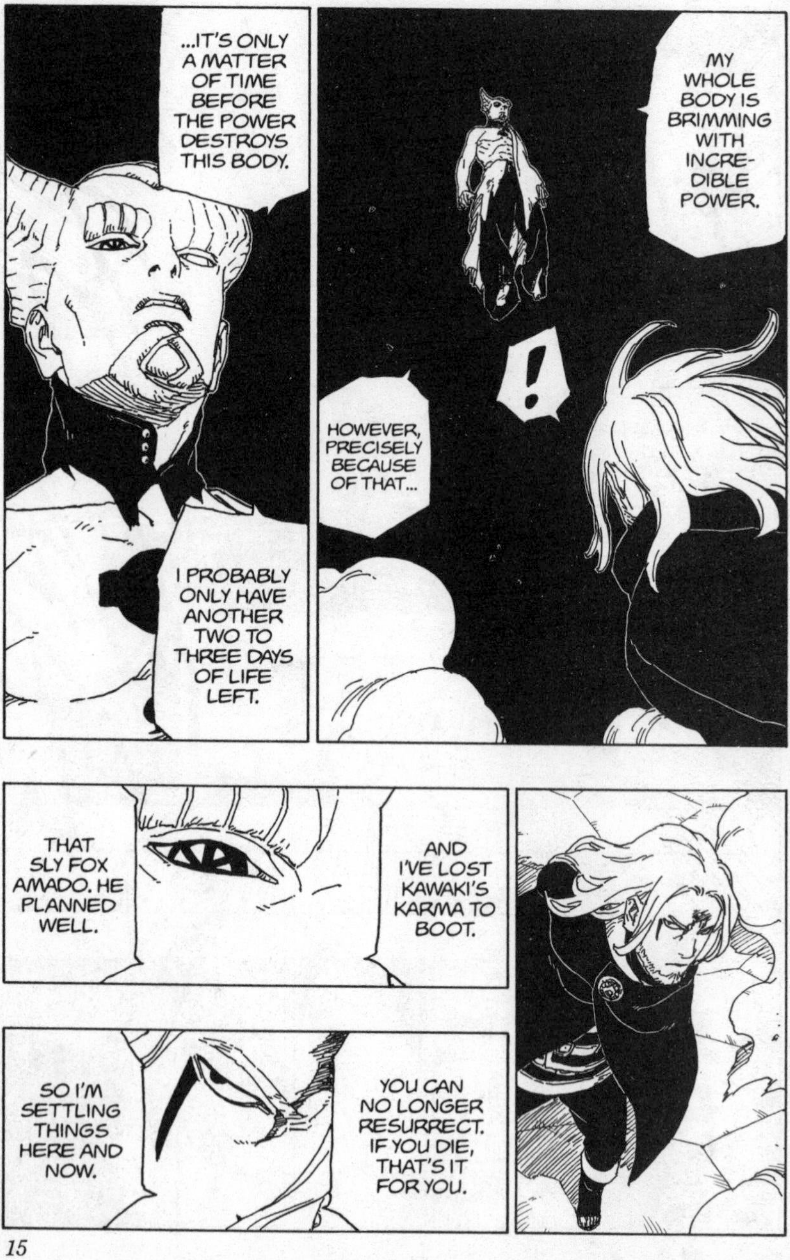
MY WHOLE BODY IS BRIMMING WITH INCREDIBLE POWER.
!
HOWEVER, PRECISELY BECAUSE OF THAT...
...IT'S ONLY A MATTER OF TIME BEFORE THE POWER DESTROYS THIS BODY.
I PROBABLY ONLY HAVE ANOTHER TWO TO THREE DAYS OF LIFE LEFT.
AND I'VE LOST KAWAKI'S KARMA TO BOOT.
THAT SLY FOX AMADO. HE PLANNED WELL.
YOU CAN NO LONGER RESURRECT. IF YOU DIE, THAT'S IT FOR YOU.
SO I'M SETTLING THINGS HERE AND NOW.

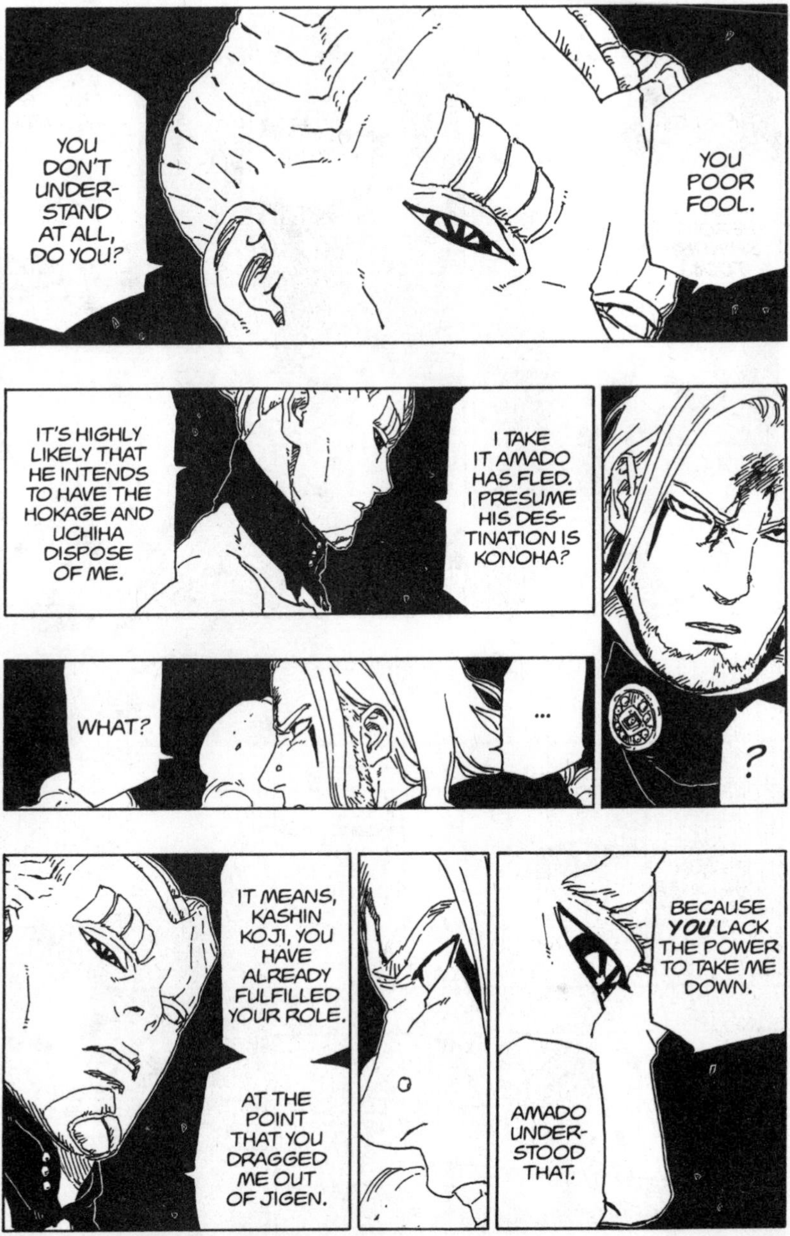
YOU POOR FOOL.
YOU DON'T UNDER-STAND AT ALL, DO YOU?
?
I TAKE IT AMADO HAS FLED. I PRESUME HIS DES-TINATION IS KONOHA?
IT'S HIGHLY LIKELY THAT HE INTENDS TO HAVE THE HOKAGE AND UCHIHA DISPOSE OF ME.
...
WHAT?
BECAUSE *YOU* LACK THE POWER TO TAKE ME DOWN.
AMADO UNDER-STOOD THAT.
IT MEANS, KASHIN KOJI, YOU HAVE ALREADY FULFILLED YOUR ROLE.
AT THE POINT THAT YOU DRAGGED ME OUT OF JIGEN.

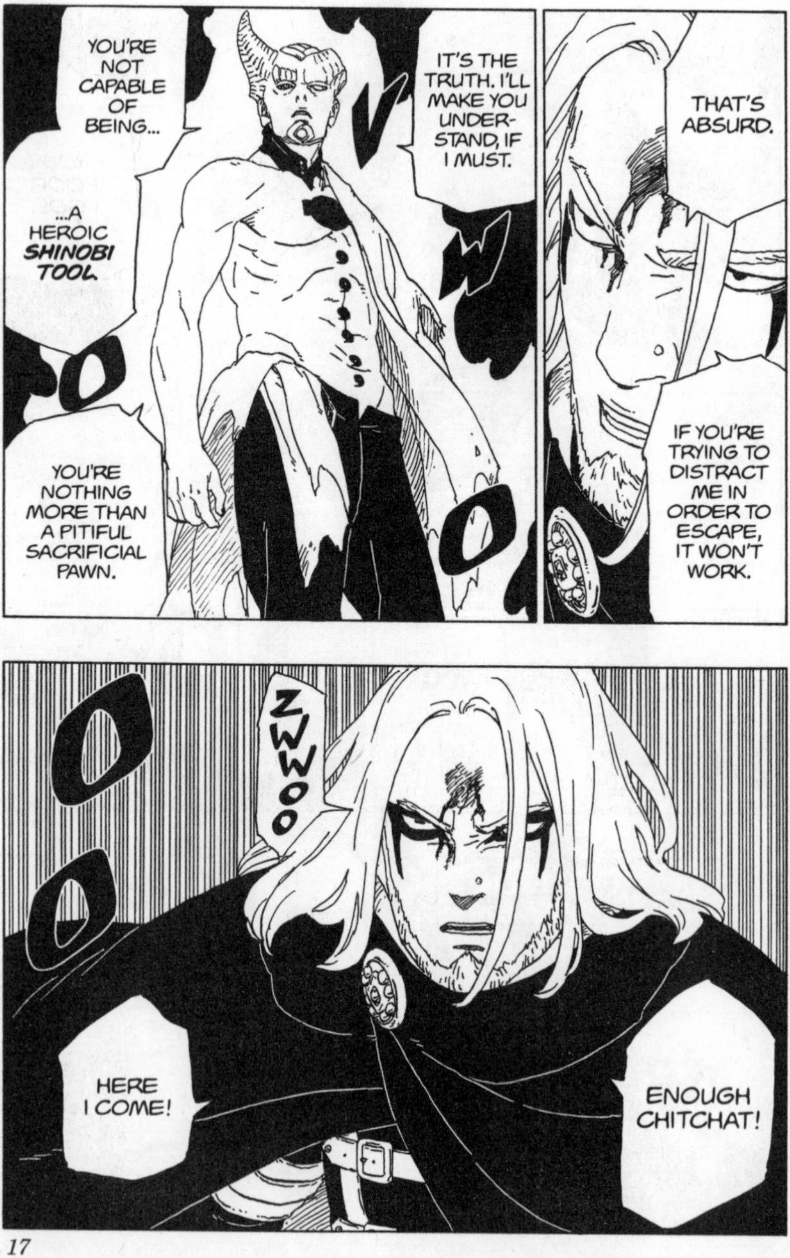
THAT'S ABSURD.
IF YOU'RE TRYING TO DISTRACT ME IN ORDER TO ESCAPE, IT WON'T WORK.
IT'S THE TRUTH. I'LL MAKE YOU UNDERSTAND, IF I MUST.
YOU'RE NOT CAPABLE OF BEING...
...A HEROIC SHINOBI TOOL.
YOU'RE NOTHING MORE THAN A PITIFUL SACRIFICIAL PAWN.
ZWWOO
ENOUGH CHITCHAT!
HERE I COME!

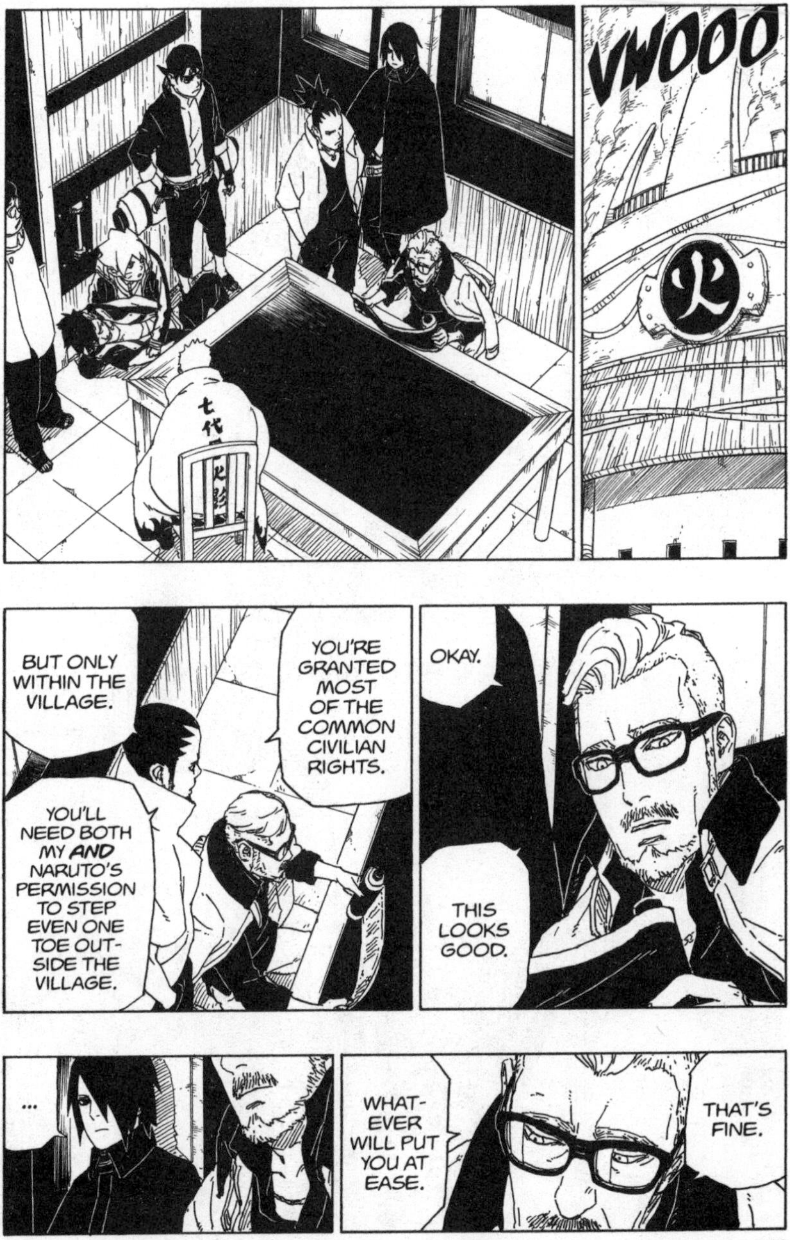
VWOOO
OKAY.
THIS LOOKS GOOD.
YOU'RE GRANTED MOST OF THE COMMON CIVILIAN RIGHTS.
BUT ONLY WITHIN THE VILLAGE.
YOU'LL NEED BOTH MY ***AND*** NARUTO'S PERMISSION TO STEP EVEN ONE TOE OUT-SIDE THE VILLAGE.
THAT'S FINE.
WHAT-EVER WILL PUT YOU AT EASE.
...

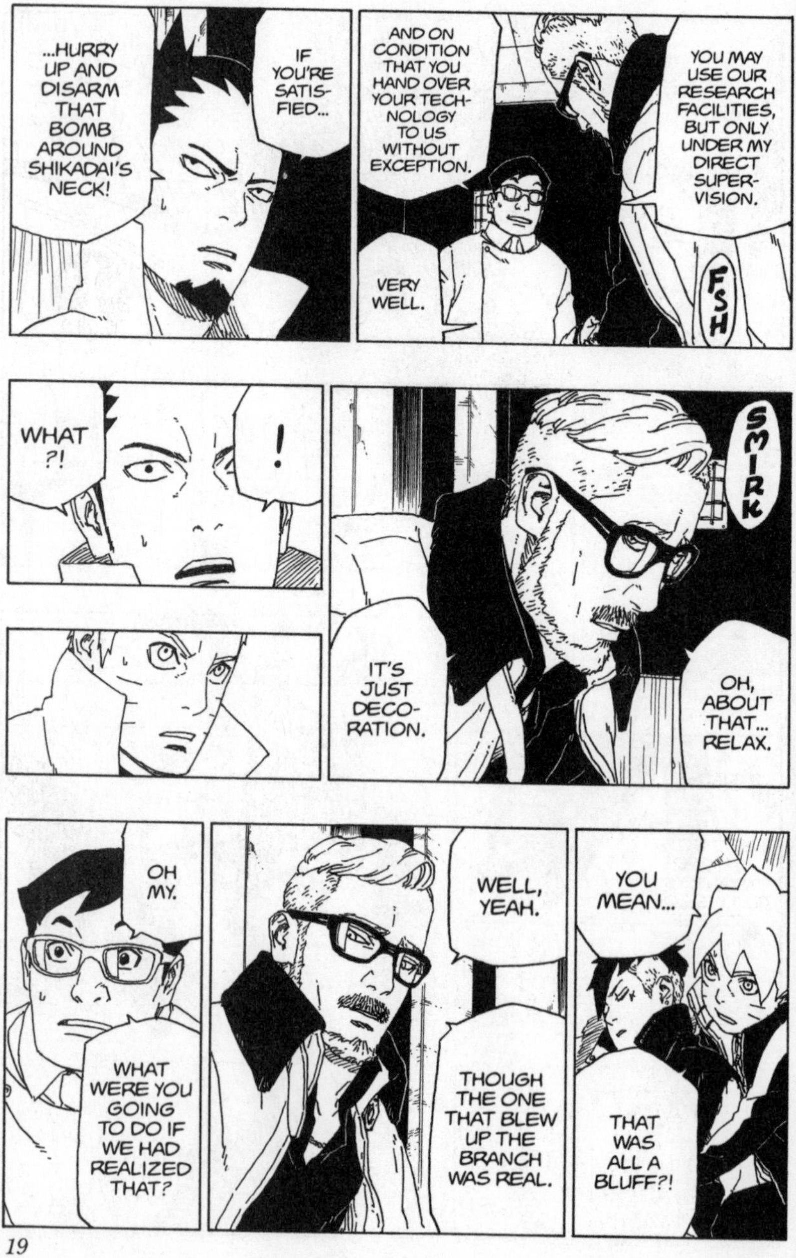
YOU MAY USE OUR RESEARCH FACILITIES, BUT ONLY UNDER MY DIRECT SUPERVISION.
AND ON CONDITION THAT YOU HAND OVER YOUR TECHNOLOGY TO US WITHOUT EXCEPTION.
FSH
VERY WELL.
IF YOU'RE SATISFIED...
...HURRY UP AND DISARM THAT BOMB AROUND SHIKADAI'S NECK!
SMIRK
OH, ABOUT THAT... RELAX.
IT'S JUST DECORATION.
!
WHAT?!
YOU MEAN...
THAT WAS ALL A BLUFF?!
WELL, YEAH.
THOUGH THE ONE THAT BLEW UP THE BRANCH WAS REAL.
OH MY.
WHAT WERE YOU GOING TO DO IF WE HAD REALIZED THAT?

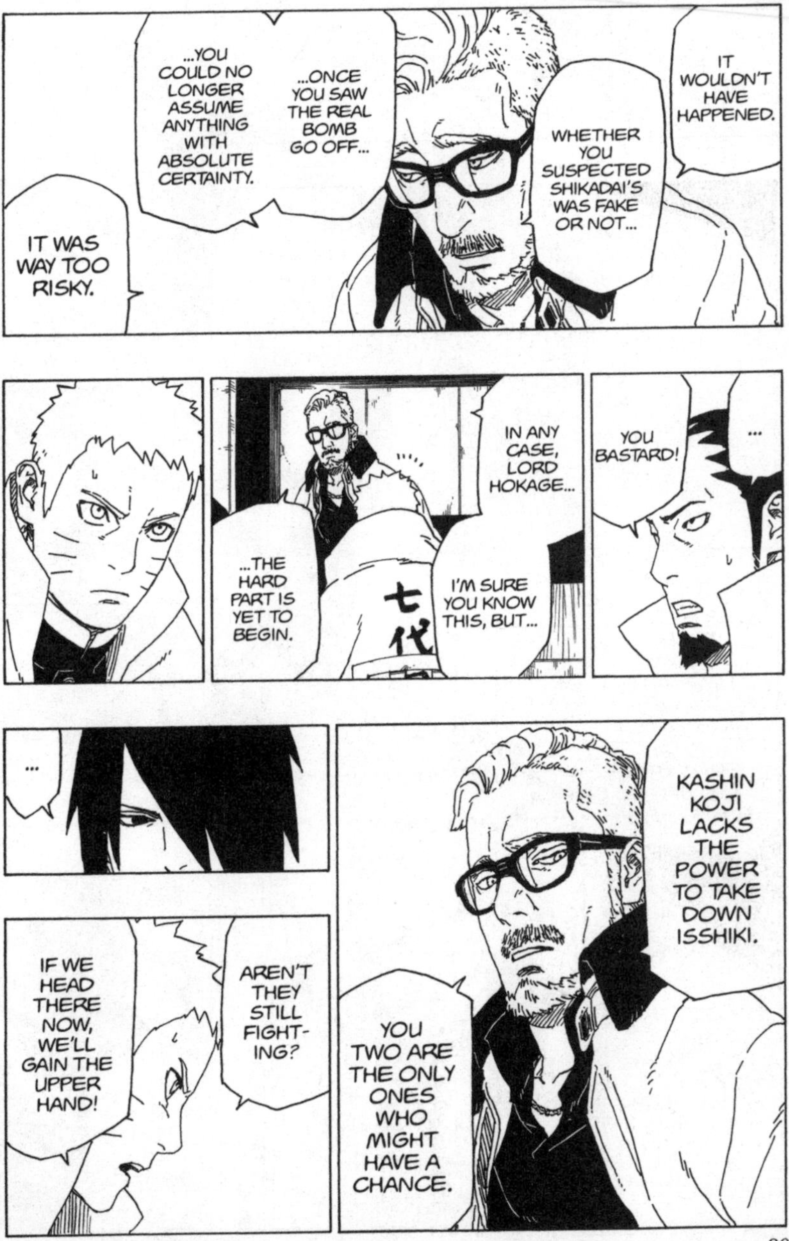
IT WOULDN'T HAVE HAPPENED.
WHETHER YOU SUSPECTED SHIKADAI'S WAS FAKE OR NOT...
...ONCE YOU SAW THE REAL BOMB GO OFF...
...YOU COULD NO LONGER ASSUME ANYTHING WITH ABSOLUTE CERTAINTY.
IT WAS WAY TOO RISKY.
...
YOU BASTARD!
IN ANY CASE, LORD HOKAGE...
I'M SURE YOU KNOW THIS, BUT...
...THE HARD PART IS YET TO BEGIN.
KASHIN KOJI LACKS THE POWER TO TAKE DOWN ISSHIKI.
YOU TWO ARE THE ONLY ONES WHO MIGHT HAVE A CHANCE.
...
AREN'T THEY STILL FIGHTING-ING?
IF WE HEAD THERE NOW, WE'LL GAIN THE UPPER HAND!

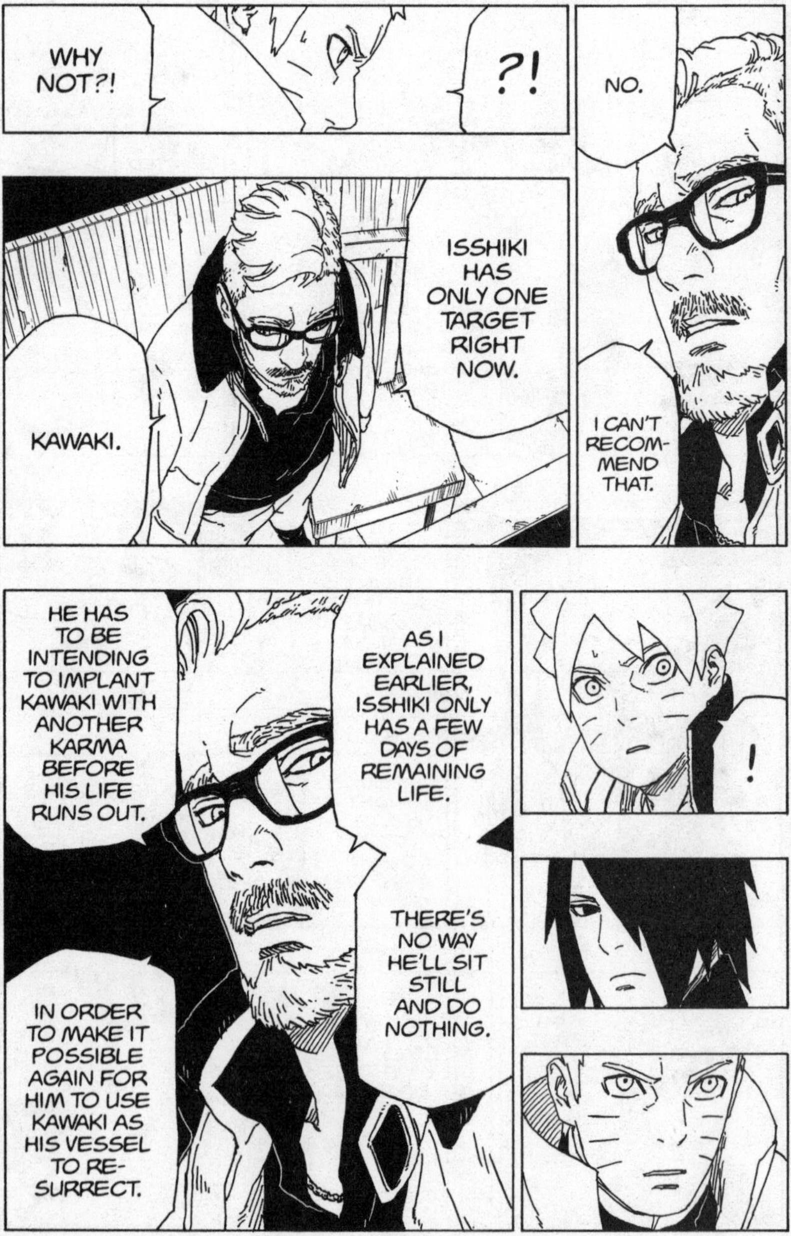
NO.
I CAN'T RECOMMEND THAT.
?!
WHY NOT?!
ISSHIKI HAS ONLY ONE TARGET RIGHT NOW.
KAWAKI.
!
AS I EXPLAINED EARLIER, ISSHIKI ONLY HAS A FEW DAYS OF REMAINING LIFE.
THERE'S NO WAY HE'LL SIT STILL AND DO NOTHING.
HE HAS TO BE INTENDING TO IMPLANT KAWAKI WITH ANOTHER KARMA BEFORE HIS LIFE RUNS OUT.
IN ORDER TO MAKE IT POSSIBLE AGAIN FOR HIM TO USE KAWAKI AS HIS VESSEL TO RE-SURRECT.

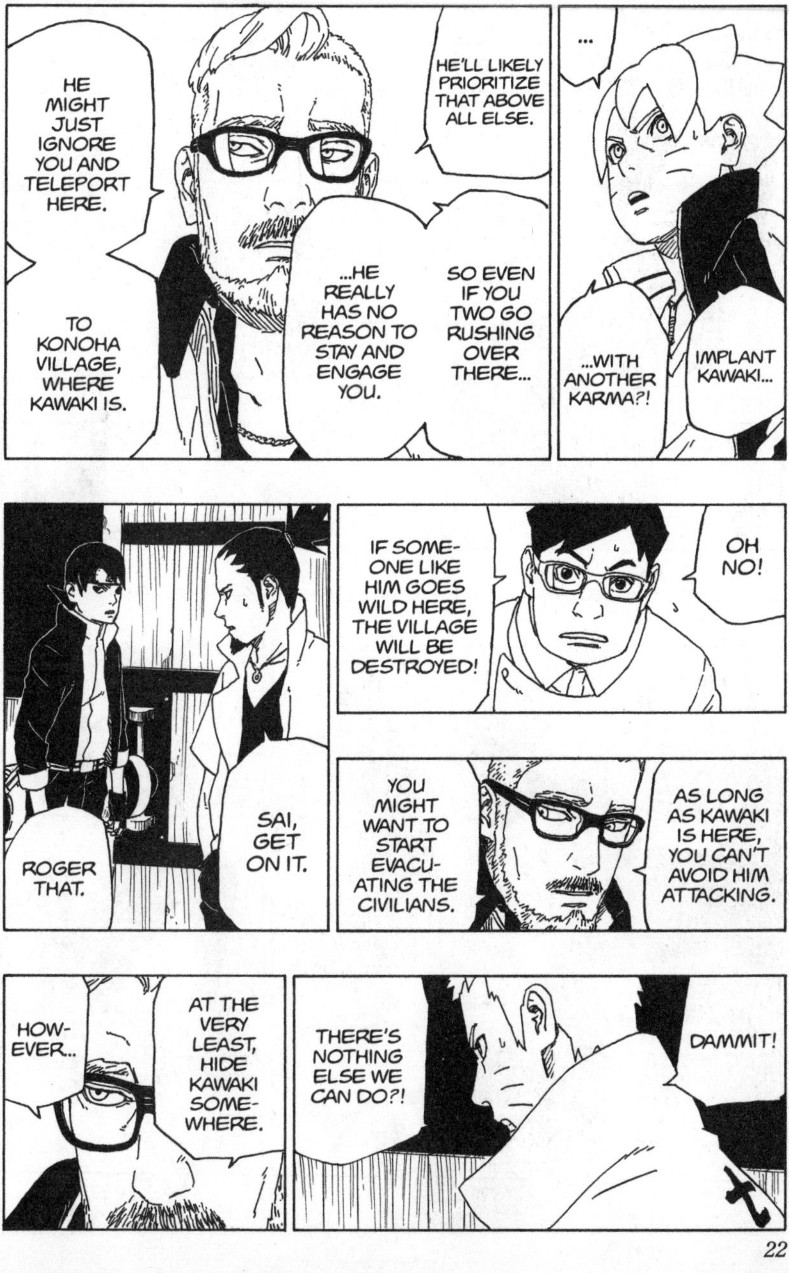
...
IMPLANT KAWAKI...
...WITH ANOTHER KARMA?!
HE'LL LIKELY PRIORITIZE THAT ABOVE ALL ELSE.
SO EVEN IF YOU TWO GO RUSHING OVER THERE...
...HE REALLY HAS NO REASON TO STAY AND ENGAGE YOU.
HE MIGHT JUST IGNORE YOU AND TELEPORT HERE.
TO KONOHA VILLAGE, WHERE KAWAKI IS.
OH NO!
IF SOME-ONE LIKE HIM GOES WILD HERE, THE VILLAGE WILL BE DESTROYED!
AS LONG AS KAWAKI IS HERE, YOU CAN'T AVOID HIM ATTACKING.
YOU MIGHT WANT TO START EVACU-ATING THE CIVILIANS.
SAI, GET ON IT.
ROGER THAT.
DAMMIT!
THERE'S NOTHING ELSE WE CAN DO?!
HOW-EVER...
AT THE VERY LEAST, HIDE KAWAKI SOME-WHERE.

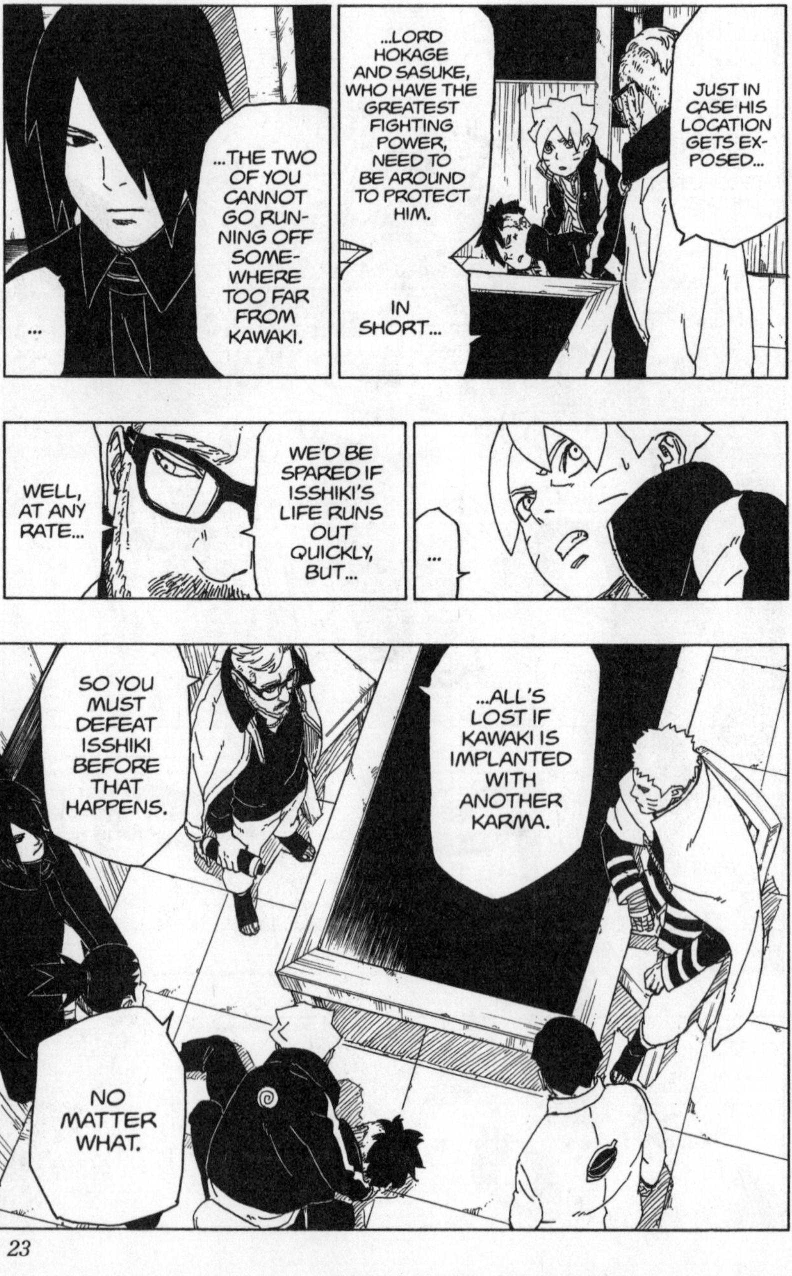
JUST IN CASE HIS LOCATION GETS EXPOSED...
...LORD HOKAGE AND SASUKE, WHO HAVE THE GREATEST FIGHTING POWER, NEED TO BE AROUND TO PROTECT HIM.
IN SHORT...
...THE TWO OF YOU CANNOT GO RUNNING OFF SOMEWHERE TOO FAR FROM KAWAKI.
...
...
WE'D BE SPARED IF ISSHIKI'S LIFE RUNS OUT QUICKLY, BUT...
WELL, AT ANY RATE...
...ALL'S LOST IF KAWAKI IS IMPLANTED WITH ANOTHER KARMA.
SO YOU MUST DEFEAT ISSHIKI BEFORE THAT HAPPENS.
NO MATTER WHAT.

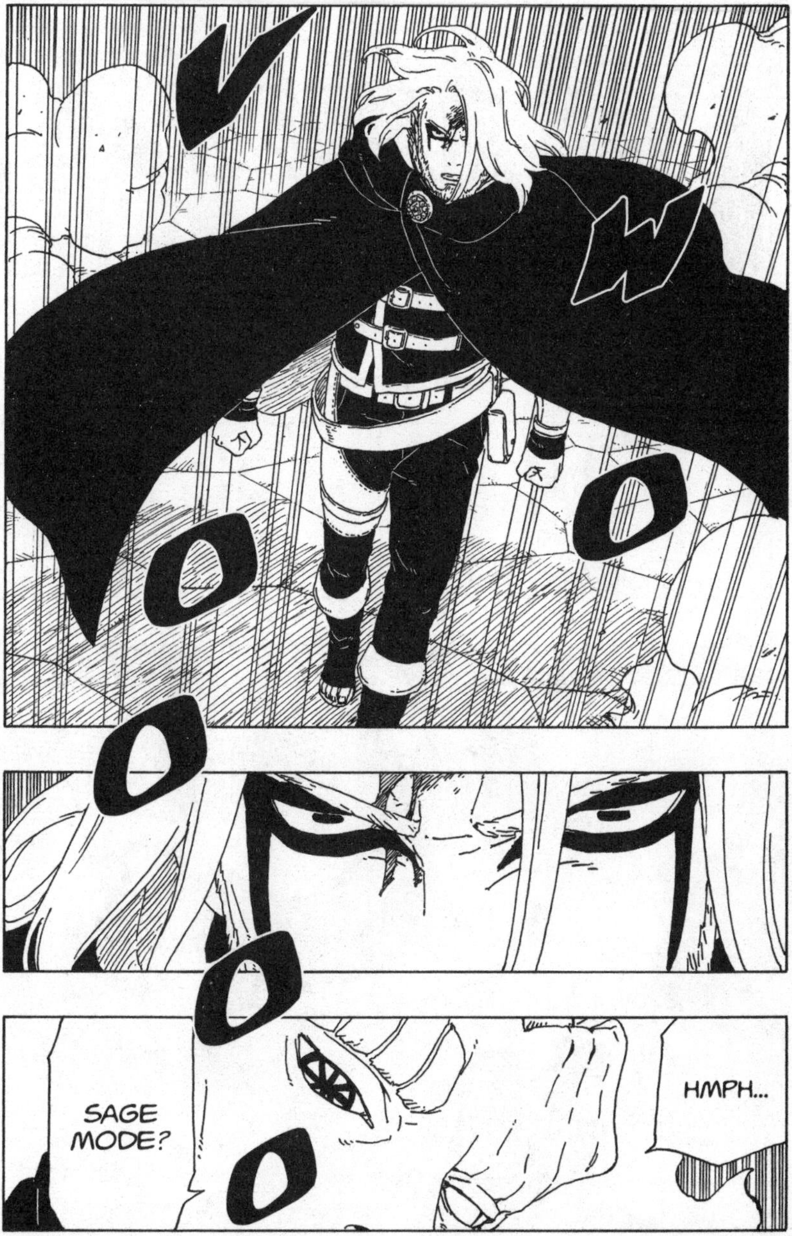
VWOOOOO
HMPH...
SAGE MODE?

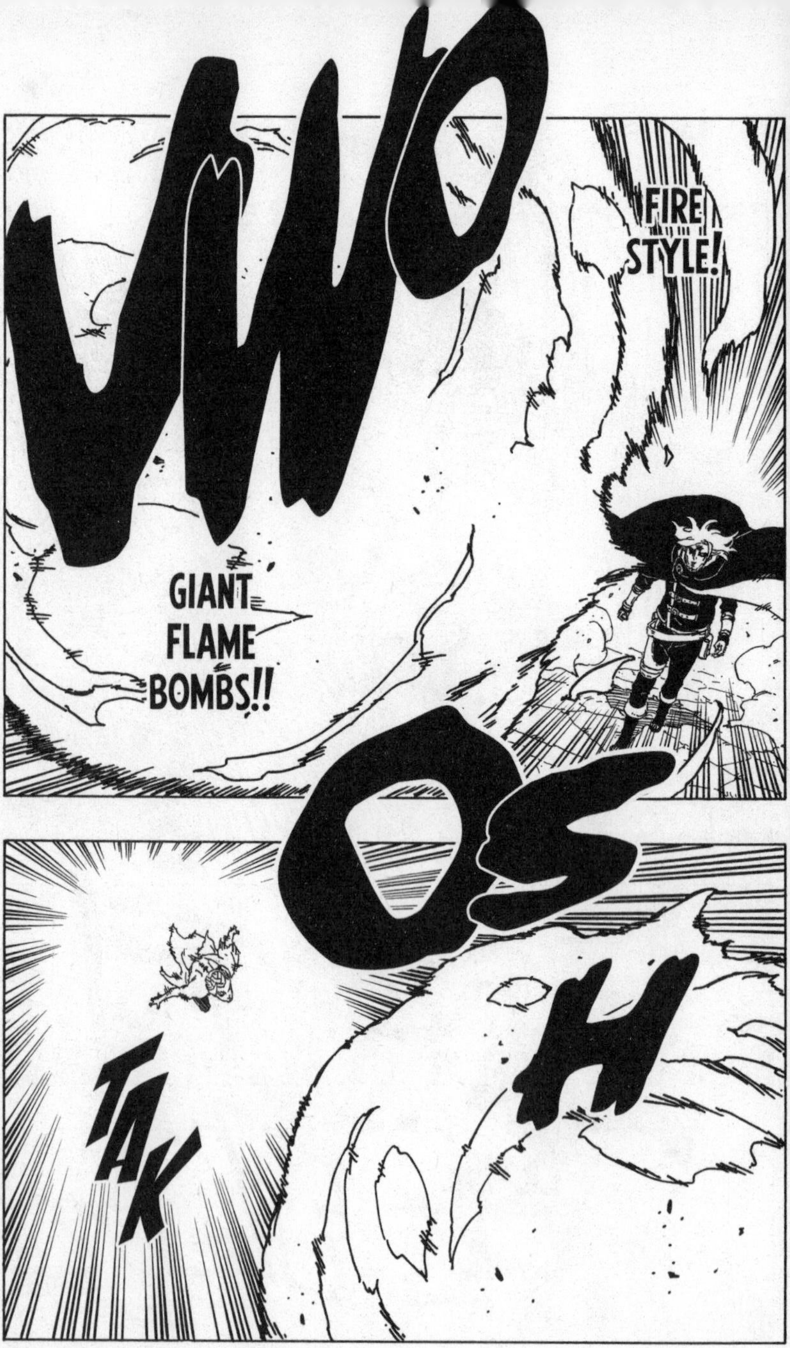
FIRE STYLE!
GIANT FLAME BOMBS!!
VWOOSH
TAK

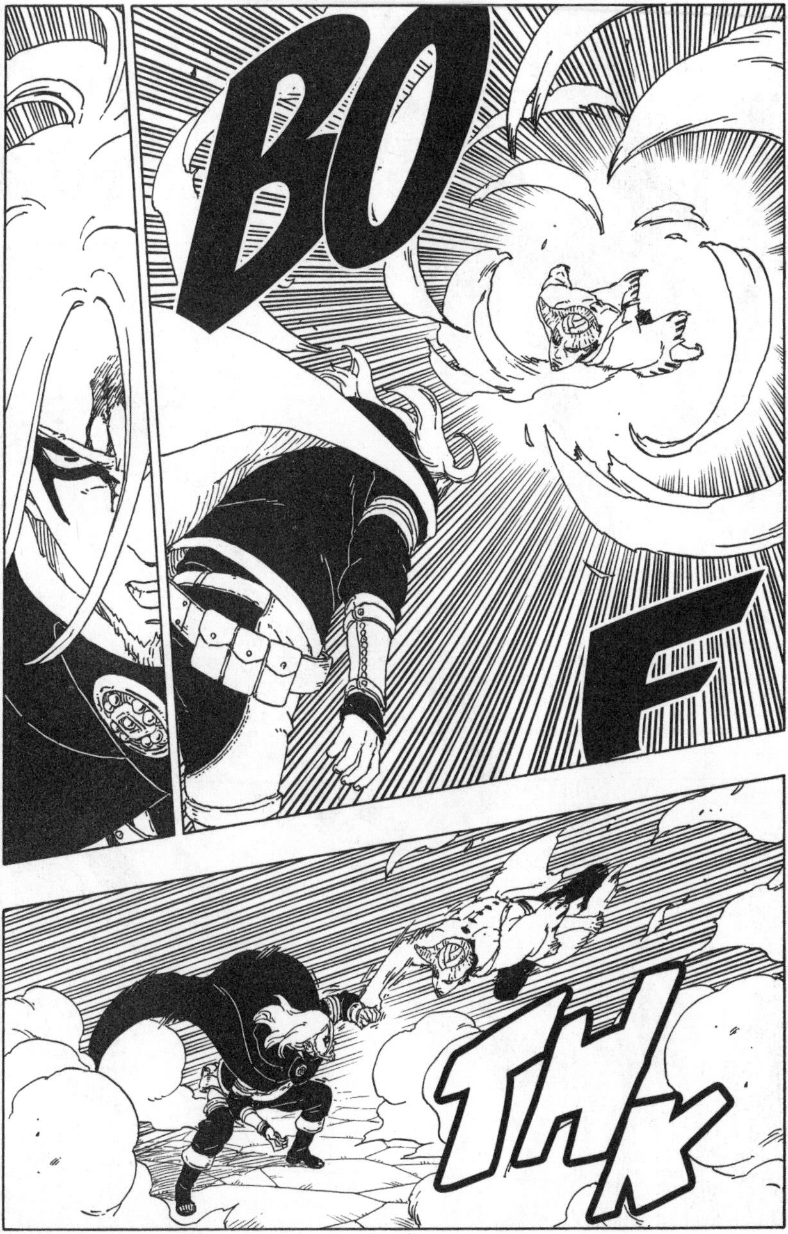
BOF
THK

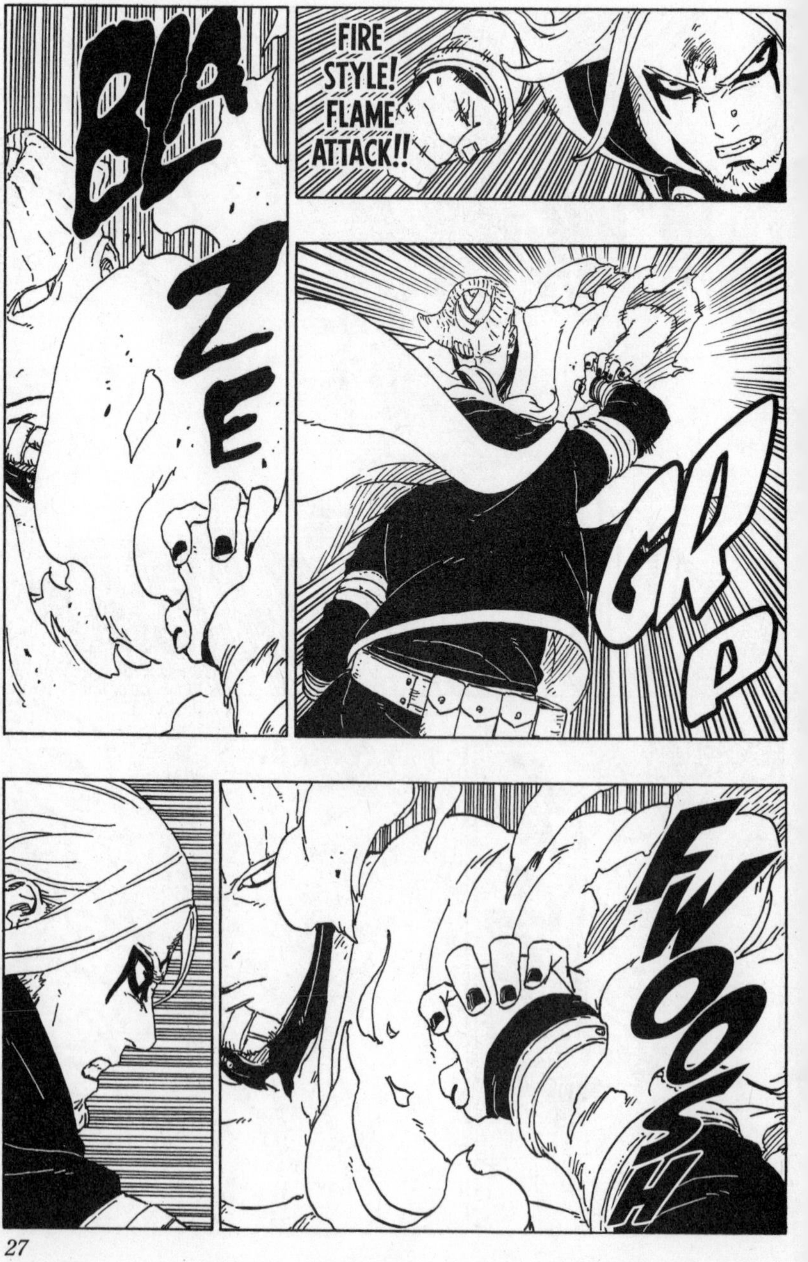
FIRE STYLE! FLAME ATTACK!!
GRIP
BLAZE
FWOOSH

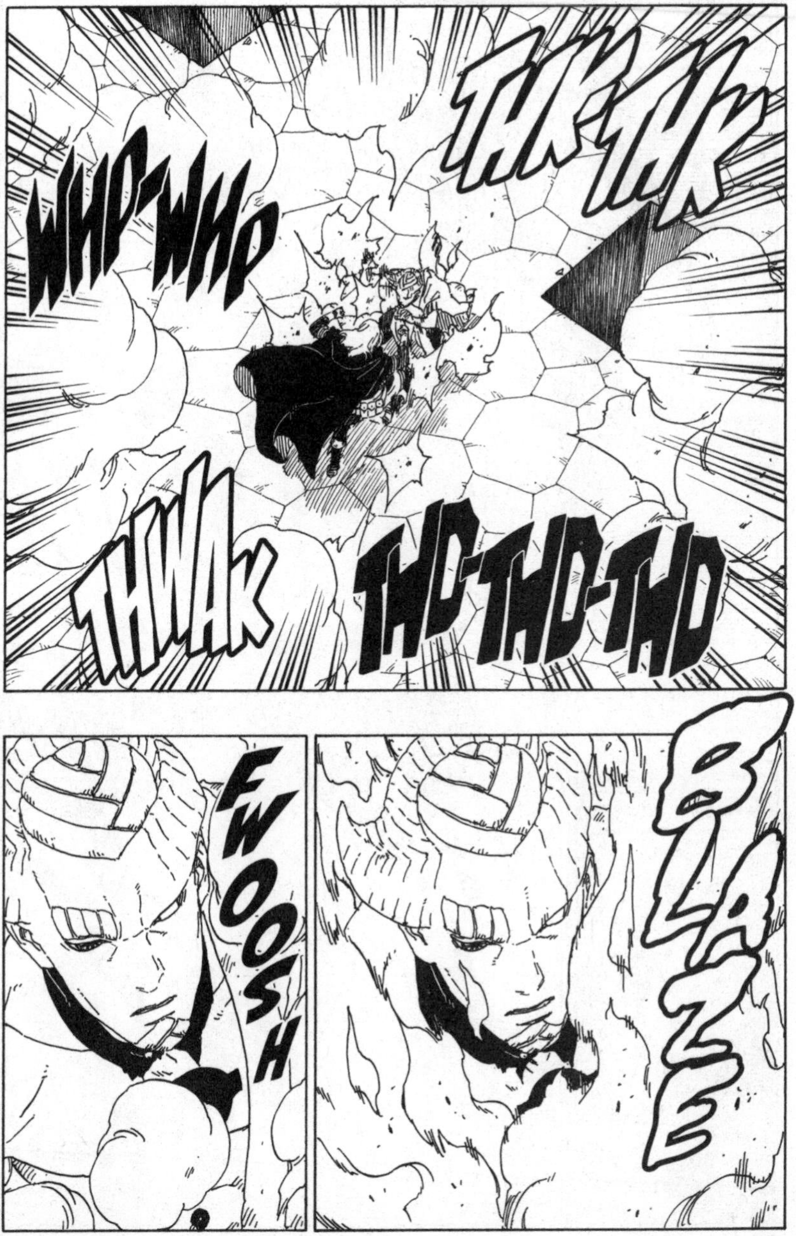
TAK-TAK
WHP-WHP
THD-THD-THD
THWAK
BLAZE
FWOOSH

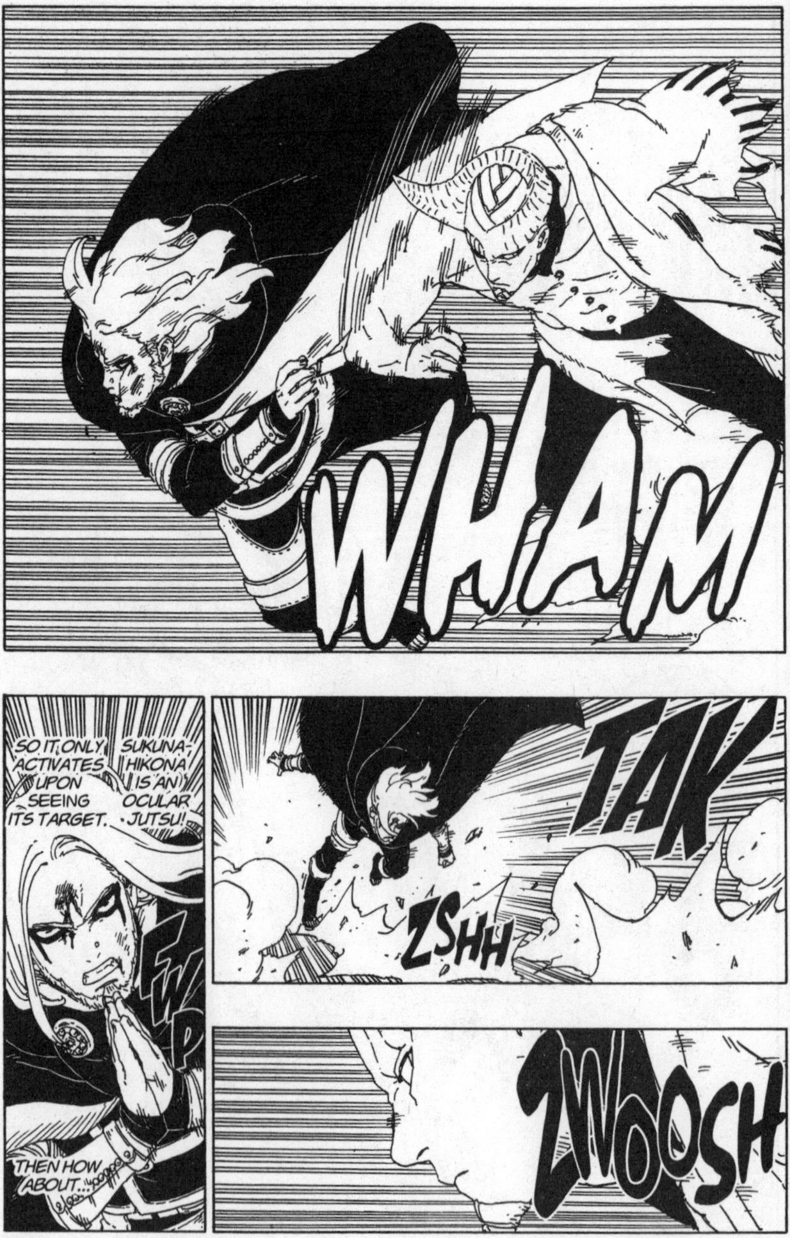
WHAM
TAK
ZSHH
ZWOOSH
SUKUNA-HIKONA IS AN OCULAR JUTSU!
SO IT ONLY ACTIVATES UPON SEEING ITS TARGET.
FWP
THEN HOW ABOUT...

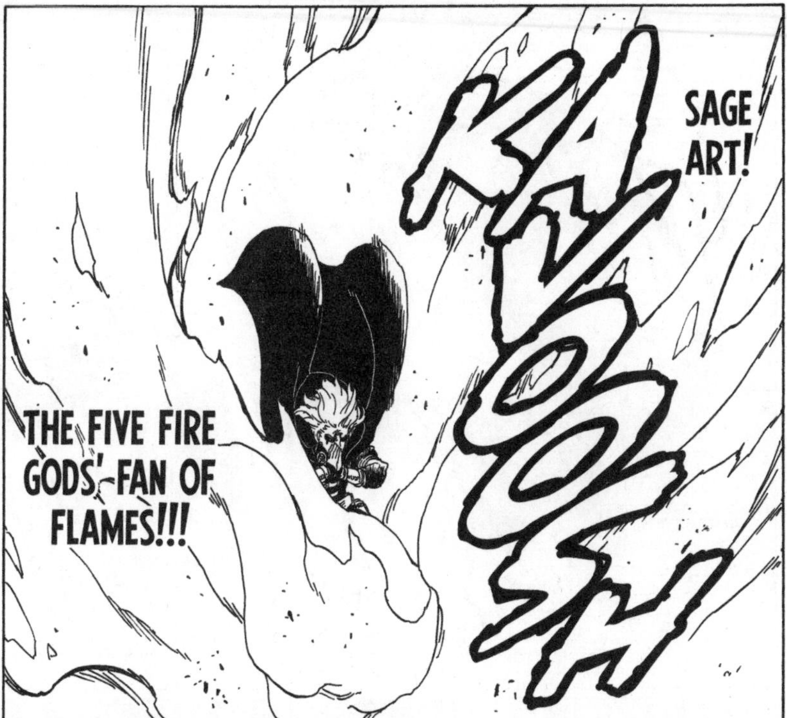
SAGE ART!
KAWOOOSH
THE FIVE FIRE GODS' FAN OF FLAMES!!!
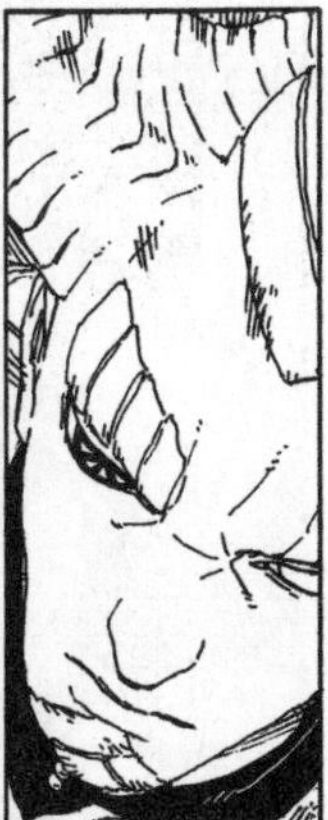
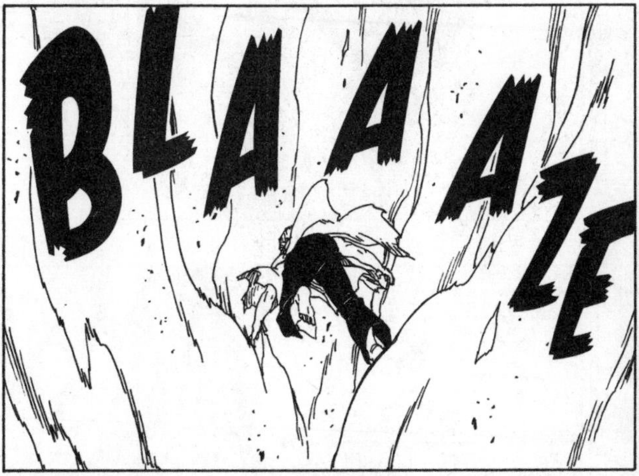
BLAAAZE

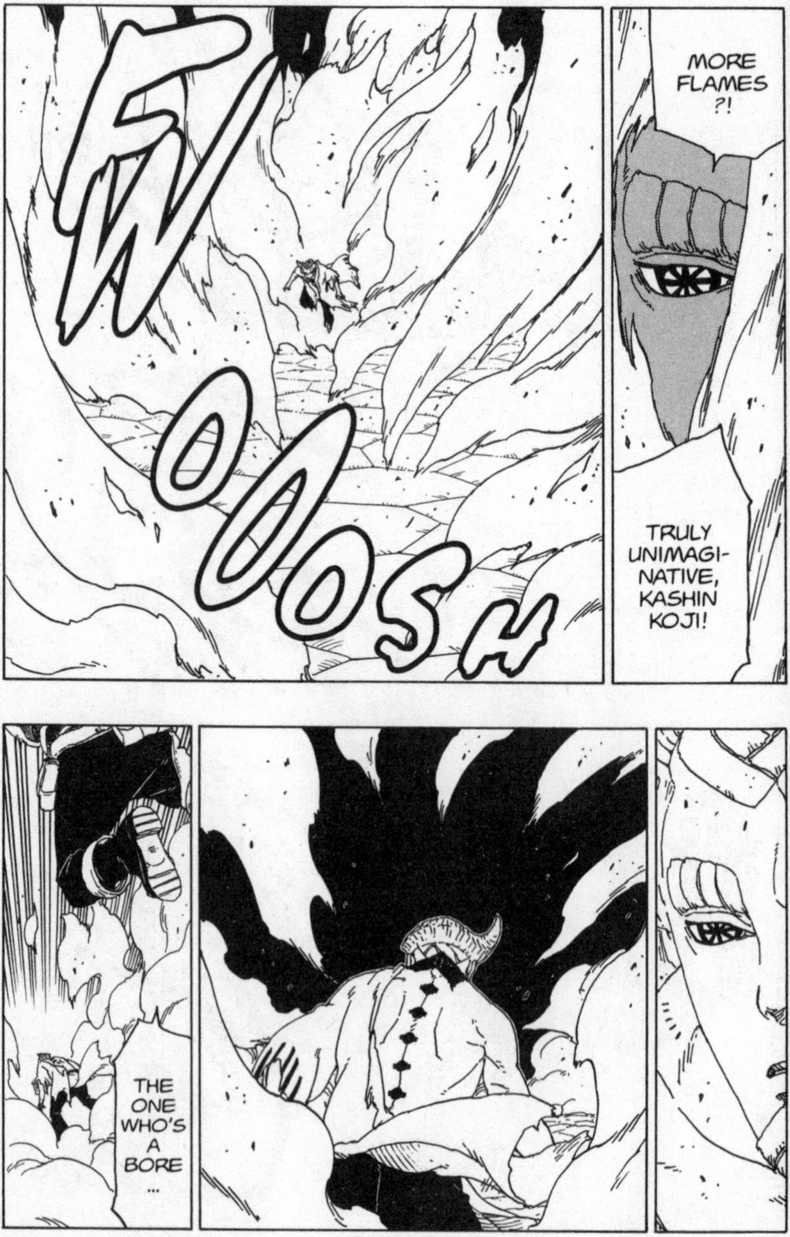
MORE FLAMES ?!
TRULY UNIMAGINATIVE, KASHIN KOJI!
FWOOOSH
THE ONE WHO'S A BORE ...

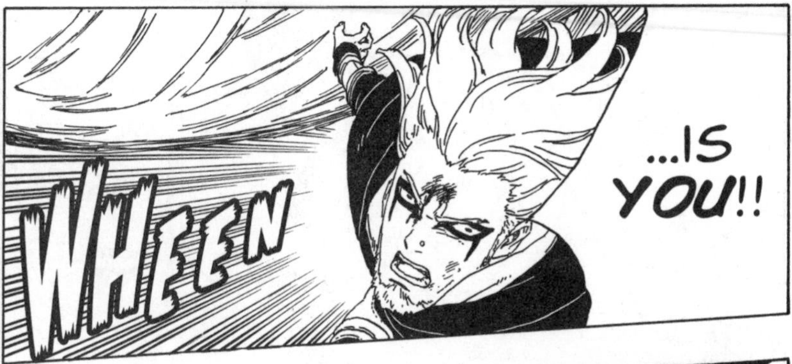
...IS YOU!!
WHEEN

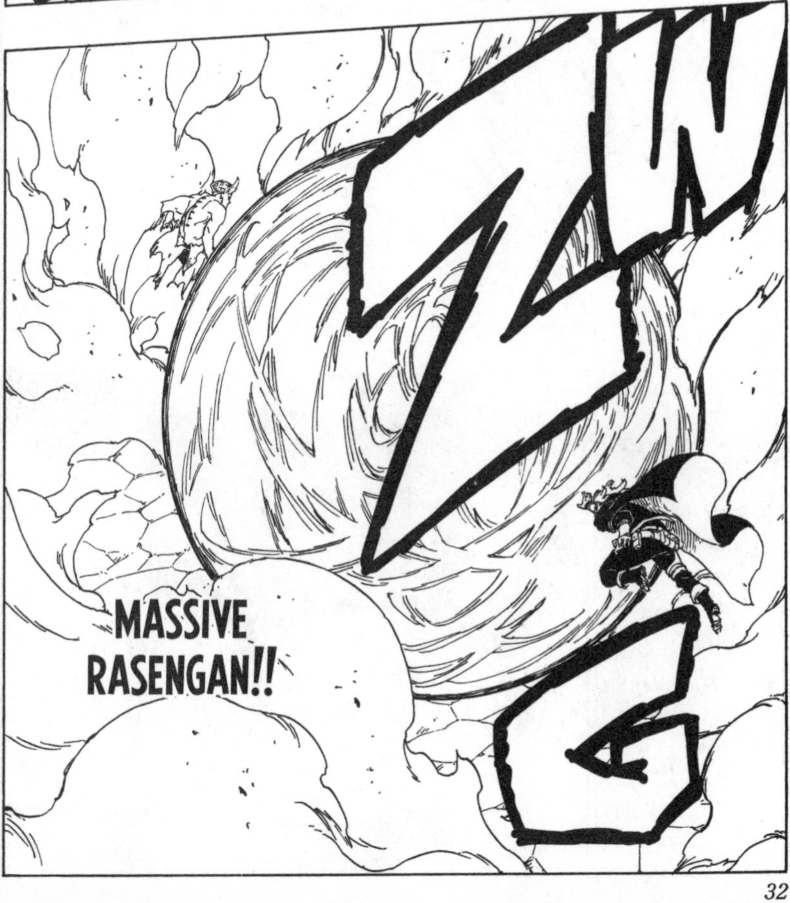
MASSIVE RASENGAN!!

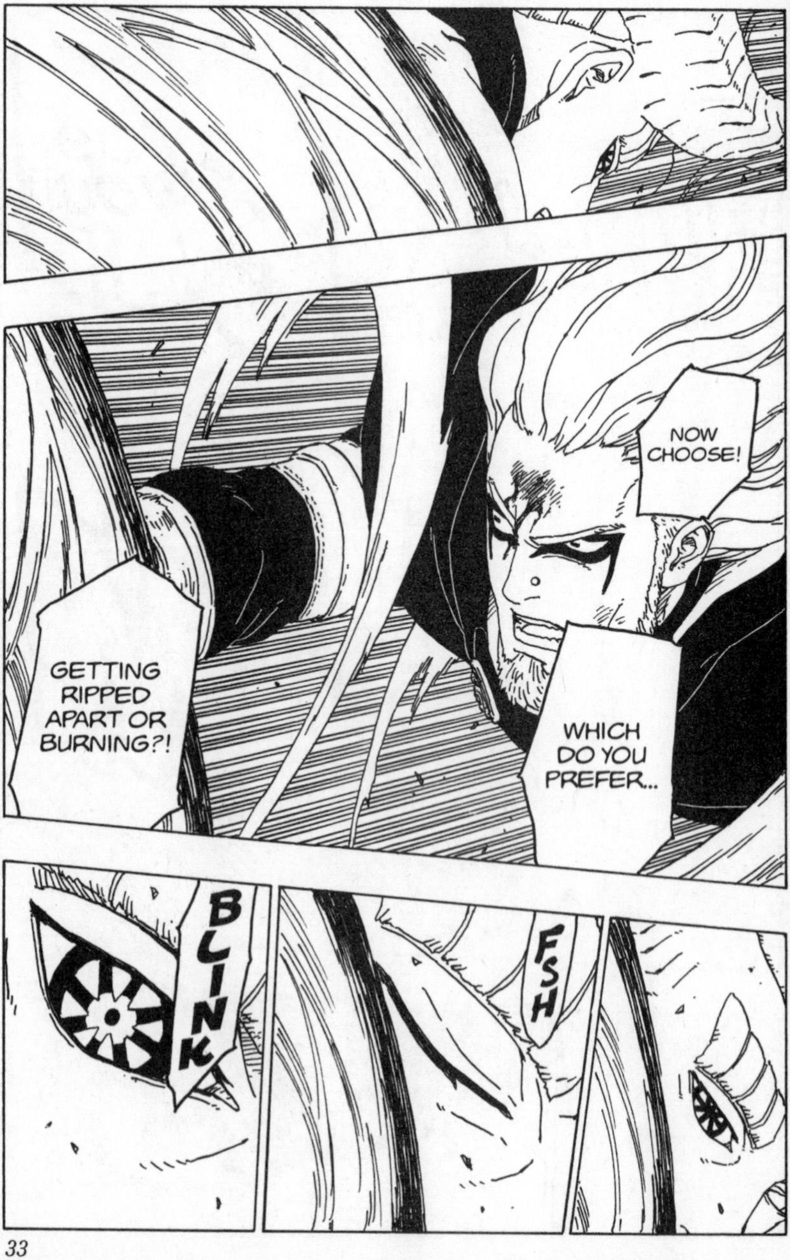
NOW CHOOSE!
WHICH DO YOU PREFER...
GETTING RIPPED APART OR BURNING?!
FSH
BLINK

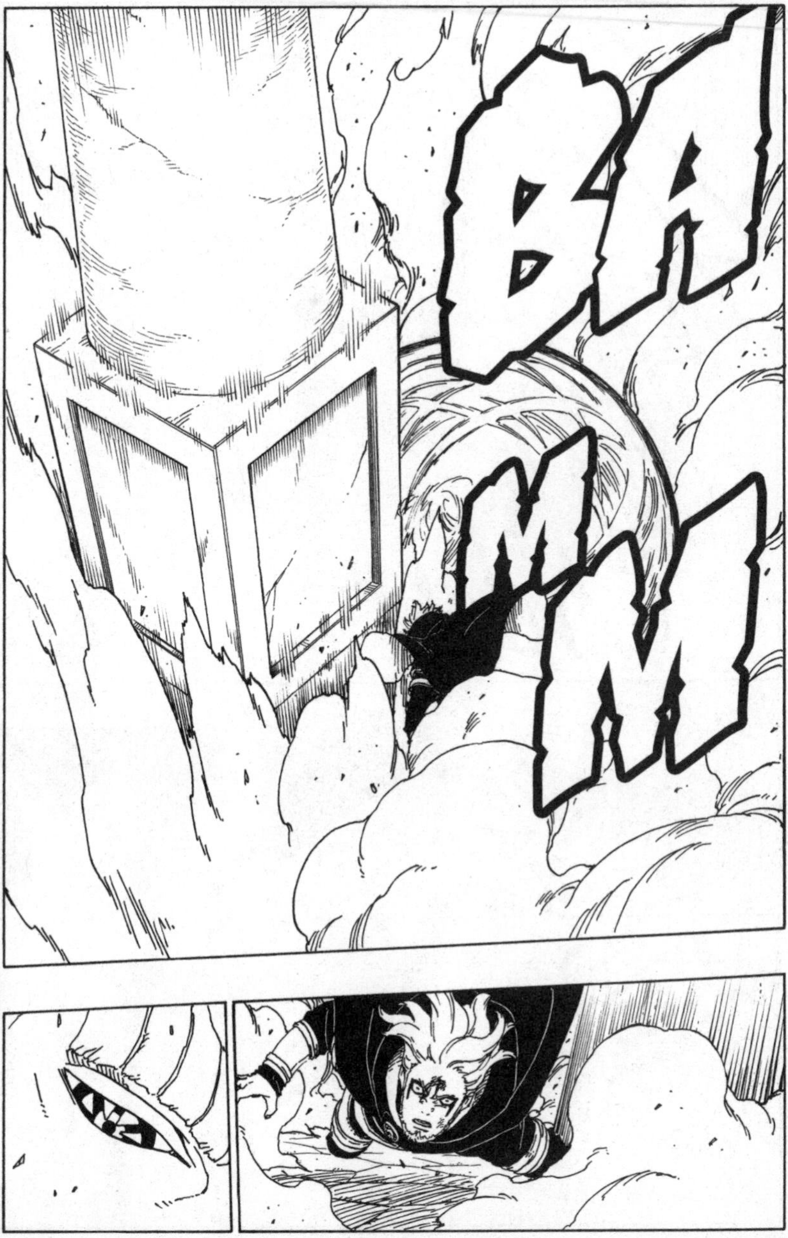
BAMM

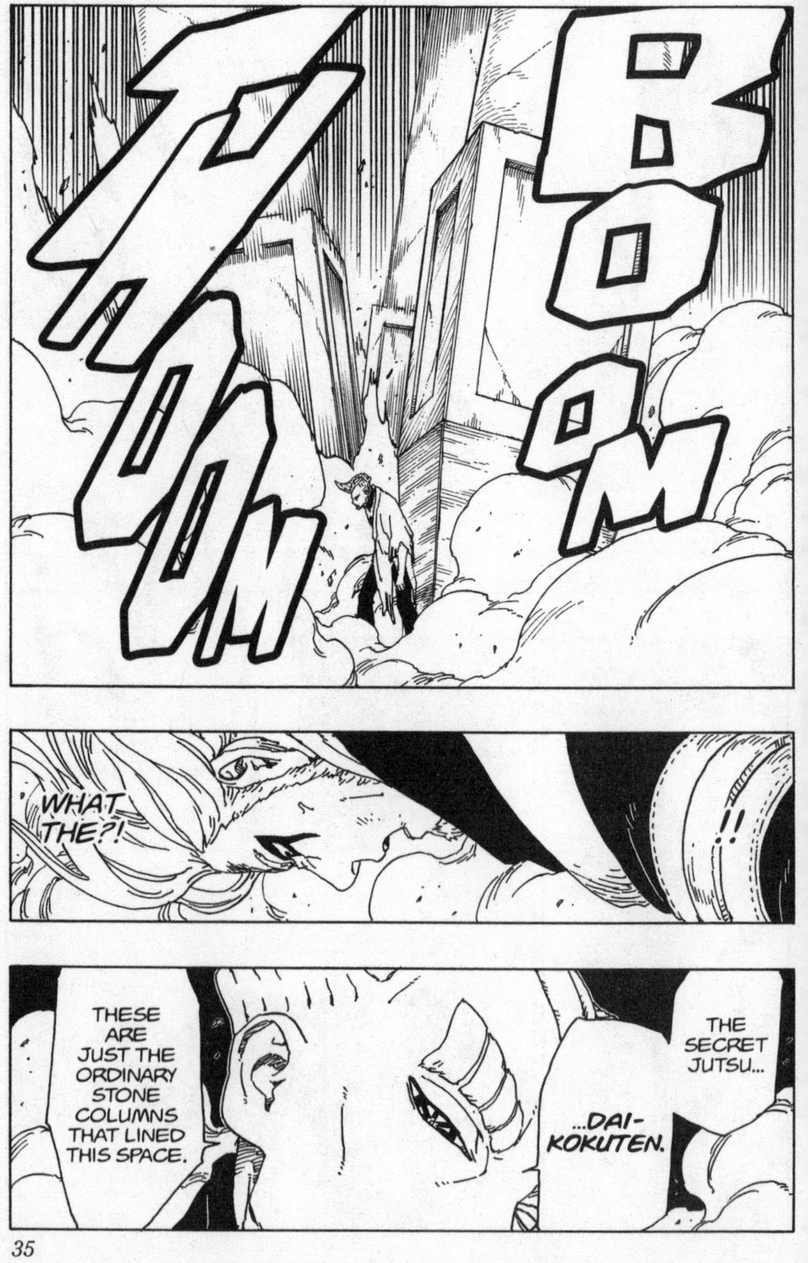
BOOM
WHAT THE?!
!!
THE SECRET JUTSU...
...DAI-KOKUTEN.
THESE ARE JUST THE ORDINARY STONE COLUMNS THAT LINED THIS SPACE.

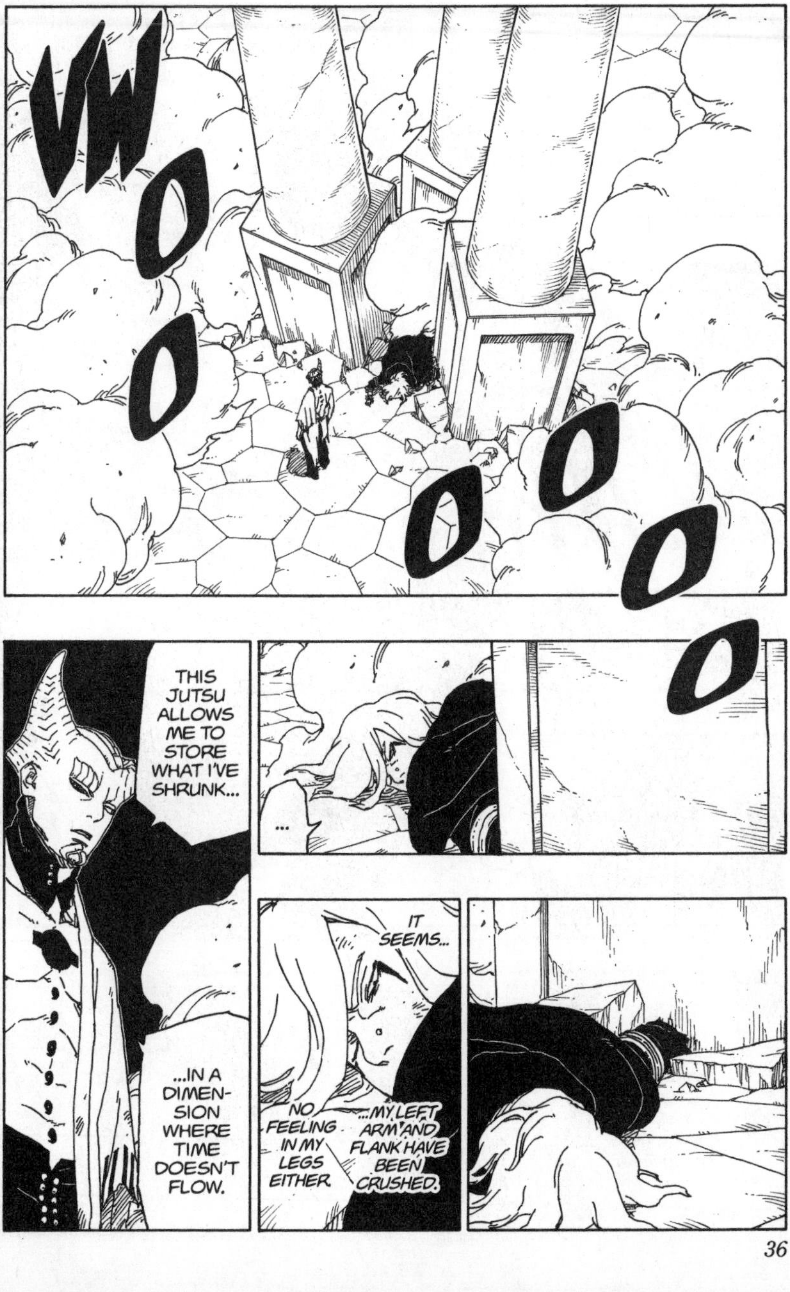
VWOOOOOO
...
IT SEEMS...
...MY LEFT ARM AND FLANK HAVE BEEN CRUSHED.
NO FEELING IN MY LEGS EITHER.
THIS JUTSU ALLOWS ME TO STORE WHAT I'VE SHRUNK...
...IN A DIMENSION WHERE TIME DOESN'T FLOW.

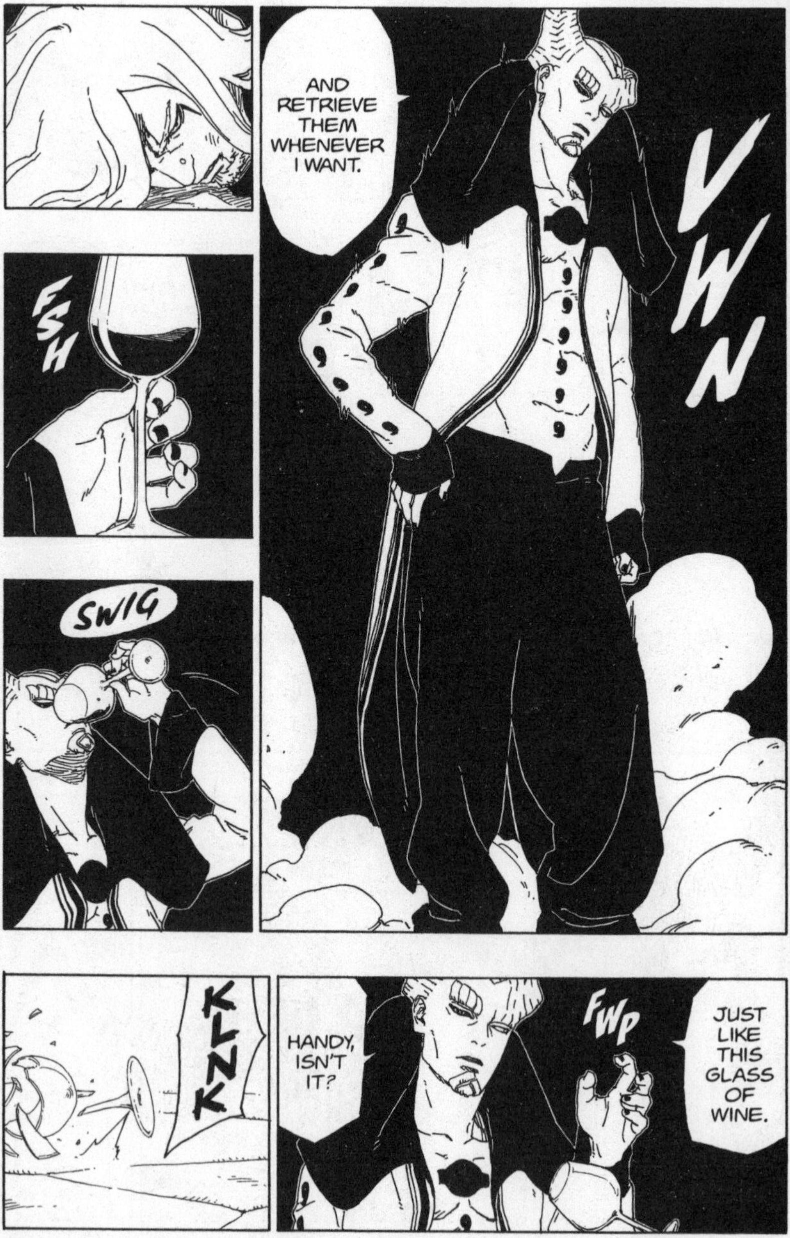

AND RETRIEVE THEM WHENEVER I WANT.
VWN
FSH
SWIG
JUST LIKE THIS GLASS OF WINE.
FWP
HANDY, ISN'T IT?
KLNK

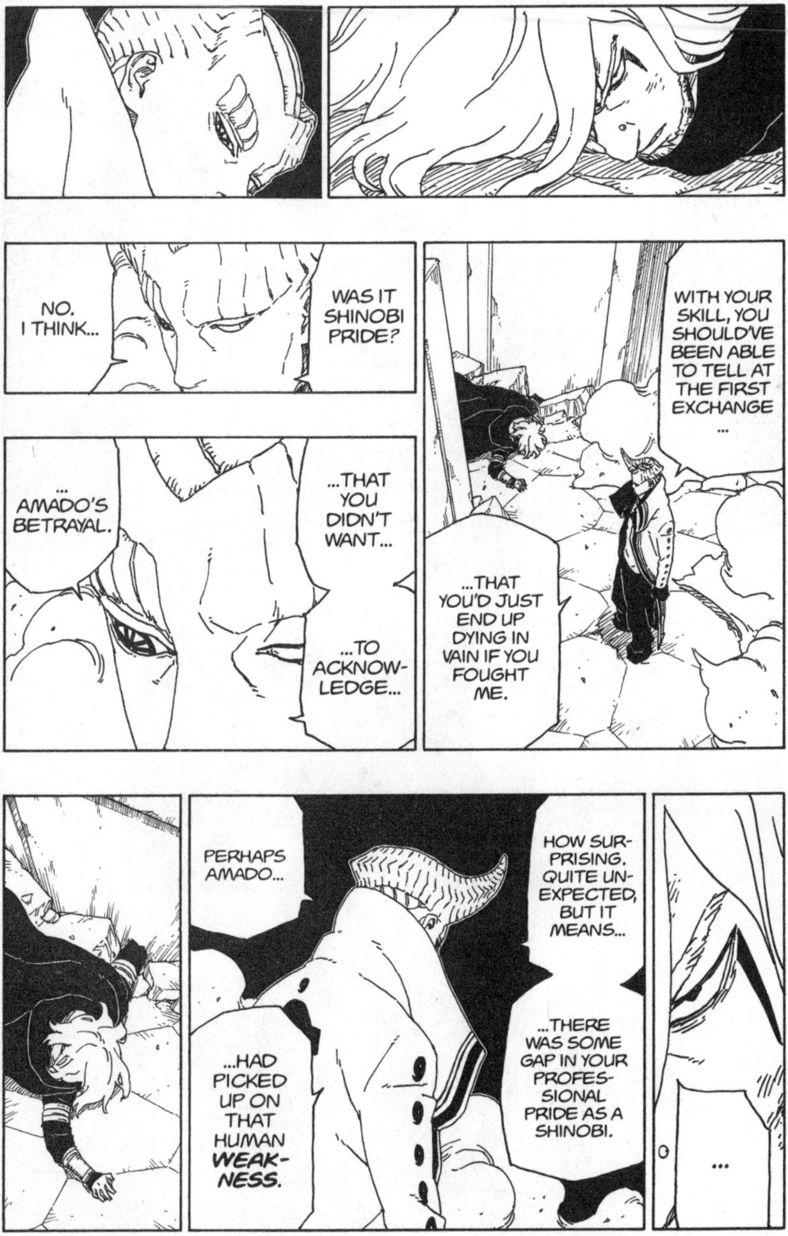
WITH YOUR SKILL, YOU SHOULD'VE BEEN ABLE TO TELL AT THE FIRST EXCHANGE ...
...THAT YOU'D JUST END UP DYING IN VAIN IF YOU FOUGHT ME.
WAS IT SHINOBI PRIDE?
NO. I THINK...
...THAT YOU DIDN'T WANT...
...TO ACKNOWLEDGE...
... AMADO'S BETRAYAL.
...
HOW SURPRISING. QUITE UNEXPECTED, BUT IT MEANS...
...THERE WAS SOME GAP IN YOUR PROFESSIONAL PRIDE AS A SHINOBI.
PERHAPS AMADO...
...HAD PICKED UP ON THAT HUMAN ***WEAKNESS.***

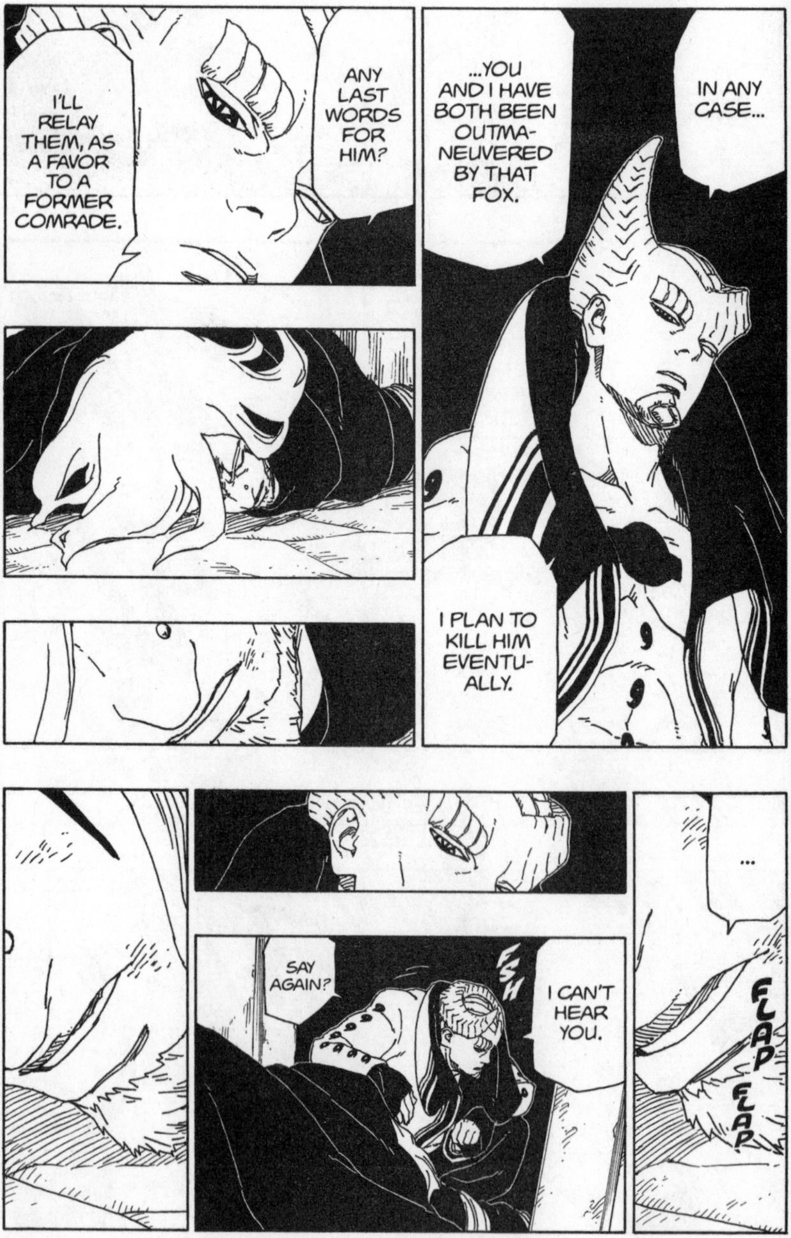
IN ANY CASE...
...YOU AND I HAVE BOTH BEEN OUTMANEUVERED BY THAT FOX.
I PLAN TO KILL HIM EVENTUALLY.
ANY LAST WORDS FOR HIM?
I'LL RELAY THEM, AS A FAVOR TO A FORMER COMRADE.
...
FLAP FLAP FLAP
I CAN'T HEAR YOU.
FSH
SAY AGAIN?

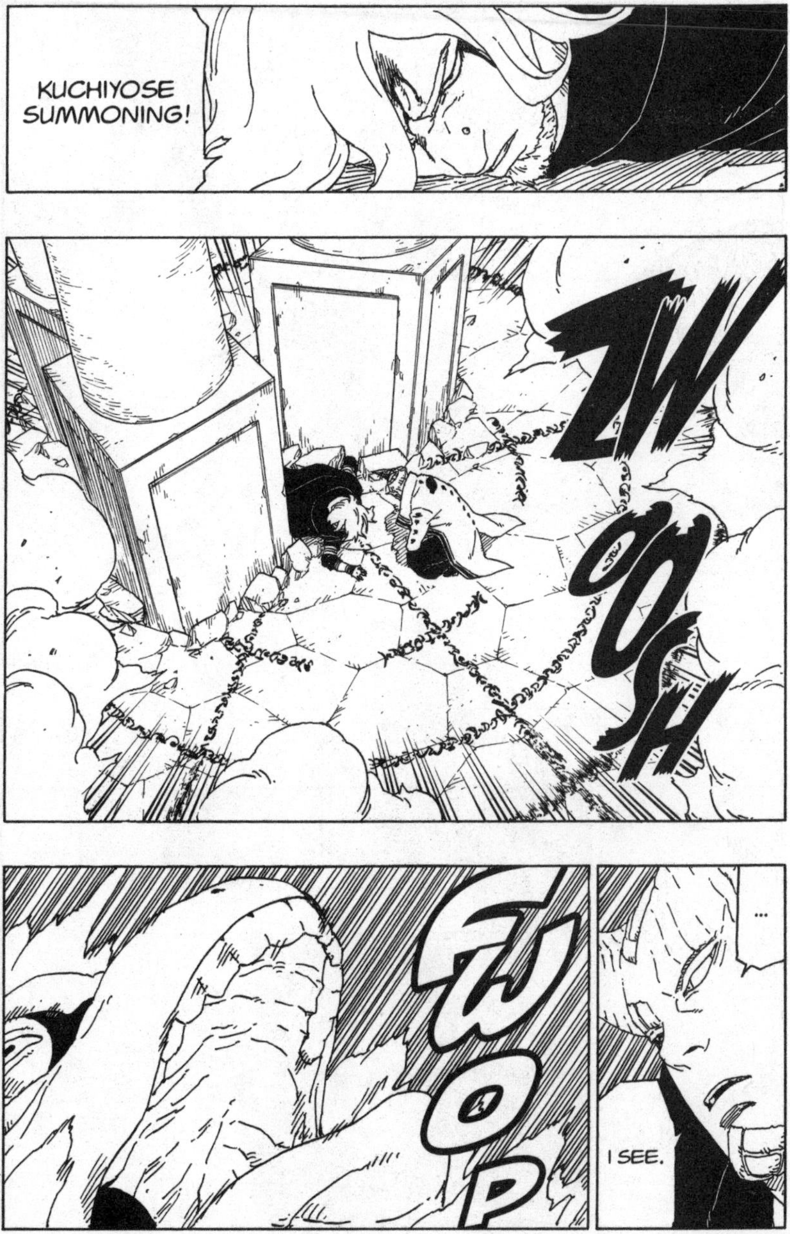
KUCHIYOSE SUMMONING!
ZWOOSH
...
I SEE.
FWOOP

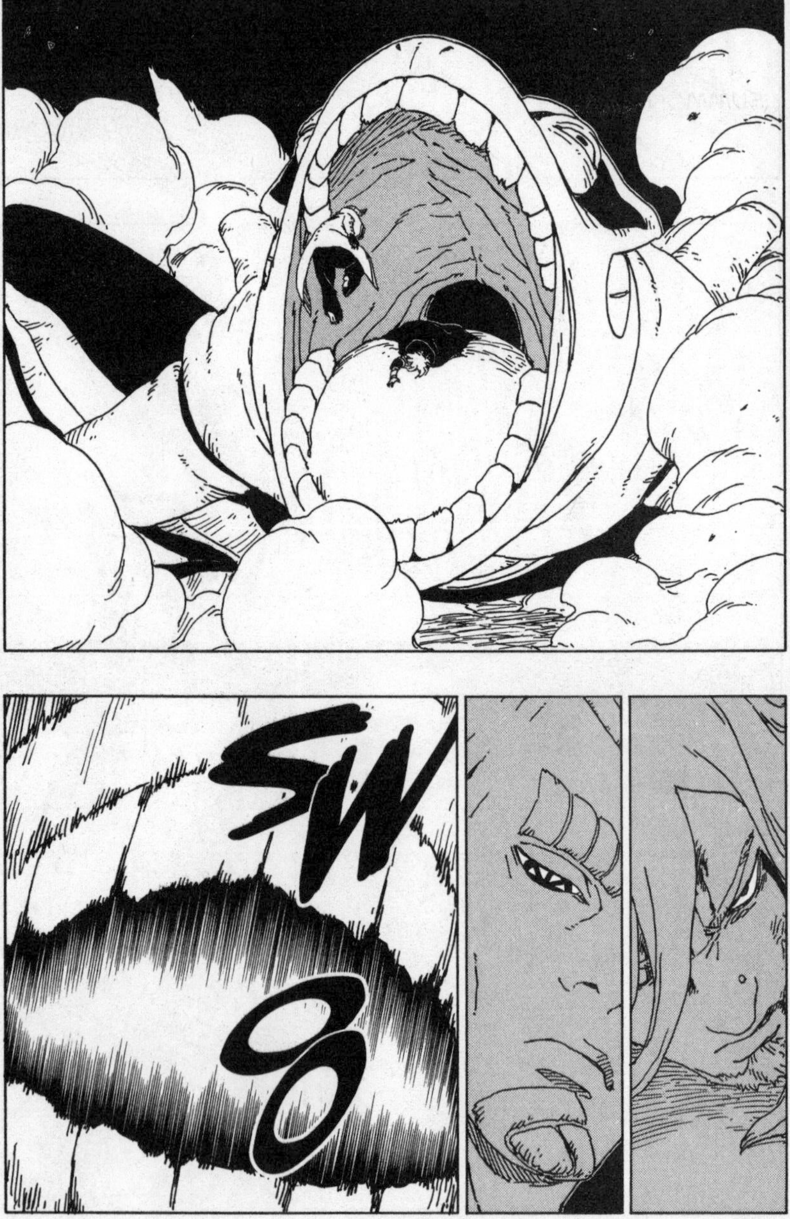
SWOO

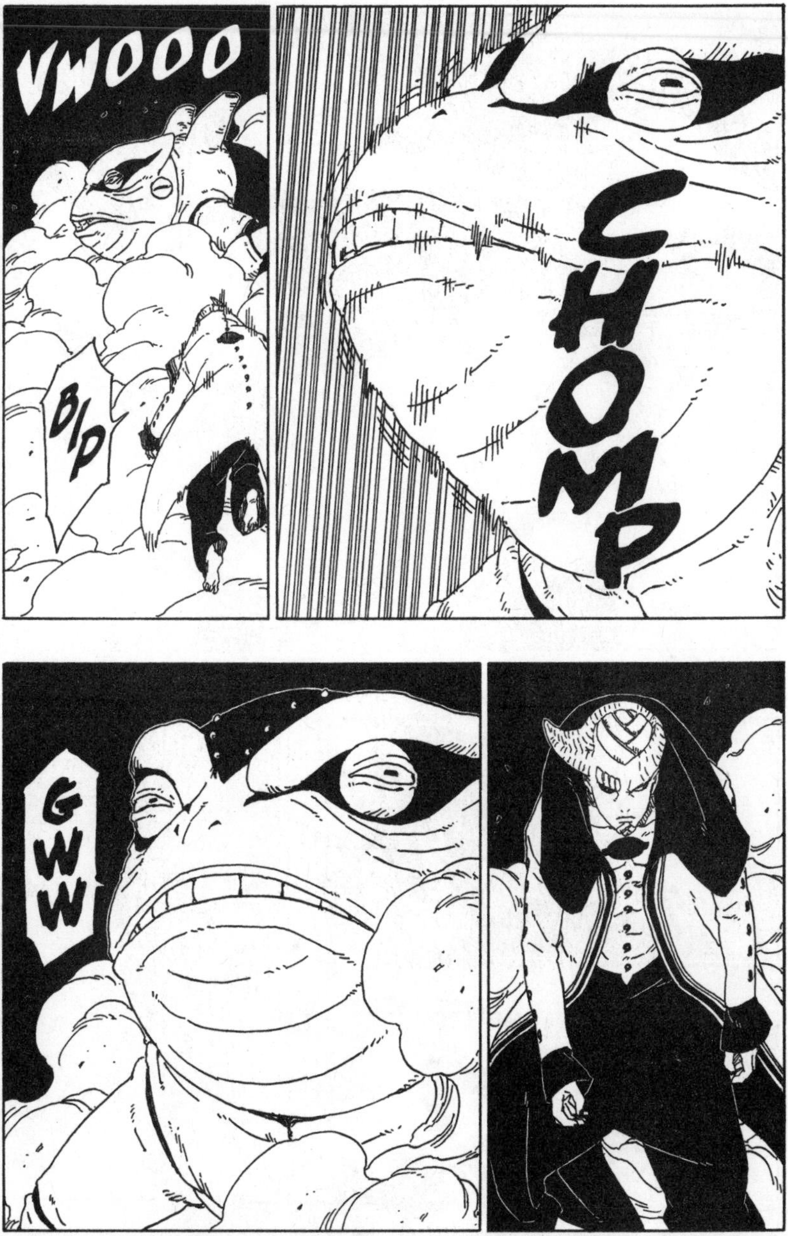
CHOMP
VWOOO
BIP
GWW

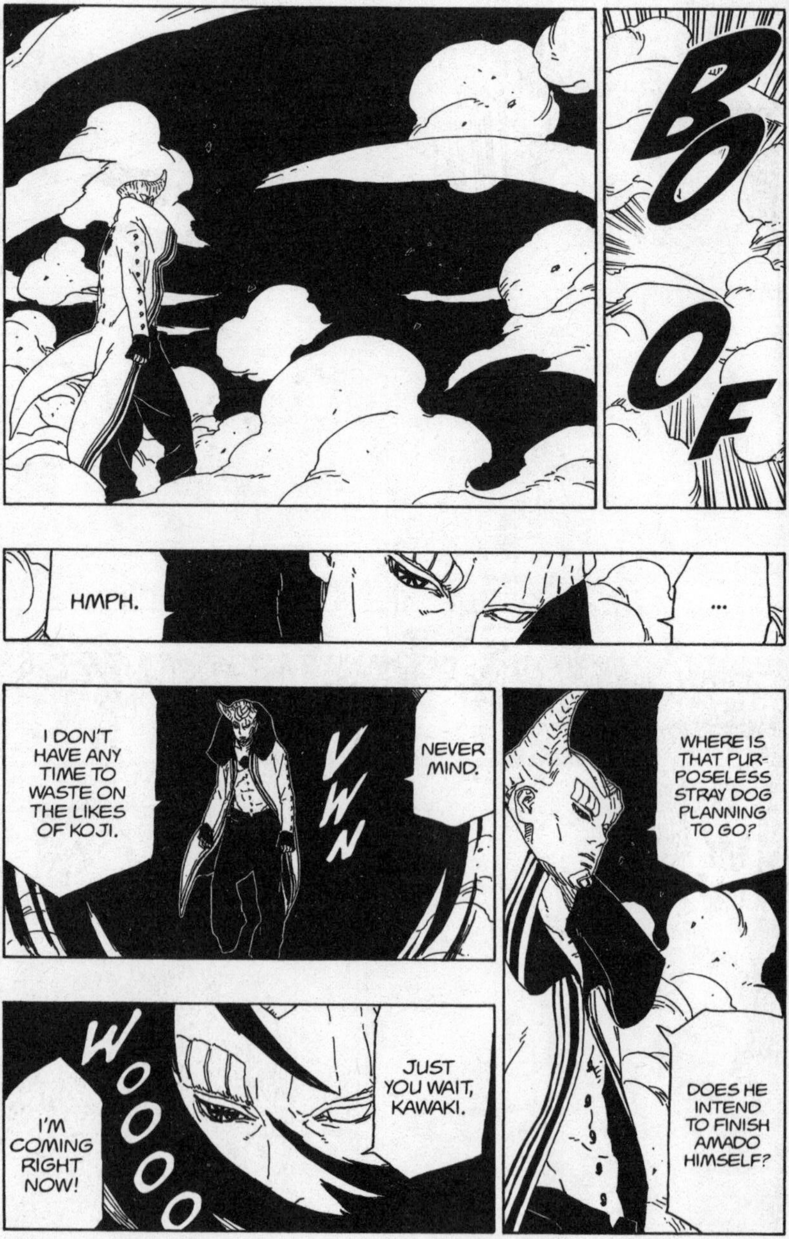
BOOOF
...
HMPH.
WHERE IS THAT PURPOSELESS STRAY DOG PLANNING TO GO?
DOES HE INTEND TO FINISH AMADO HIMSELF?
NEVER MIND.
VWN
I DON'T HAVE ANY TIME TO WASTE ON THE LIKES OF KOJI.
JUST YOU WAIT, KAWAKI.
WOOOO
I'M COMING RIGHT NOW!

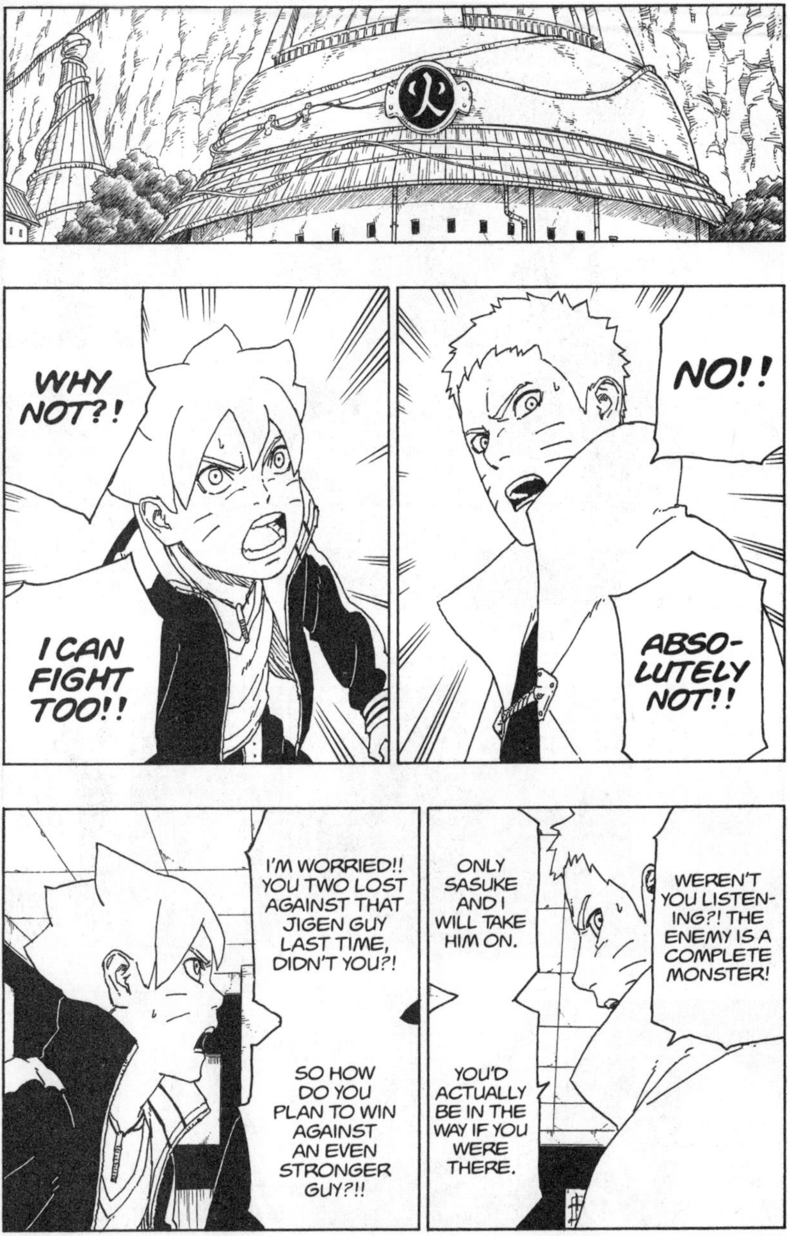
NO!!
ABSOLUTELY NOT!!
WHY NOT?!
I CAN FIGHT TOO!!
WEREN'T YOU LISTENING?! THE ENEMY IS A COMPLETE MONSTER!
ONLY SASUKE AND I WILL TAKE HIM ON.
YOU'D ACTUALLY BE IN THE WAY IF YOU WERE THERE.
I'M WORRIED!! YOU TWO LOST AGAINST THAT JIGEN GUY LAST TIME, DIDN'T YOU?!
SO HOW DO YOU PLAN TO WIN AGAINST AN EVEN STRONGER GUY?!!

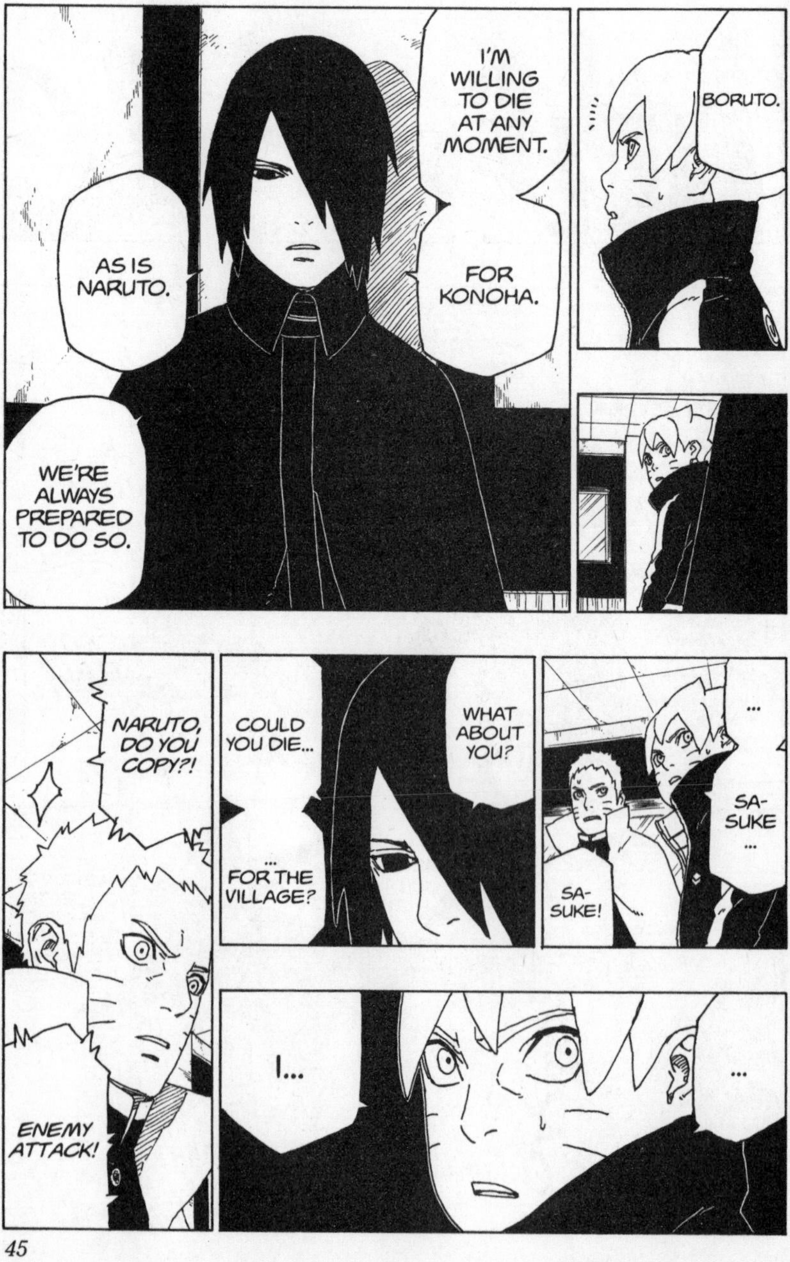
BORUTO.
I'M WILLING TO DIE AT ANY MOMENT.
FOR KONOHA.
AS IS NARUTO.
WE'RE ALWAYS PREPARED TO DO SO.
...
SA-SUKE ...
SA-SUKE!
WHAT ABOUT YOU?
COULD YOU DIE...
... FOR THE VILLAGE?
...
I...
NARUTO, DO YOU COPY?!
ENEMY ATTACK!

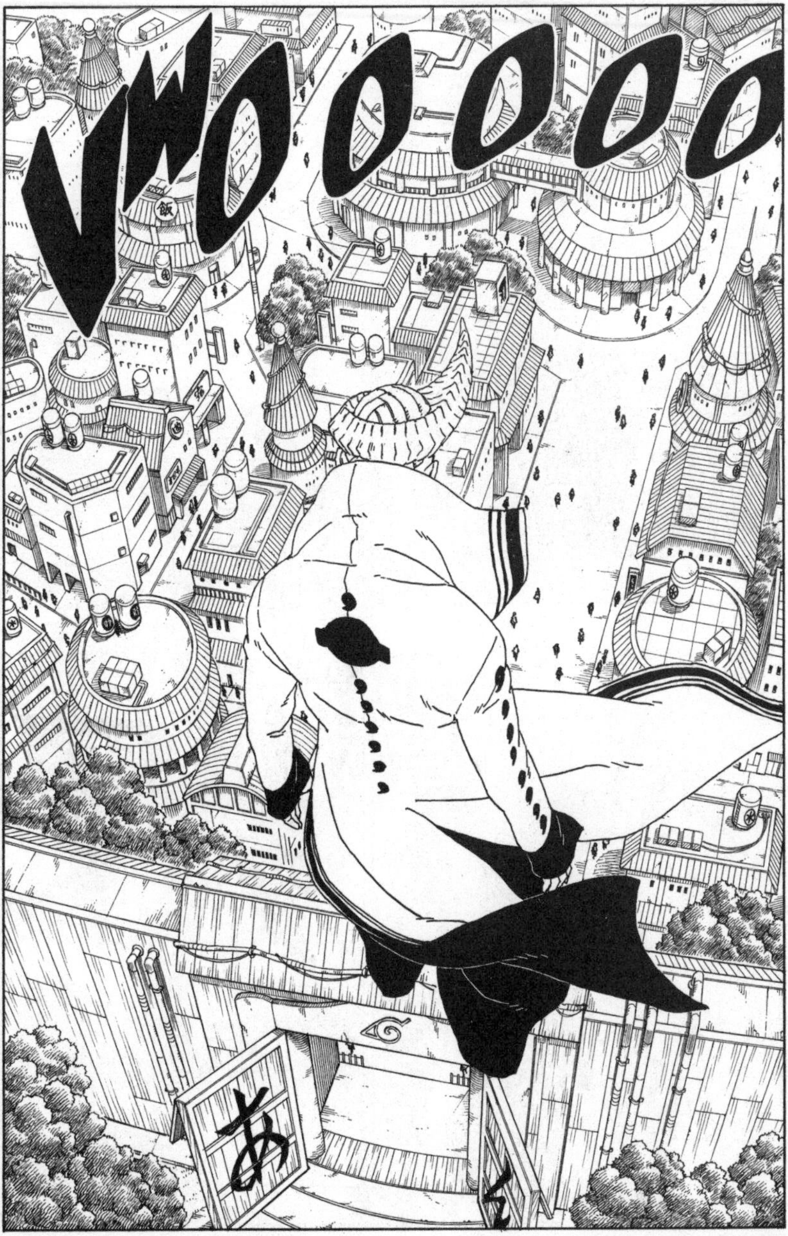
VWOOOOOO
飯
あ

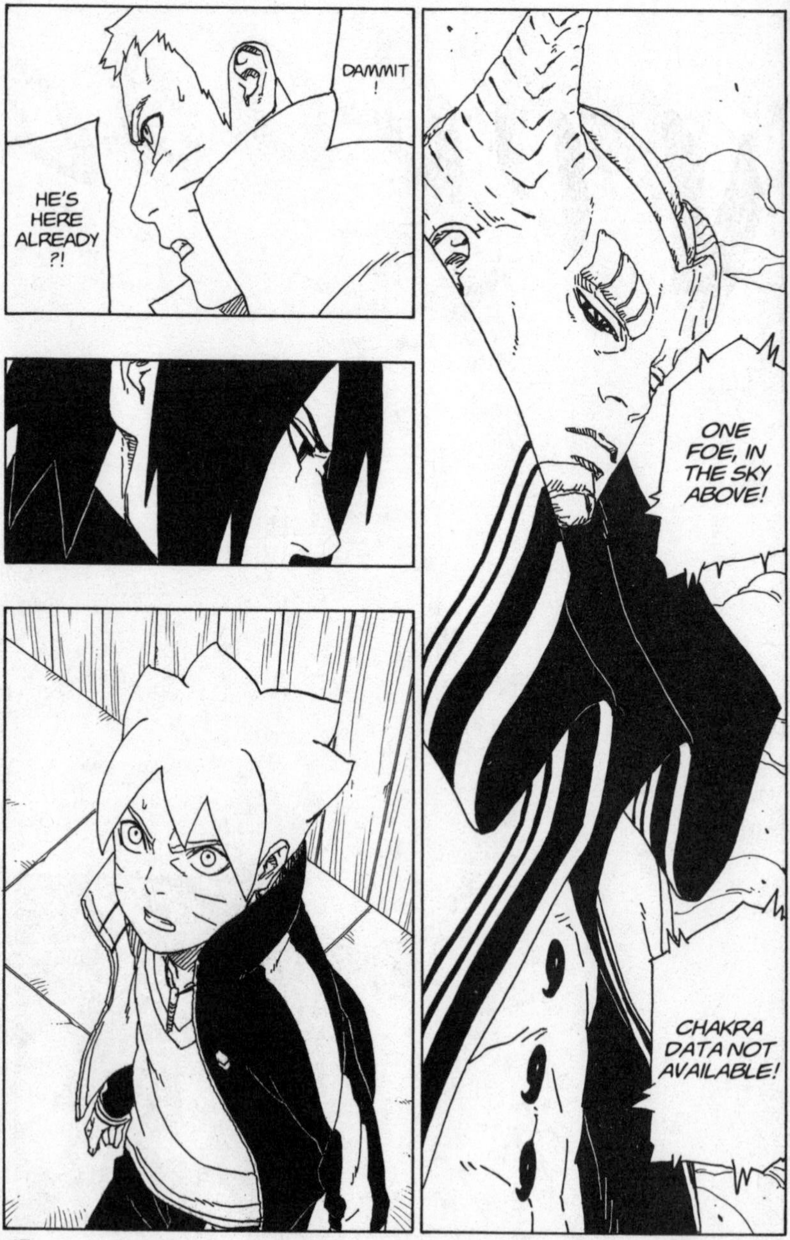
ONE FOE, IN THE SKY ABOVE!
CHAKRA DATA NOT AVAILABLE!
DAMMIT!
HE'S HERE ALREADY?!

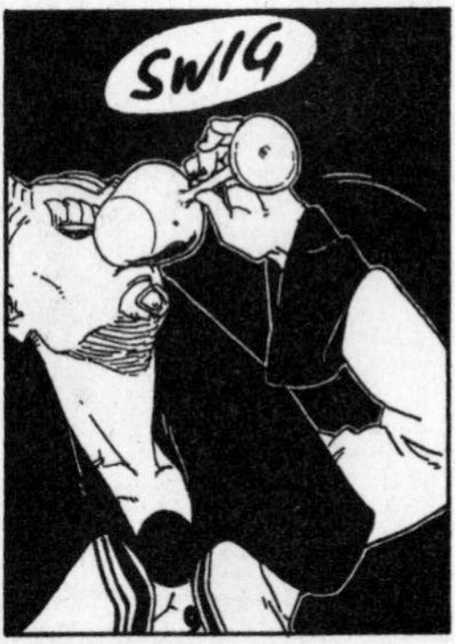
SWIG

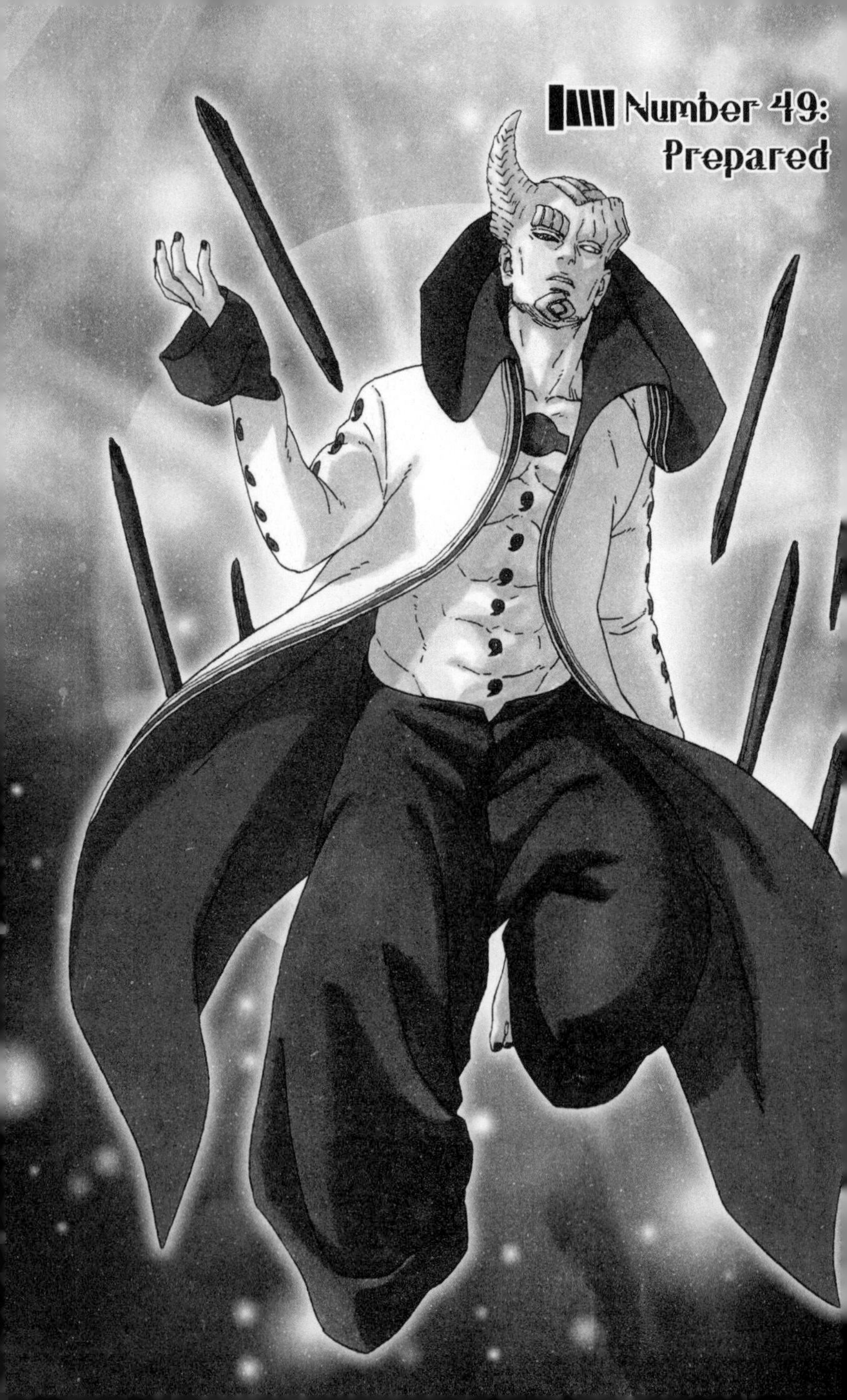
Number 49:
Prepared

BORUTO
-NARUTO NEXT GENERATIONS-

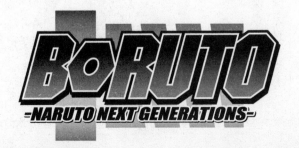

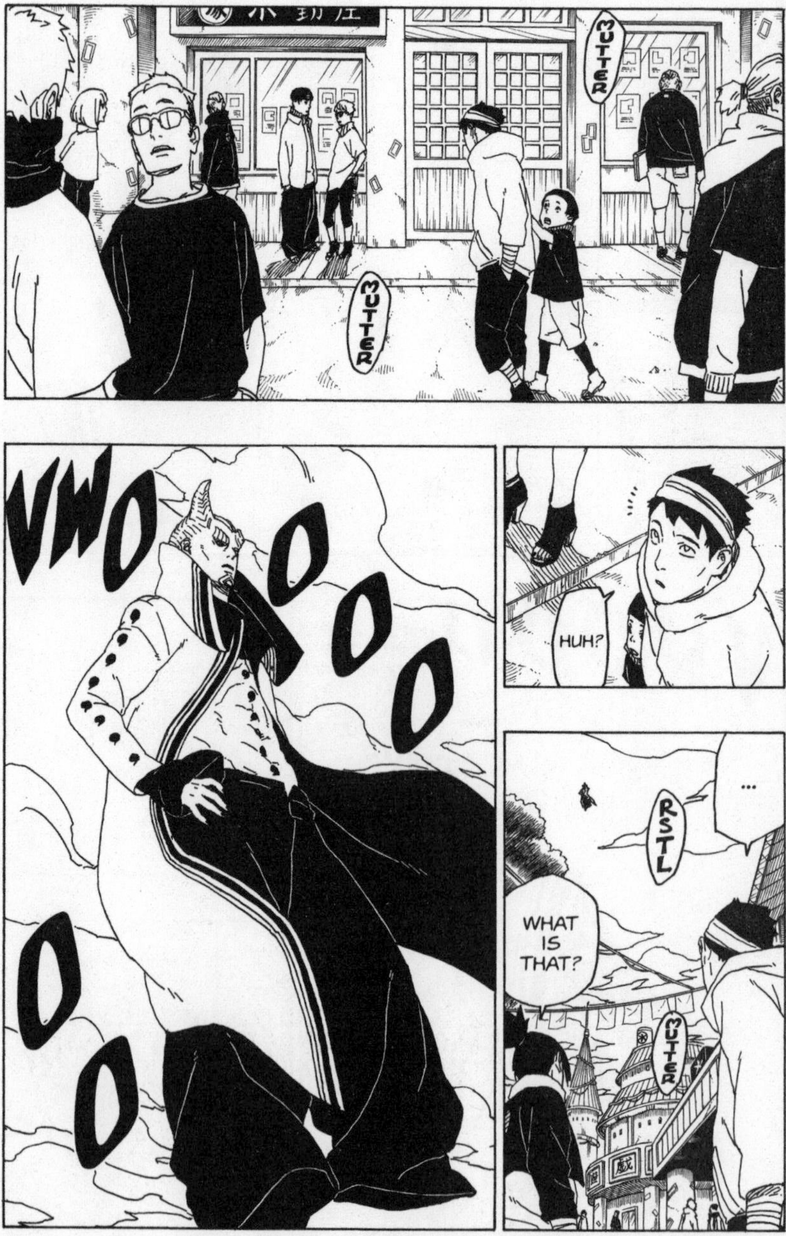

MUTTER
MUTTER
HUH?
...
RSTL
WHAT IS THAT?
MUTTER
VWOOOOOO

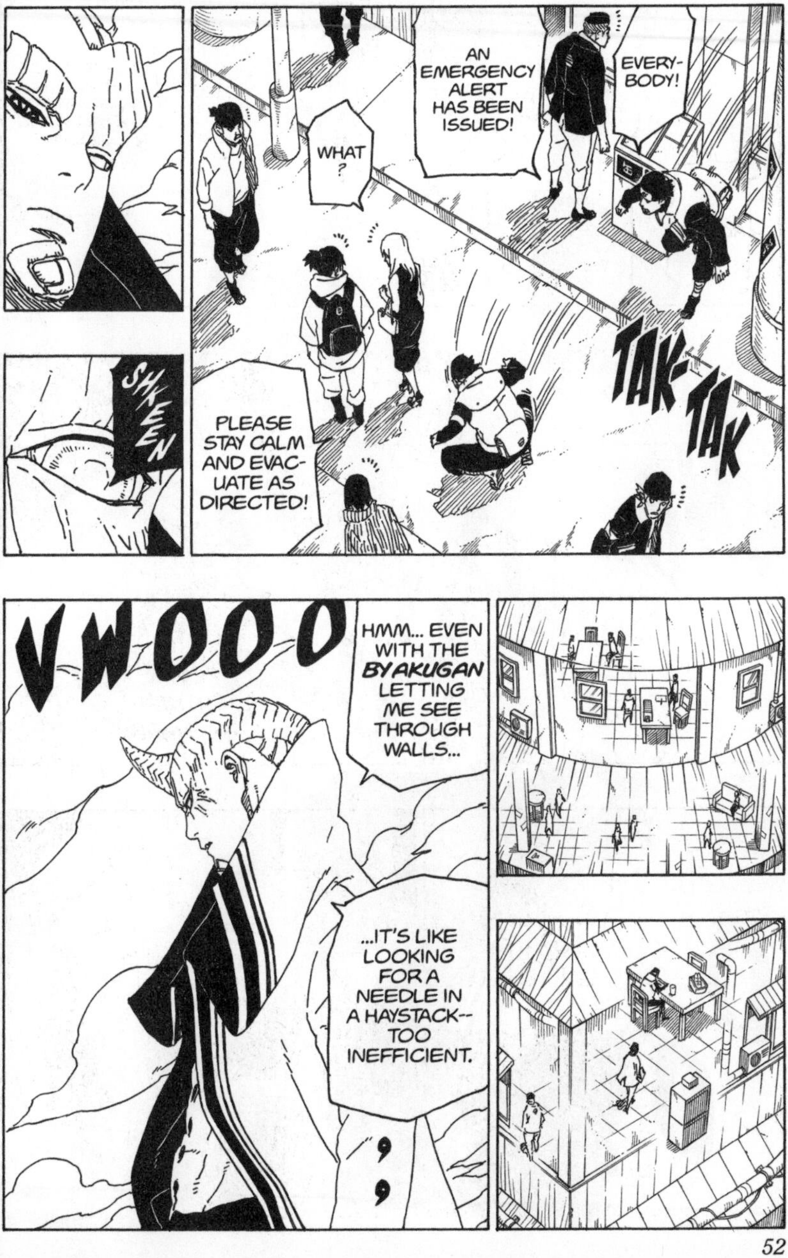
EVERY-BODY!
AN EMERGENCY ALERT HAS BEEN ISSUED!
WHAT?
TAK-TAK
PLEASE STAY CALM AND EVAC-UATE AS DIRECTED!
SHKEEN
HMM... EVEN WITH THE **BYAKUGAN** LETTING ME SEE THROUGH WALLS...
...IT'S LIKE LOOKING FOR A NEEDLE IN A HAYSTACK--TOO INEFFICIENT.
VWOOO

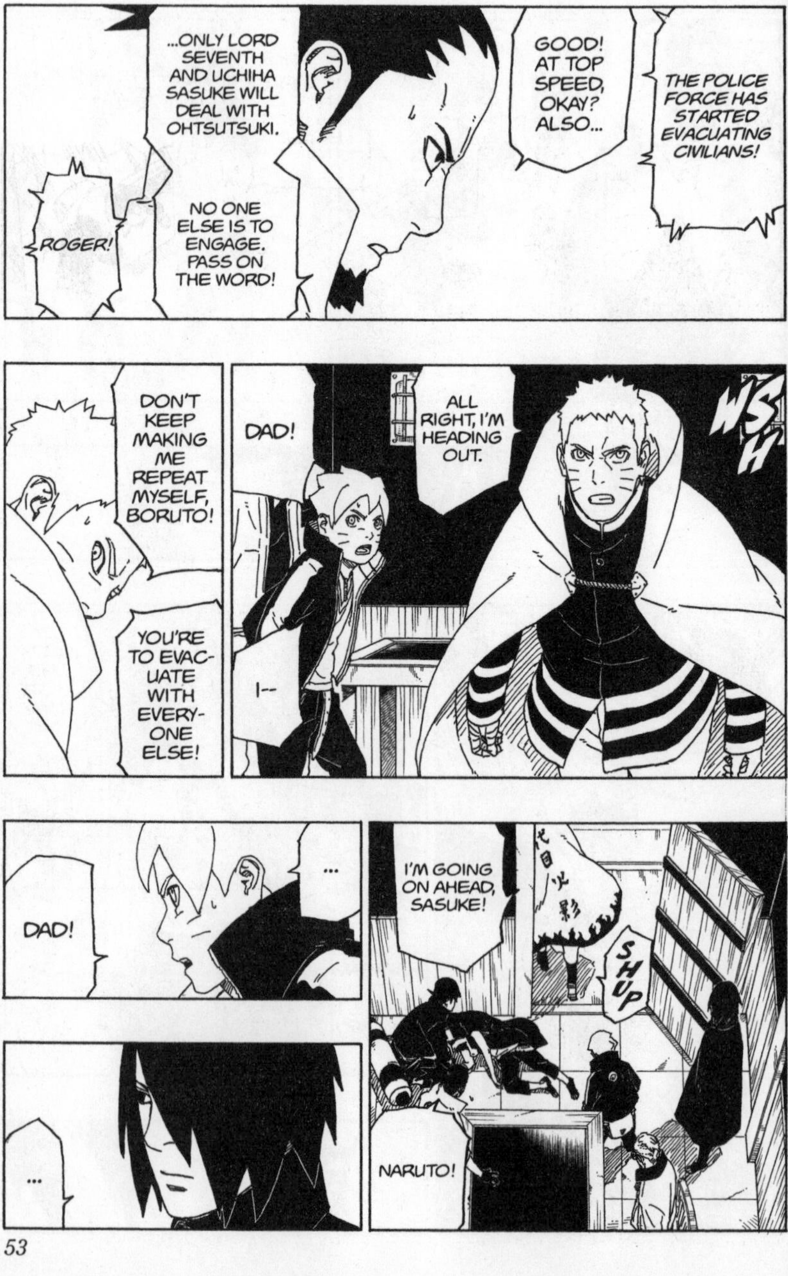
THE POLICE FORCE HAS STARTED EVACUATING CIVILIANS!
GOOD! AT TOP SPEED, OKAY? ALSO...
...ONLY LORD SEVENTH AND UCHIHA SASUKE WILL DEAL WITH OHTSUTSUKI.
NO ONE ELSE IS TO ENGAGE. PASS ON THE WORD!
ROGER!
WSH
ALL RIGHT, I'M HEADING OUT.
DAD!
I--
DON'T KEEP MAKING ME REPEAT MYSELF, BORUTO!
YOU'RE TO EVACUATE WITH EVERYONE ELSE!
I'M GOING ON AHEAD, SASUKE!
代目火影
SHUP
NARUTO!
...
DAD!
...

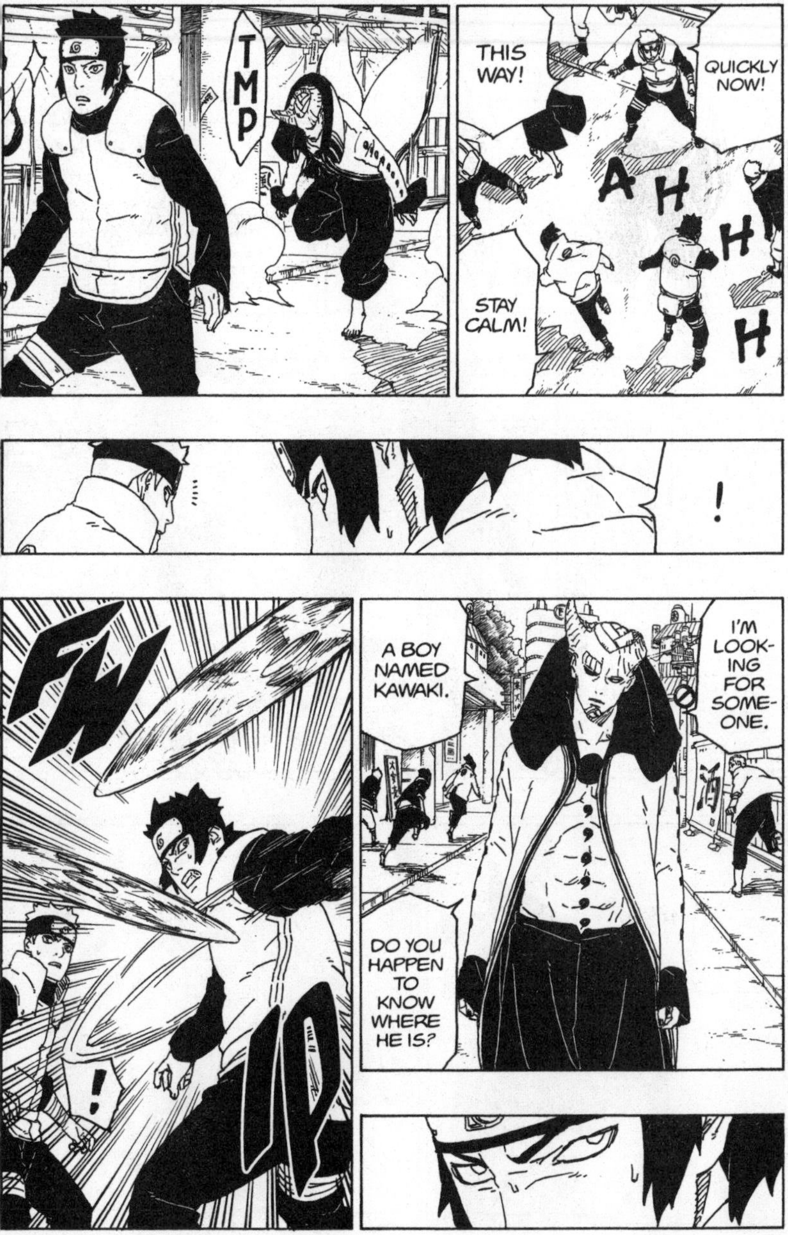
QUICKLY NOW!
THIS WAY!
AHHHH
STAY CALM!
TMP
!
I'M LOOKING FOR SOMEONE.
A BOY NAMED KAWAKI.
DO YOU HAPPEN TO KNOW WHERE HE IS?
FW
!

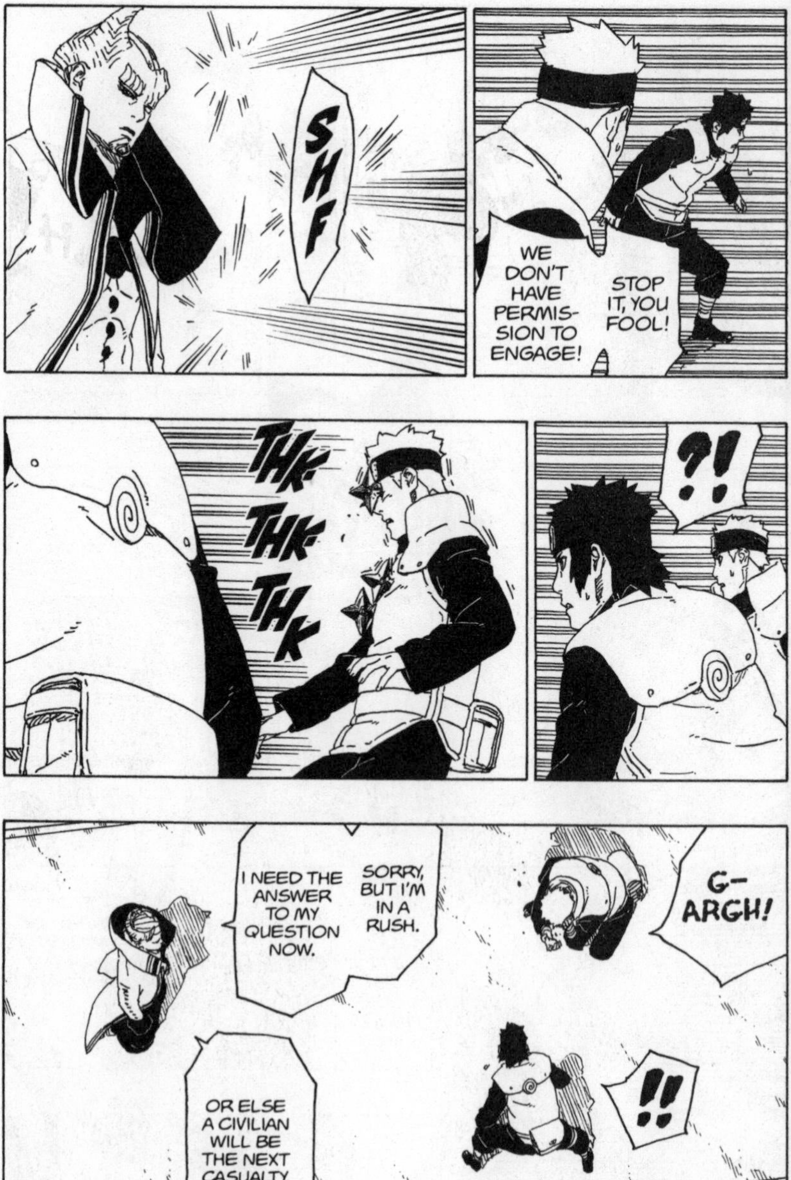
STOP IT, YOU FOOL!
WE DON'T HAVE PERMISSION TO ENGAGE!
SHF
?!!
THK THK THK
G-ARGH!
SORRY, BUT I'M IN A RUSH.
I NEED THE ANSWER TO MY QUESTION NOW.
!!
OR ELSE A CIVILIAN WILL BE THE NEXT CASUALTY.

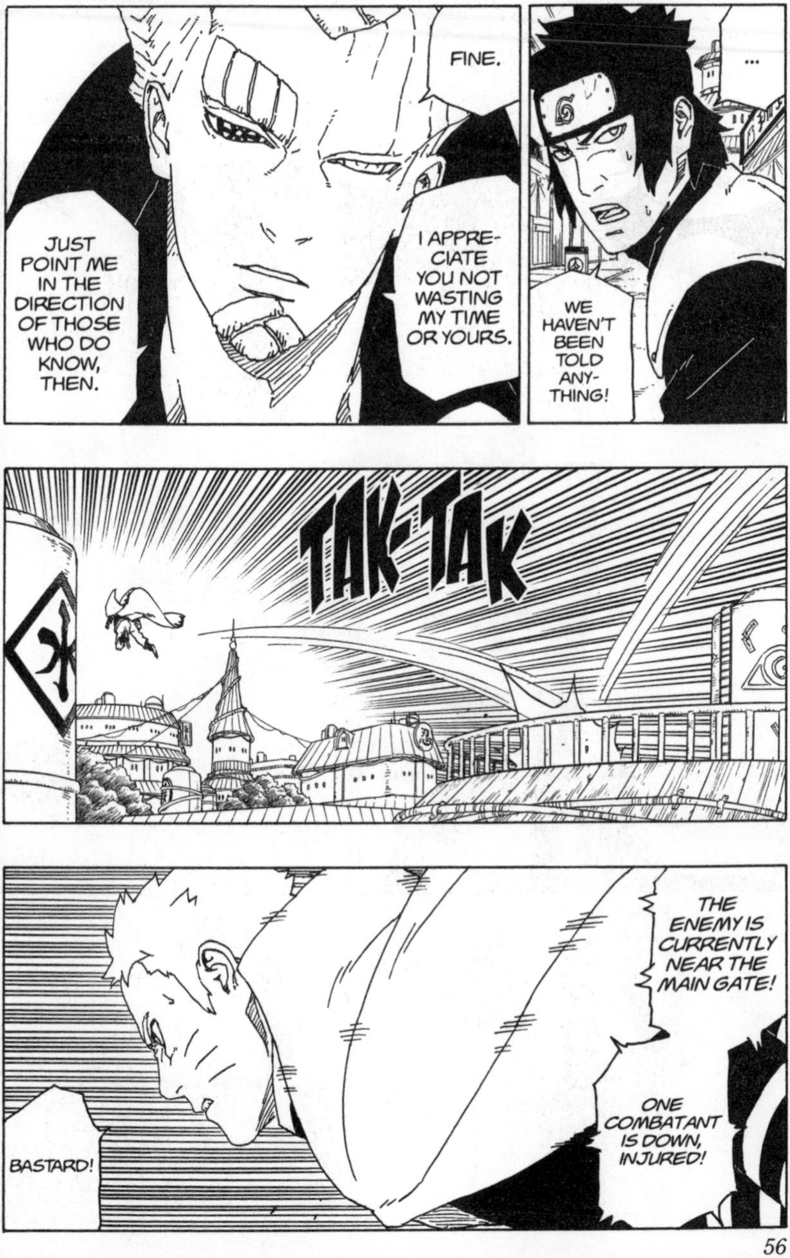
...
WE HAVEN'T BEEN TOLD ANYTHING!
FINE.
I APPRECIATE YOU NOT WASTING MY TIME OR YOURS.
JUST POINT ME IN THE DIRECTION OF THOSE WHO DO KNOW, THEN.
TAK-TAK
THE ENEMY IS CURRENTLY NEAR THE MAIN GATE!
ONE COMBATANT IS DOWN, INJURED!
BASTARD!

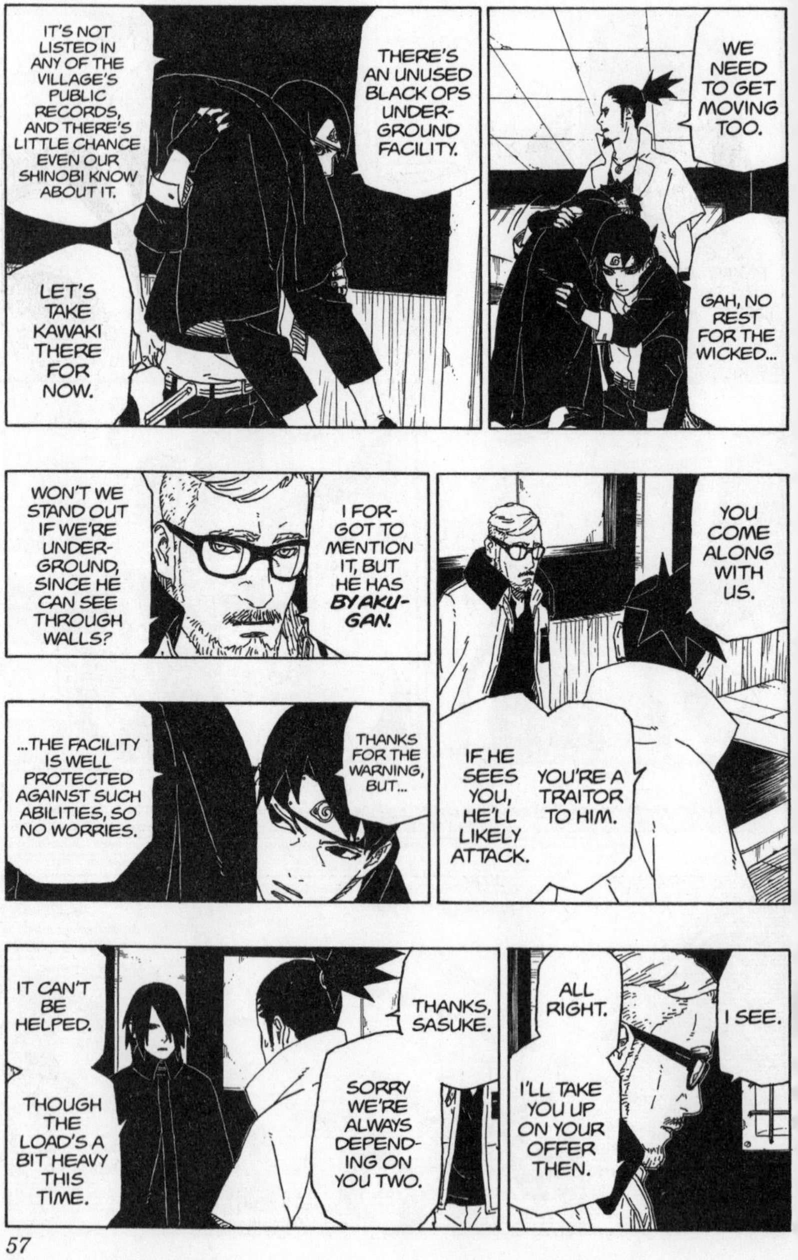
WE NEED TO GET MOVING TOO.
GAH, NO REST FOR THE WICKED...
THERE'S AN UNUSED BLACK OPS UNDER-GROUND FACILITY.
IT'S NOT LISTED IN ANY OF THE VILLAGE'S PUBLIC RECORDS, AND THERE'S LITTLE CHANCE EVEN OUR SHINOBI KNOW ABOUT IT.
LET'S TAKE KAWAKI THERE FOR NOW.
YOU COME ALONG WITH US.
YOU'RE A TRAITOR TO HIM.
IF HE SEES YOU, HE'LL LIKELY ATTACK.
I FOR-GOT TO MENTION IT, BUT HE HAS ***BYAKU-GAN.***
WON'T WE STAND OUT IF WE'RE UNDER-GROUND, SINCE HE CAN SEE THROUGH WALLS?
THANKS FOR THE WARNING, BUT...
...THE FACILITY IS WELL PROTECTED AGAINST SUCH ABILITIES, SO NO WORRIES.
I SEE.
ALL RIGHT.
I'LL TAKE YOU UP ON YOUR OFFER THEN.
THANKS, SASUKE.
SORRY WE'RE ALWAYS DEPEND-ING ON YOU TWO.
IT CAN'T BE HELPED.
THOUGH THE LOAD'S A BIT HEAVY THIS TIME.

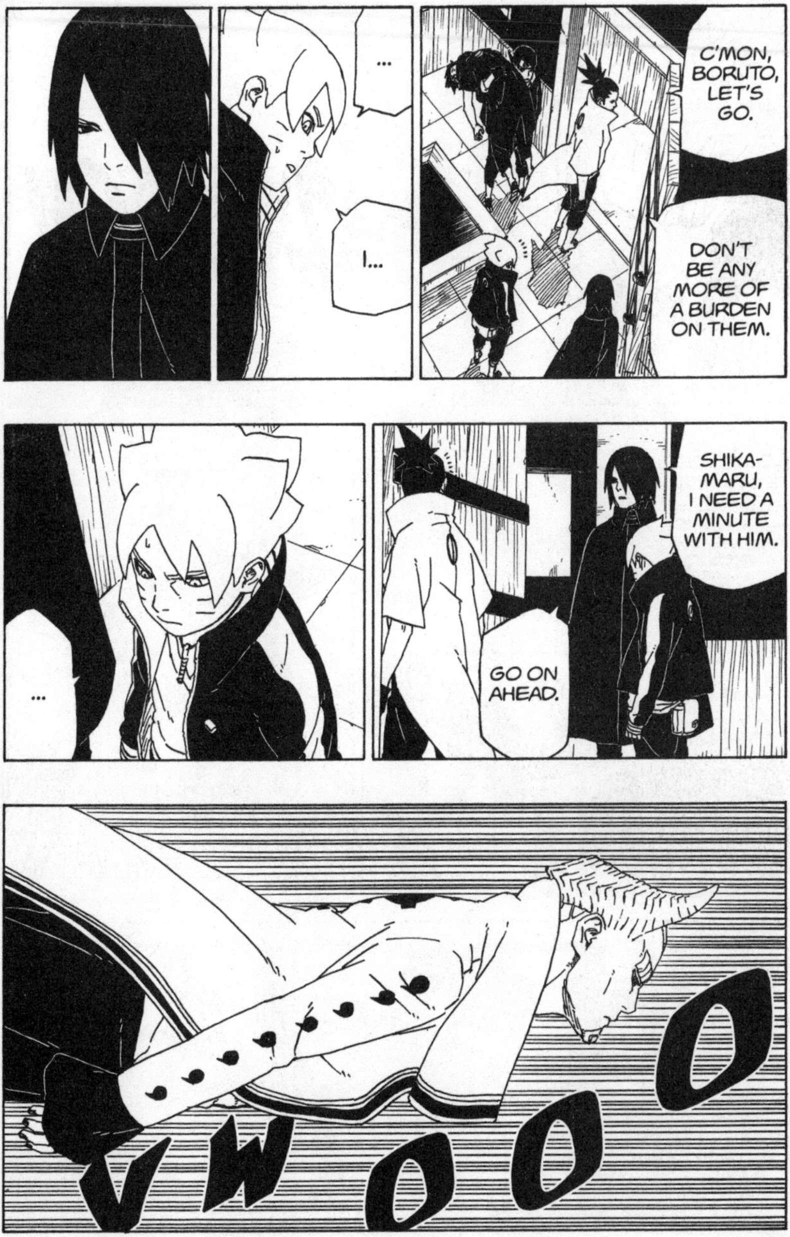
C'MON, BORUTO, LET'S GO.
DON'T BE ANY MORE OF A BURDEN ON THEM.
...
I...
SHIKA-MARU, I NEED A MINUTE WITH HIM.
GO ON AHEAD.
...
VWOOOO

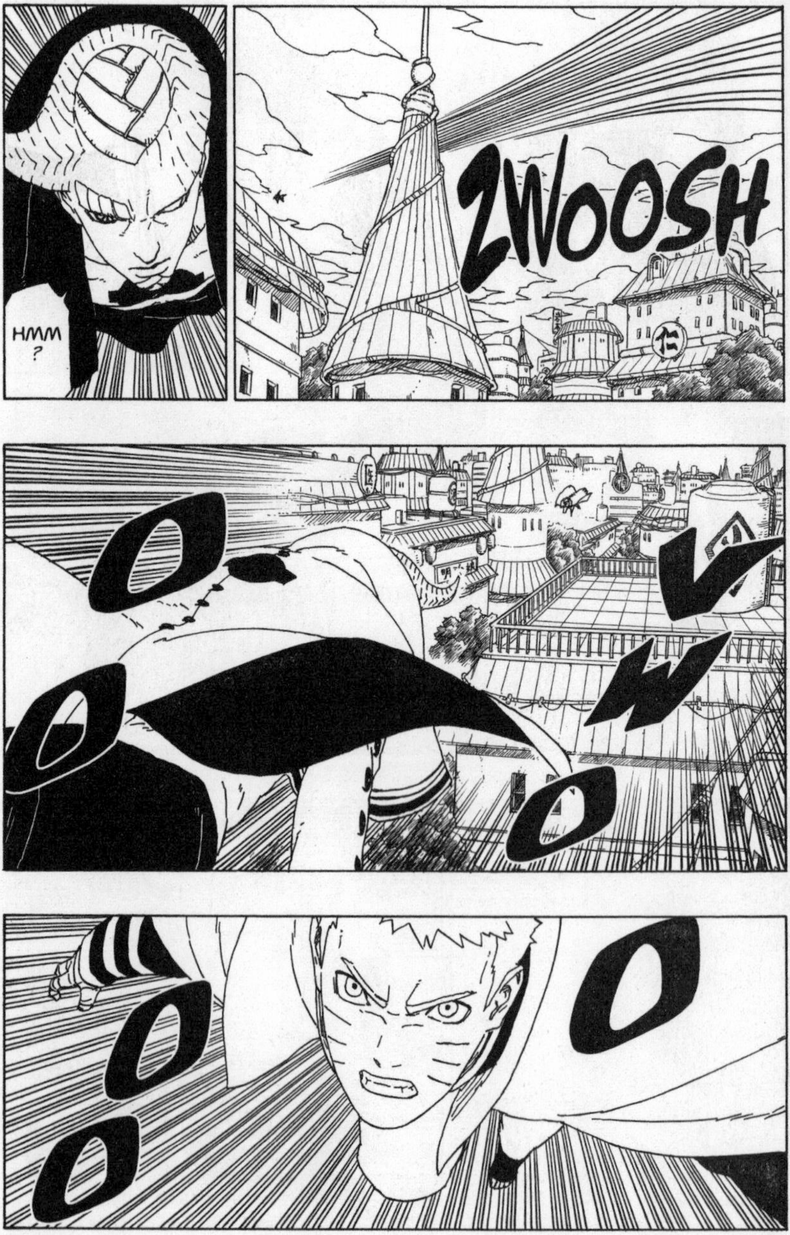
ZWOOSH
HMM ?
VWOOO
OOOO

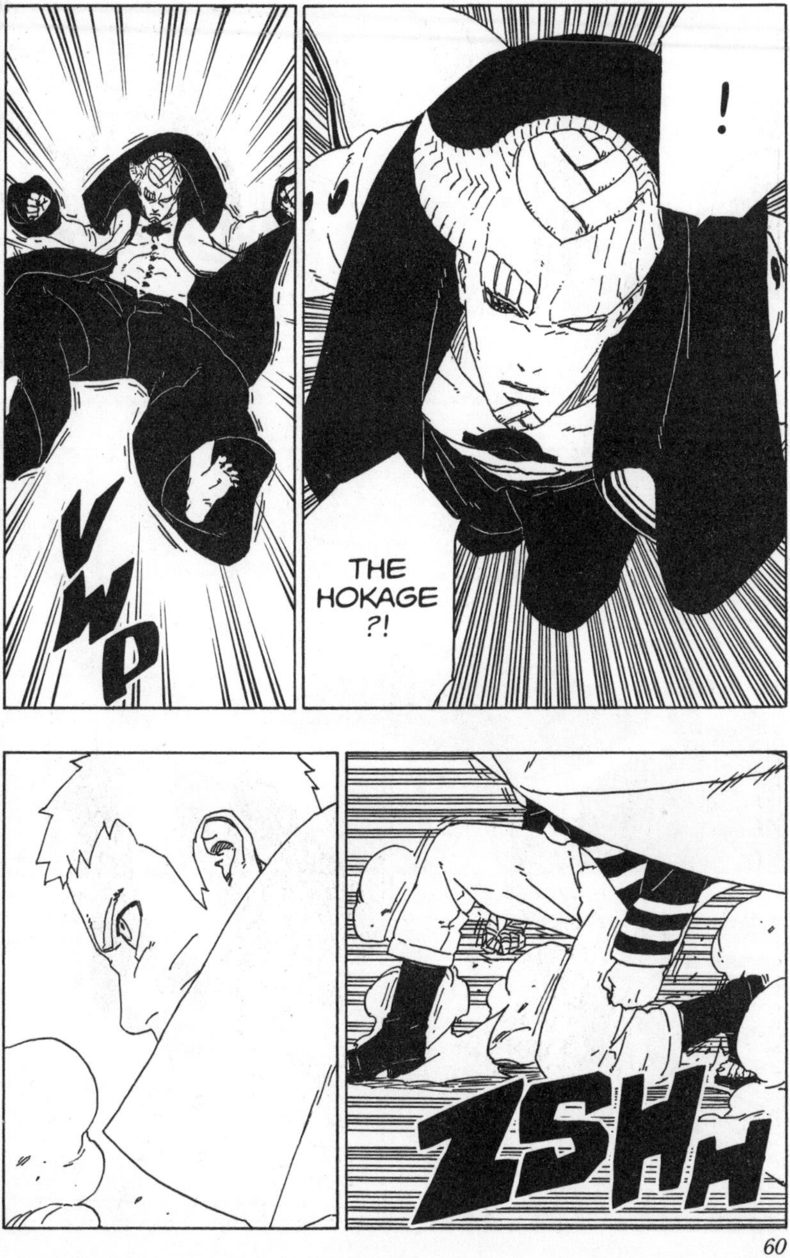
!
THE HOKAGE ?!
VWP
ZSHH

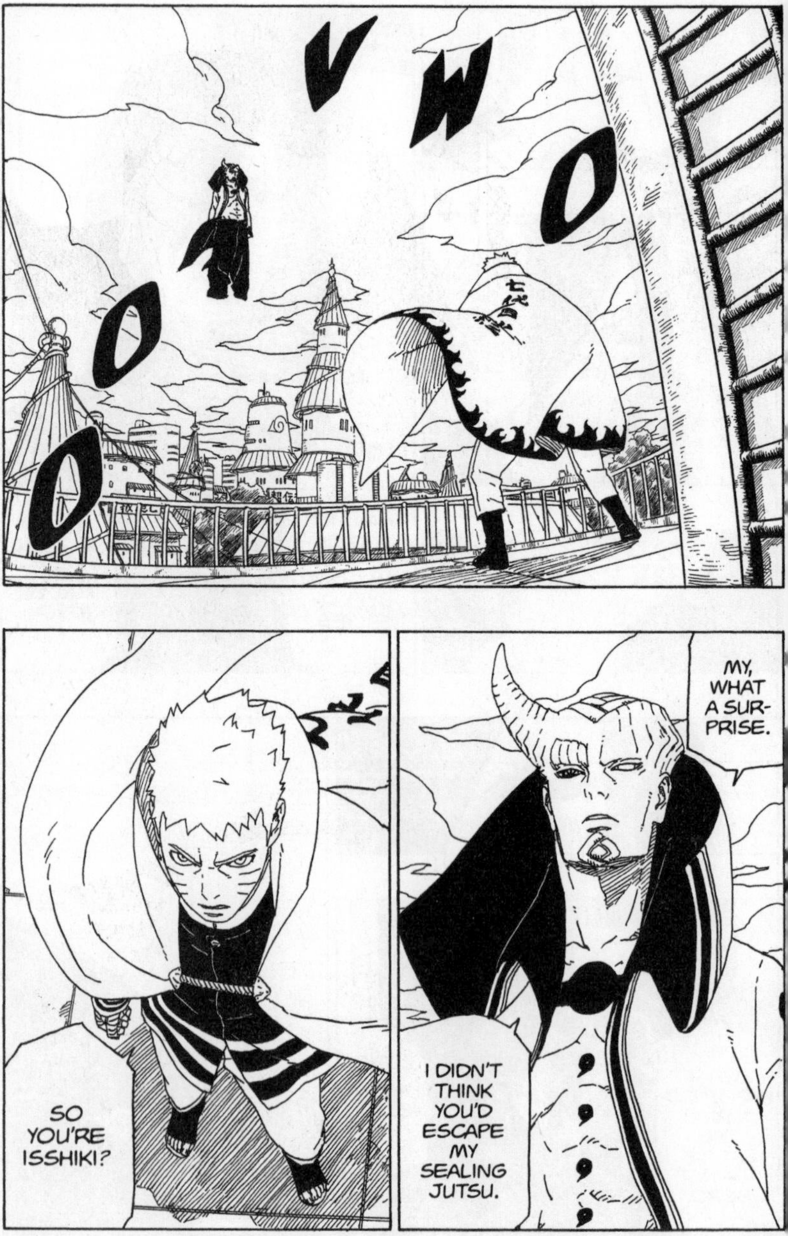
VWOOO
MY, WHAT A SURPRISE.
I DIDN'T THINK YOU'D ESCAPE MY SEALING JUTSU.
SO YOU'RE ISSHIKI?

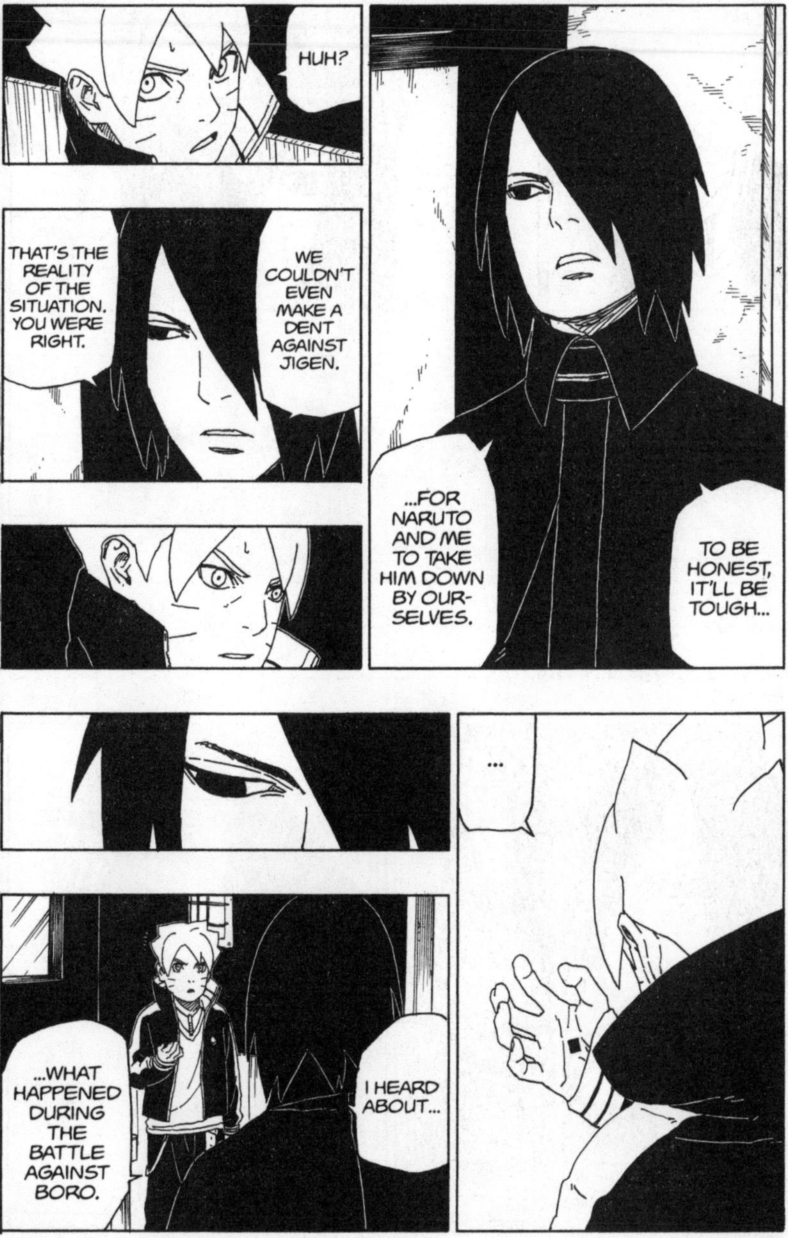

TO BE HONEST, IT'LL BE TOUGH...
...FOR NARUTO AND ME TO TAKE HIM DOWN BY OUR-SELVES.
HUH?
WE COULDN'T EVEN MAKE A DENT AGAINST JIGEN.
THAT'S THE REALITY OF THE SITUATION. YOU WERE RIGHT.
...
I HEARD ABOUT...
...WHAT HAPPENED DURING THE BATTLE AGAINST BORO.

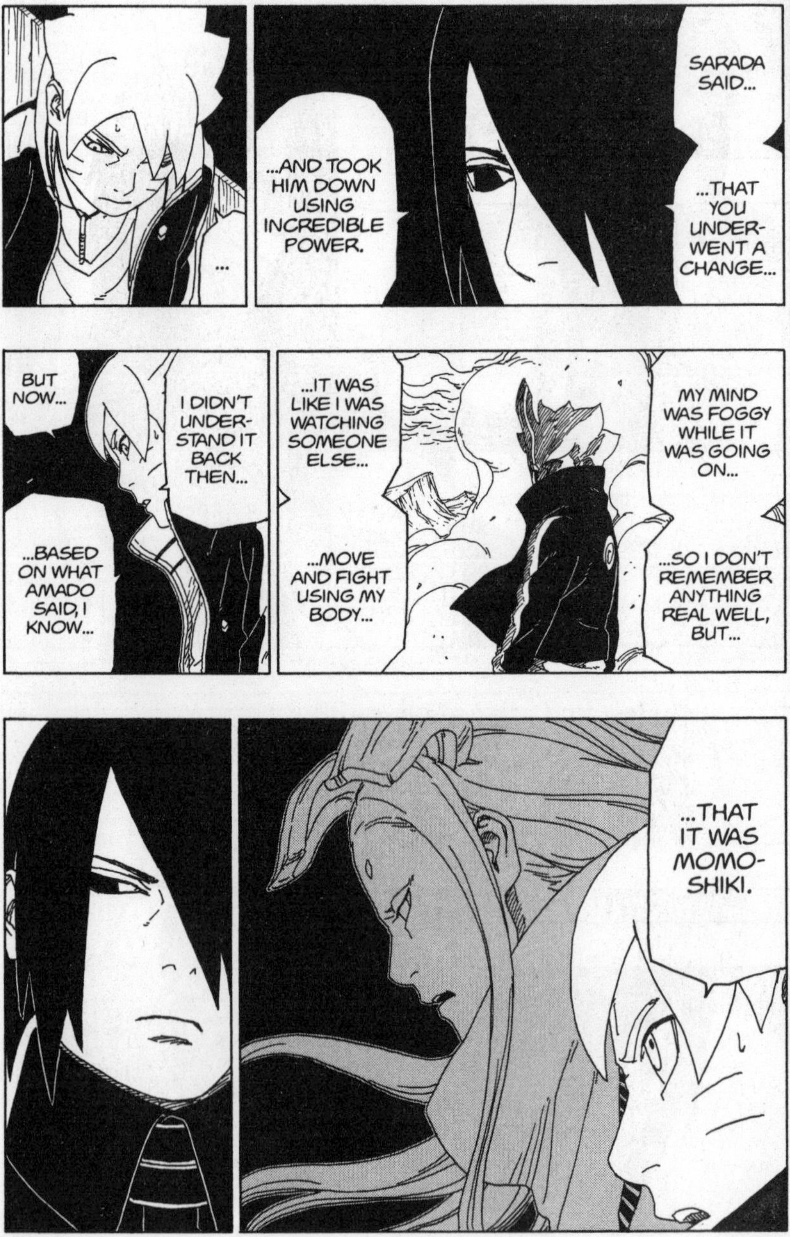
SARADA SAID...
...THAT YOU UNDER-WENT A CHANGE...
...AND TOOK HIM DOWN USING INCREDIBLE POWER.
...
MY MIND WAS FOGGY WHILE IT WAS GOING ON...
...SO I DON'T REMEMBER ANYTHING REAL WELL, BUT...
...IT WAS LIKE I WAS WATCHING SOMEONE ELSE...
...MOVE AND FIGHT USING MY BODY...
I DIDN'T UNDER-STAND IT BACK THEN...
BUT NOW...
...BASED ON WHAT AMADO SAID, I KNOW...
...THAT IT WAS MOMO-SHIKI.

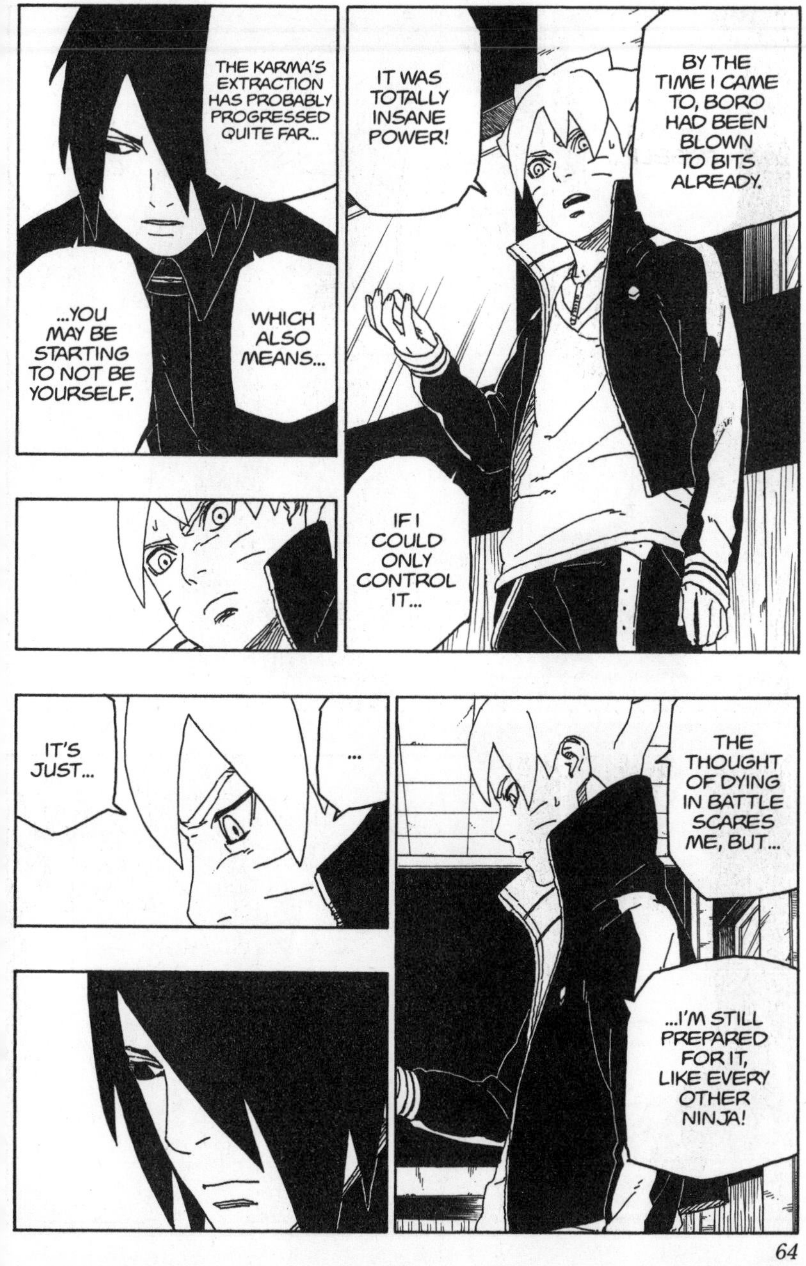
BY THE TIME I CAME TO, BORO HAD BEEN BLOWN TO BITS ALREADY.
IT WAS TOTALLY INSANE POWER!
IF I COULD ONLY CONTROL IT...
THE KARMA'S EXTRACTION HAS PROBABLY PROGRESSED QUITE FAR...
WHICH ALSO MEANS...
...YOU MAY BE STARTING TO NOT BE YOURSELF.
THE THOUGHT OF DYING IN BATTLE SCARES ME, BUT...
...I'M STILL PREPARED FOR IT, LIKE EVERY OTHER NINJA!
...
IT'S JUST...

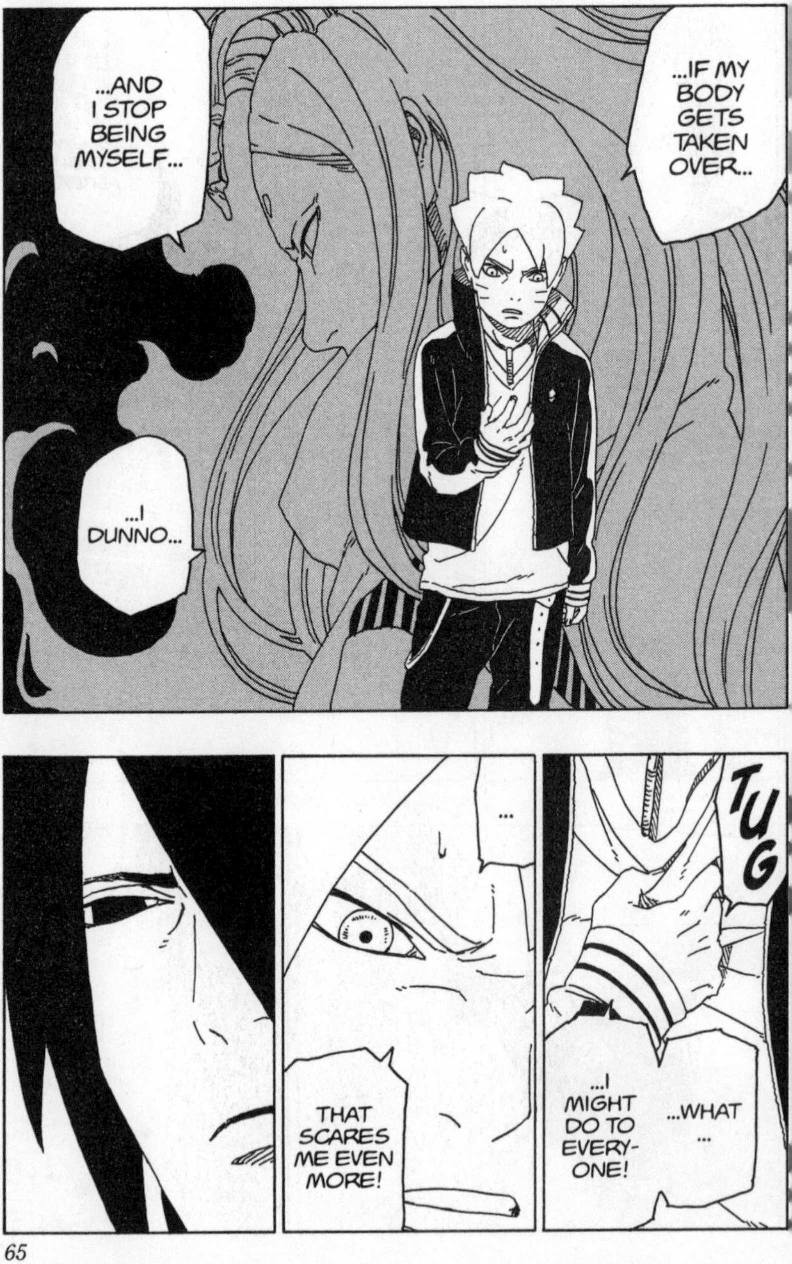
...IF MY BODY GETS TAKEN OVER...
...AND I STOP BEING MYSELF...
...I DUNNO...
TUG
...WHAT ...
...I MIGHT DO TO EVERY-ONE!
...
THAT SCARES ME EVEN MORE!

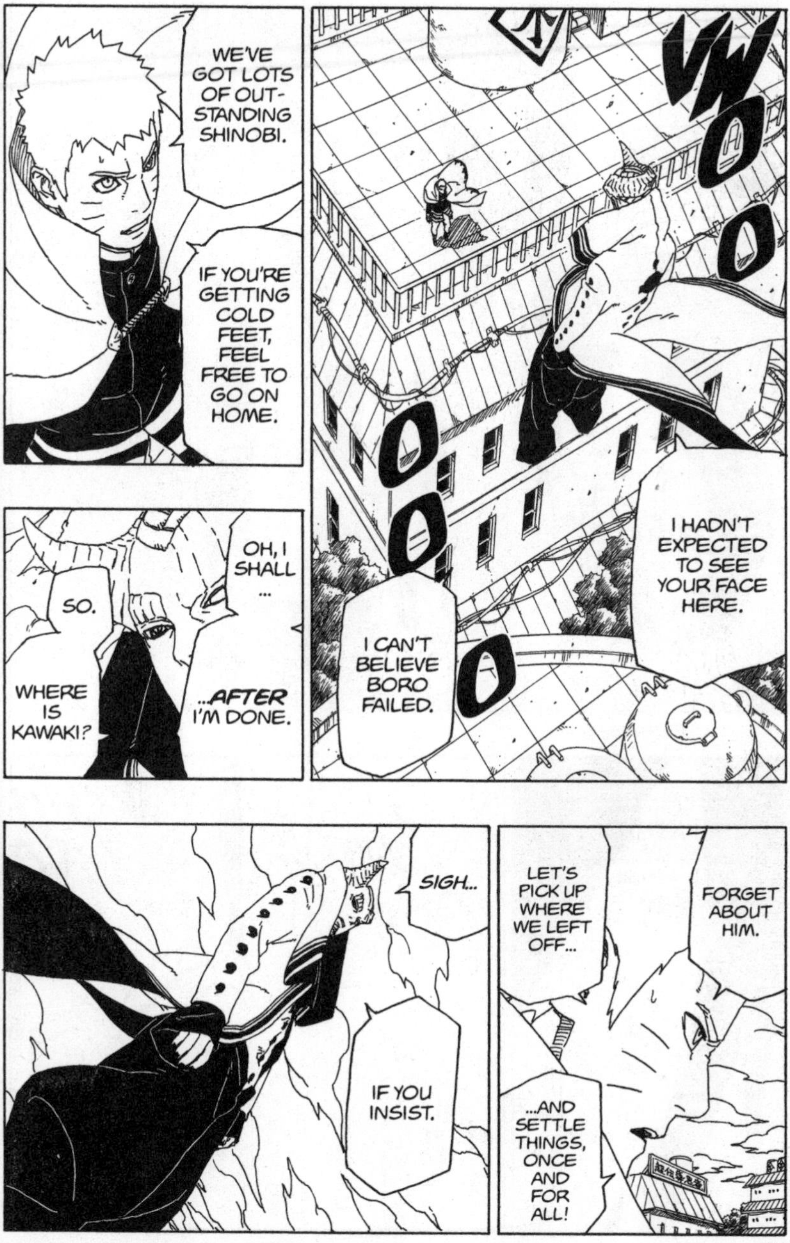
VWOOOOOOO
I HADN'T EXPECTED TO SEE YOUR FACE HERE.
I CAN'T BELIEVE BORO FAILED.
WE'VE GOT LOTS OF OUT-STANDING SHINOBI.
IF YOU'RE GETTING COLD FEET, FEEL FREE TO GO ON HOME.
OH, I SHALL ...
...*AFTER* I'M DONE.
SO.
WHERE IS KAWAKI?
FORGET ABOUT HIM.
LET'S PICK UP WHERE WE LEFT OFF...
...AND SETTLE THINGS, ONCE AND FOR ALL!
SIGH...
IF YOU INSIST.

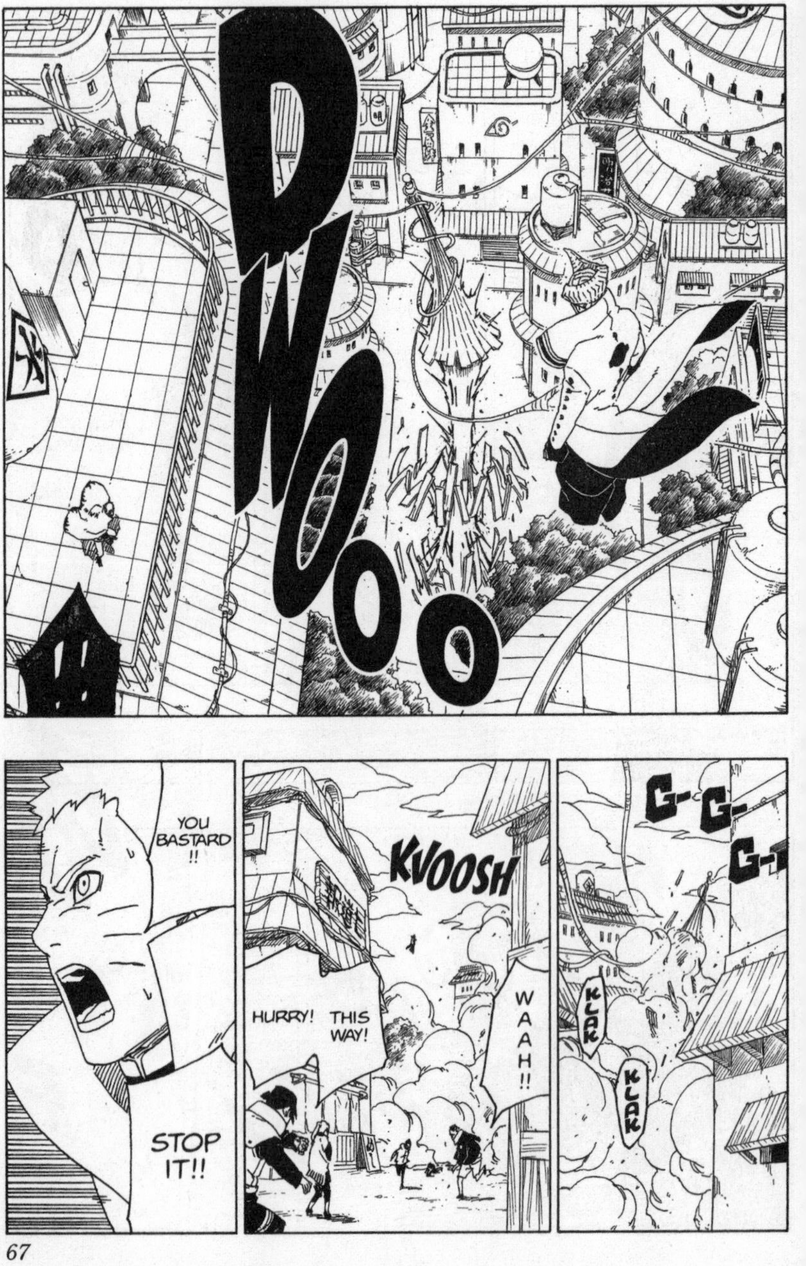
DWOOOO
G-G-G-
KLAK
KLAK
KVOOSH
WAAAH!!
HURRY!
THIS WAY!
YOU BASTARD!!
STOP IT!!

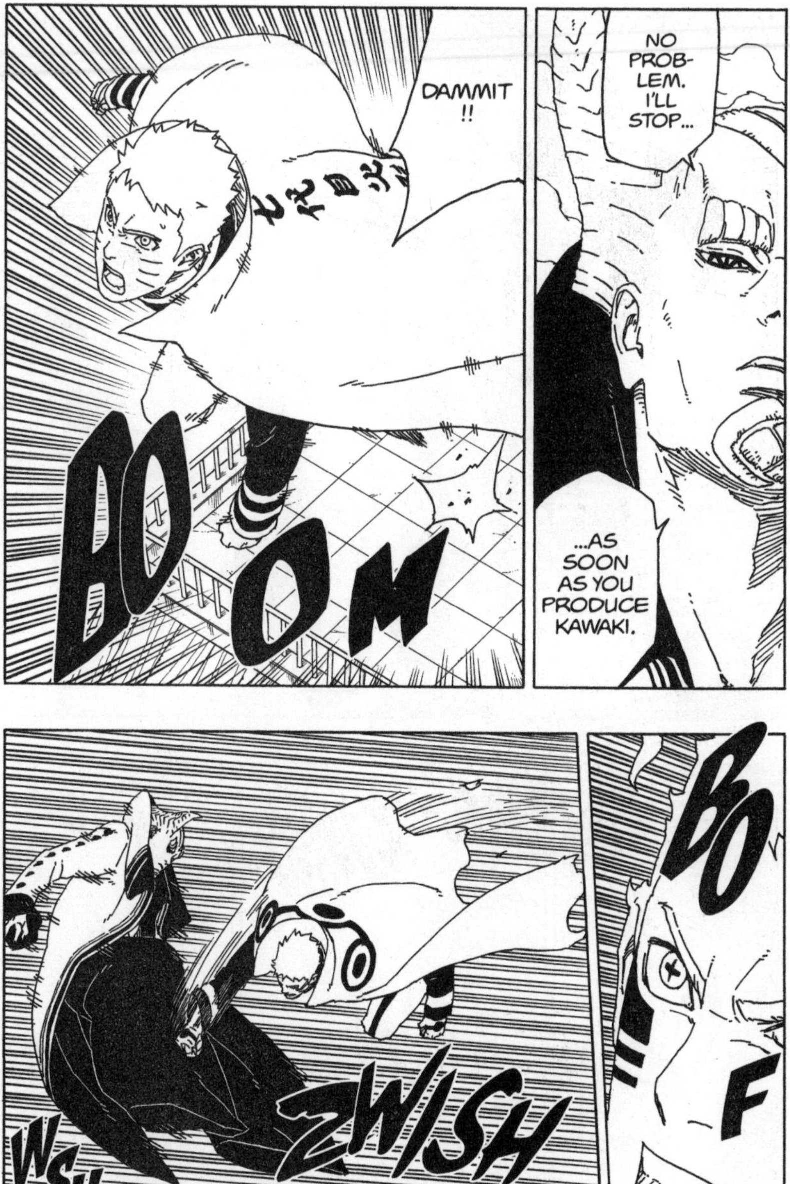
NO PROBLEM. I'LL STOP...
...AS SOON AS YOU PRODUCE KAWAKI.
DAMMIT!!
BOOM
BO
F
ZWISH
WSH

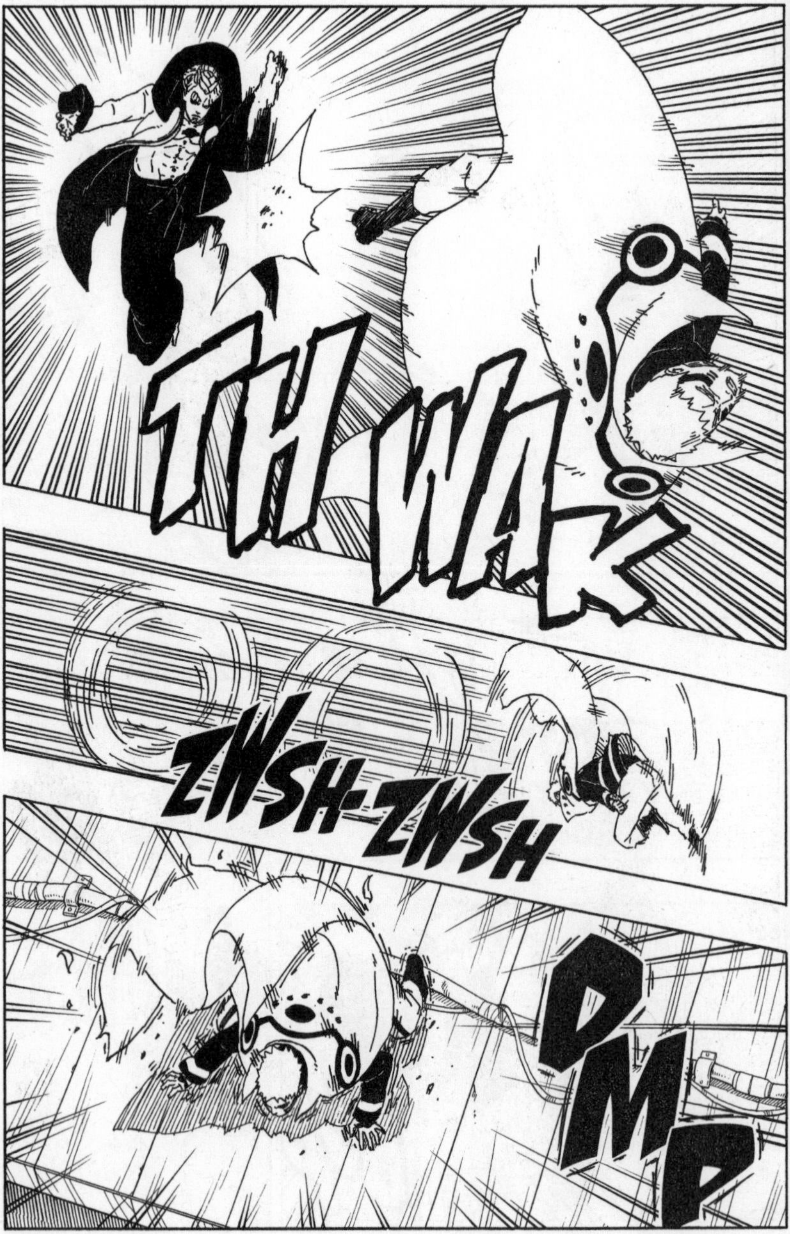
THWAK
ZWSH-ZWSH
DMP

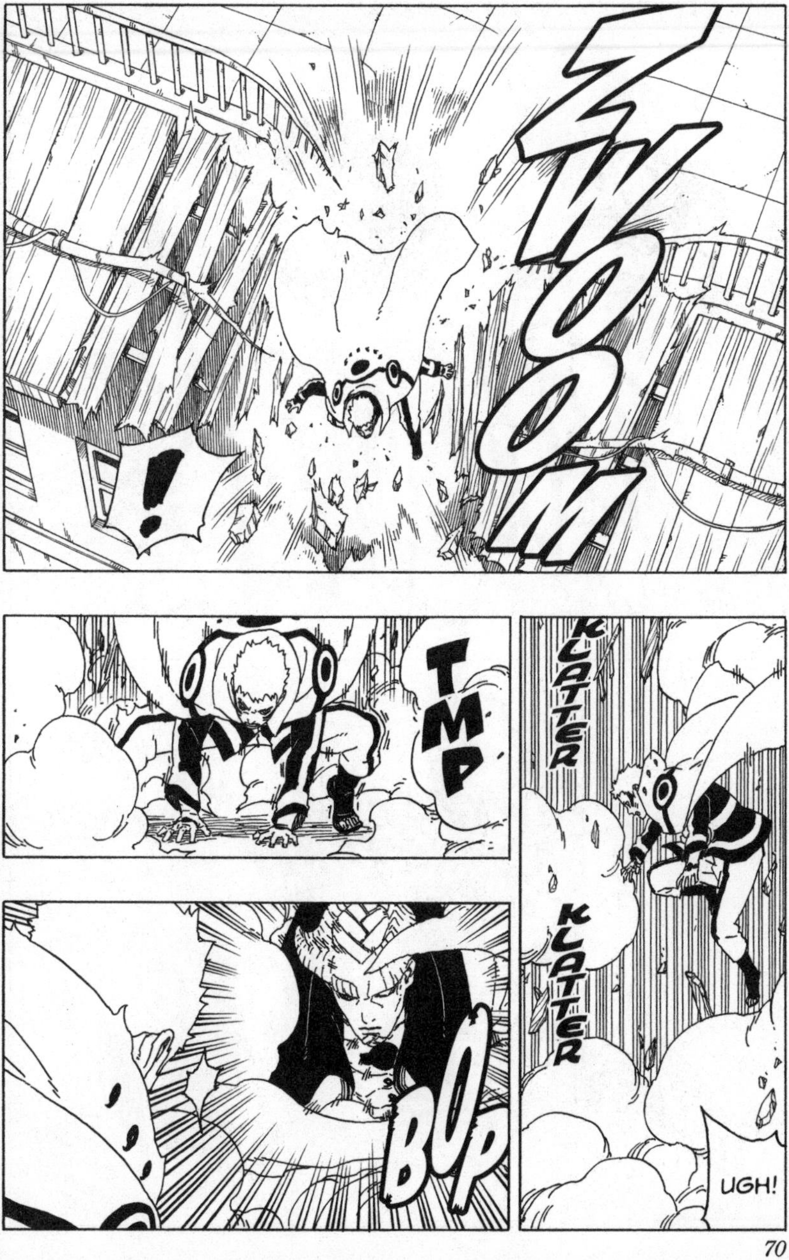
ZWOOOM
!
KLATTER
KLATTER
UGH!
TMP
BOP

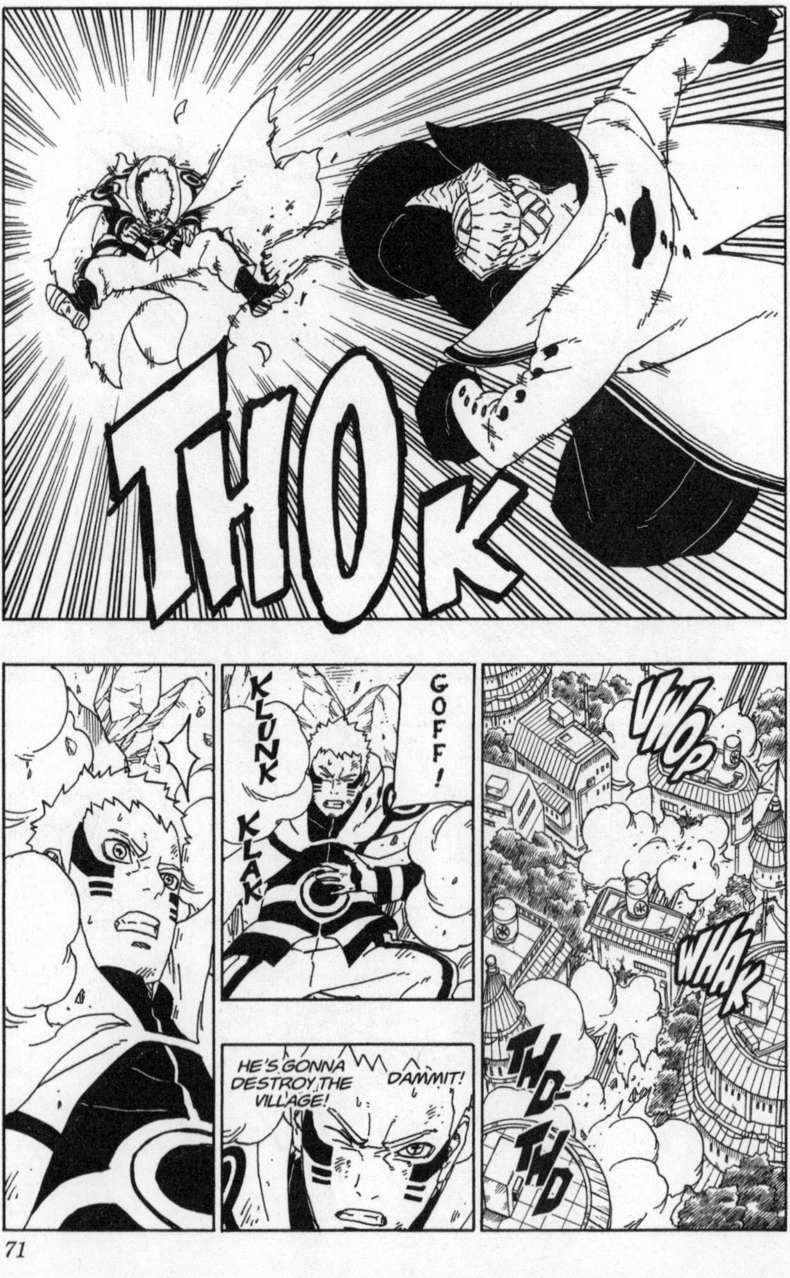
THOK
VWOP
WHAK
THD-THD
GOFF!
KLUNK
KLAK
DAMMIT!
HE'S GONNA DESTROY THE VILLAGE!

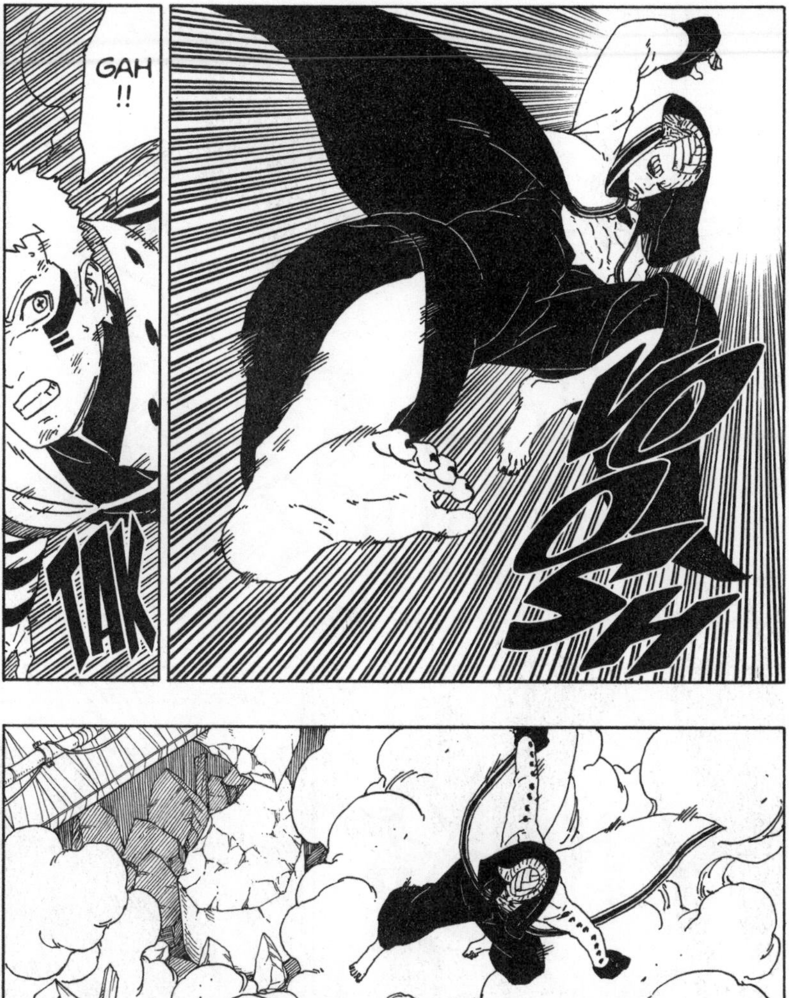
WOOSH
GAH!!
TAK
TAT

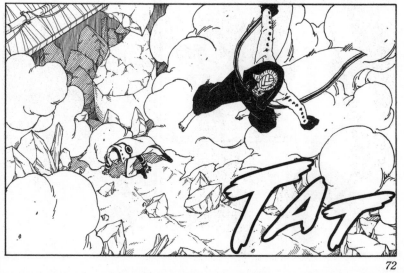

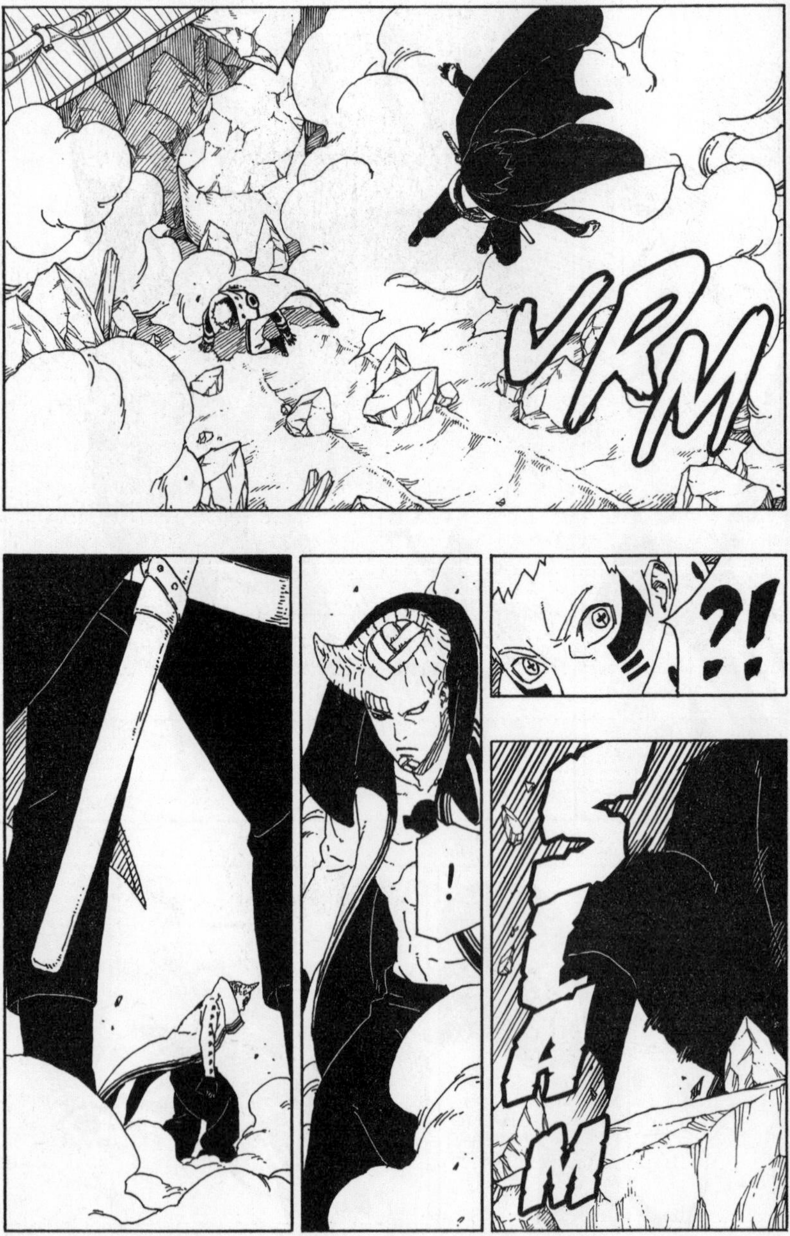
VRM
?!
SLAM
!

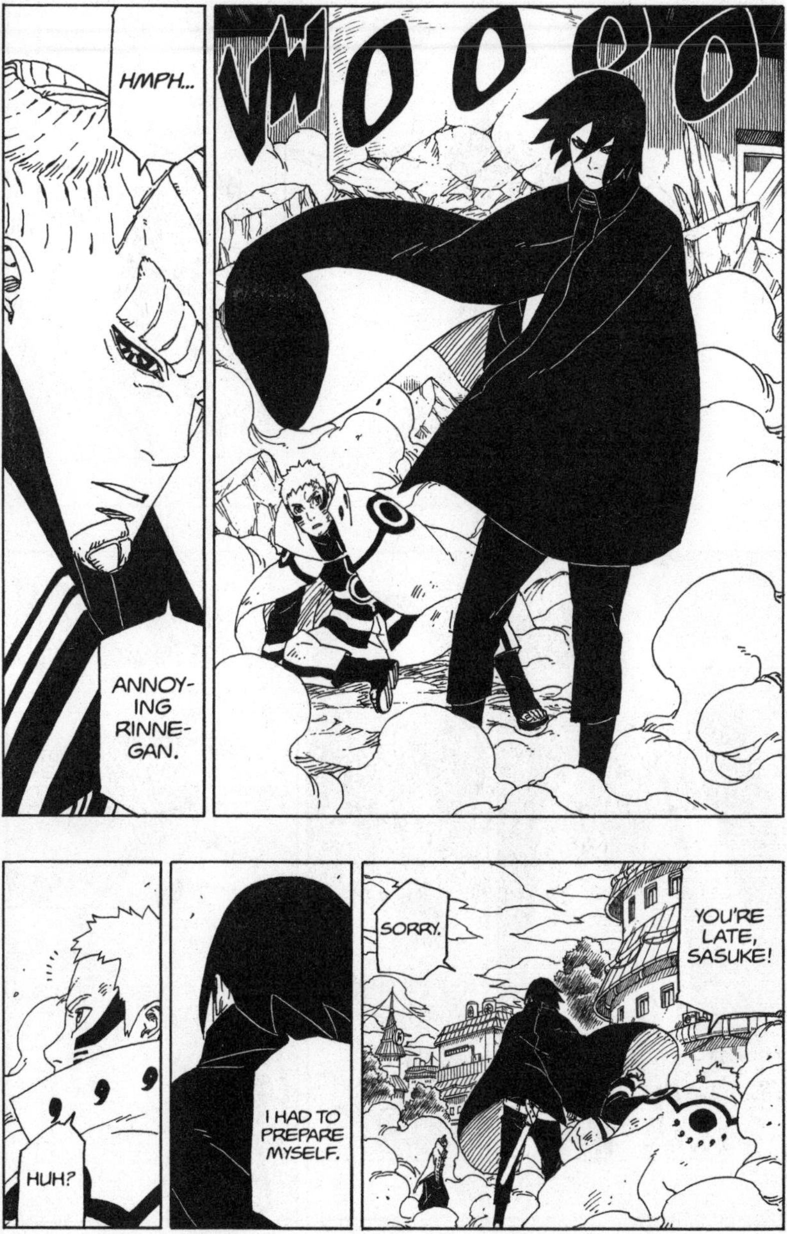
VWOOOO
HMPH...
ANNOY-ING RINNE-GAN.
YOU'RE LATE, SASUKE!
SORRY.
I HAD TO PREPARE MYSELF.
HUH?

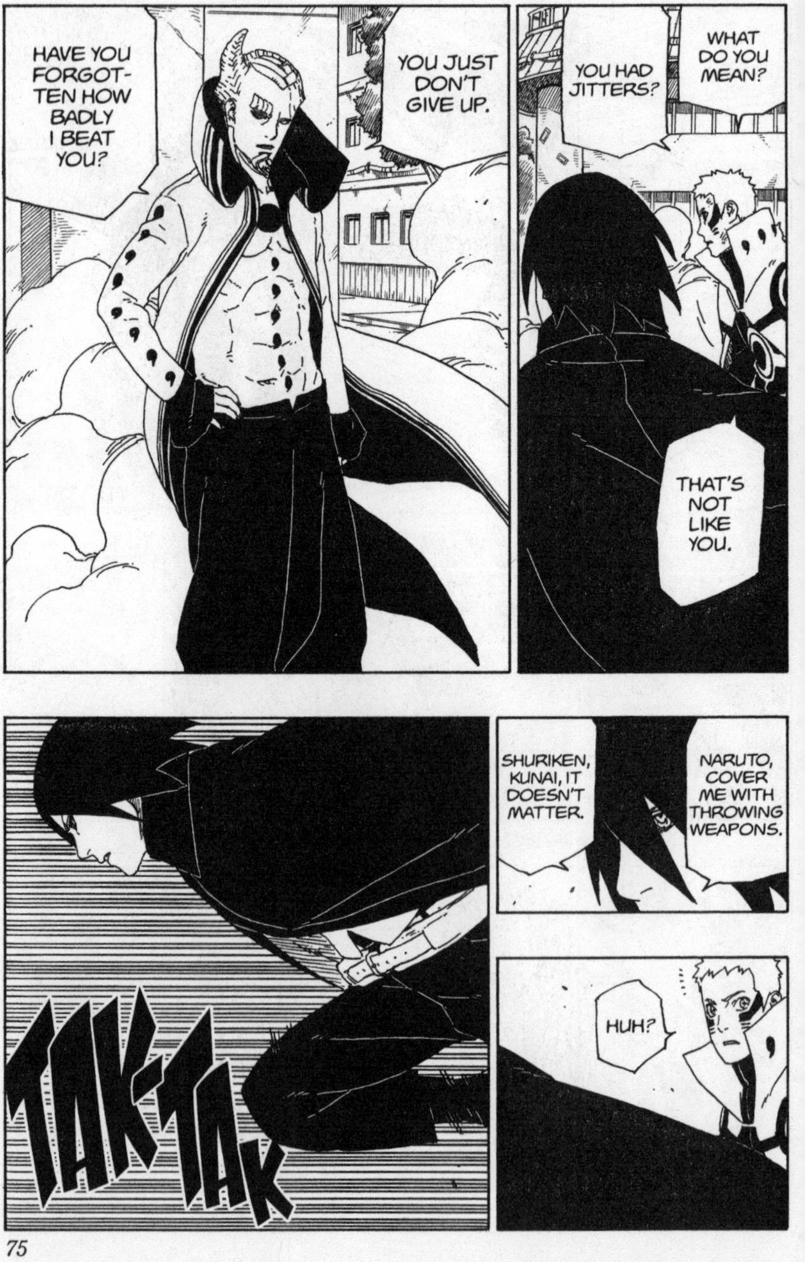
WHAT DO YOU MEAN?
YOU HAD JITTERS?
THAT'S NOT LIKE YOU.
YOU JUST DON'T GIVE UP.
HAVE YOU FORGOTTEN HOW BADLY I BEAT YOU?
NARUTO, COVER ME WITH THROWING WEAPONS.
SHURIKEN, KUNAI, IT DOESN'T MATTER.
HUH?
TAK-TAK

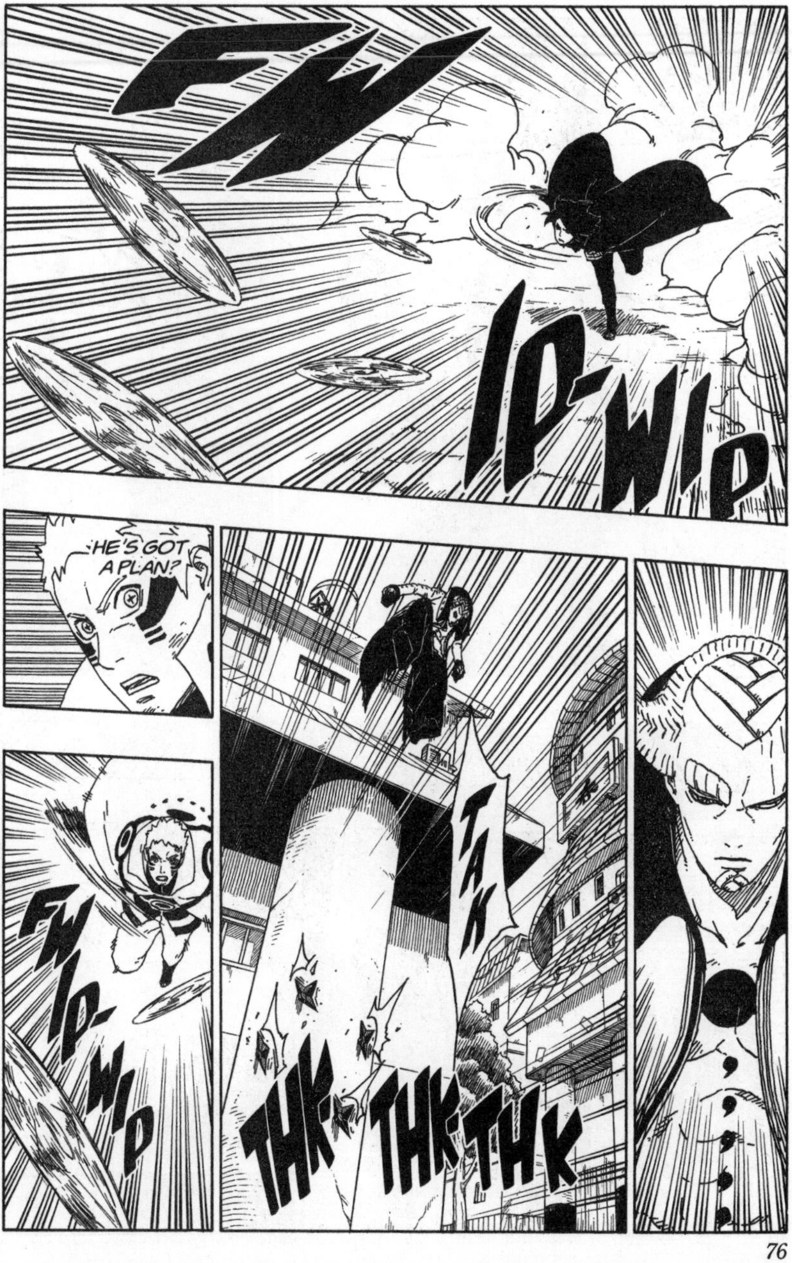
FWIP-WIP
TAK
THK-THK-THK
HE'S GOT A PLAN?
FWIP-WIP

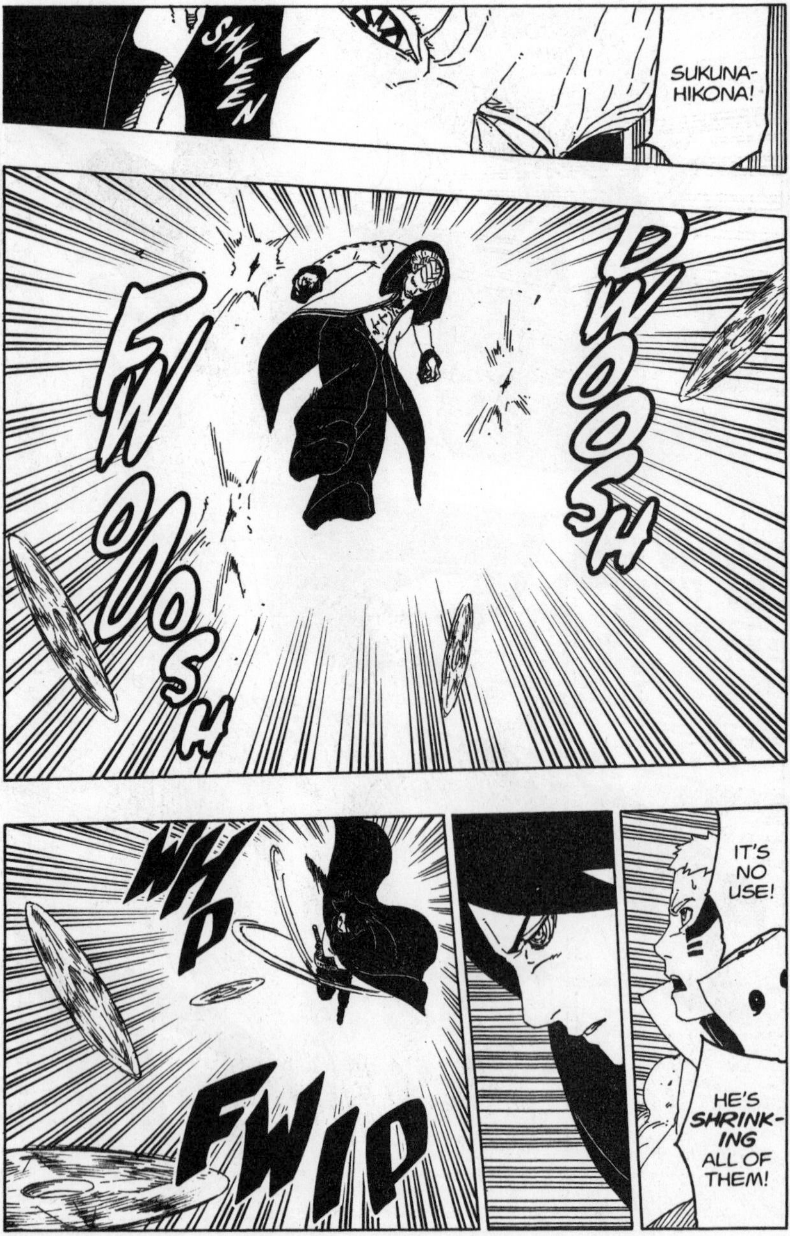
SUKUNA-HIKONA!
SHKEEN
DWOOOSH
FWOOOOSH
IT'S NO USE!
HE'S **SHRINKING** ALL OF THEM!
WHP
FWIP

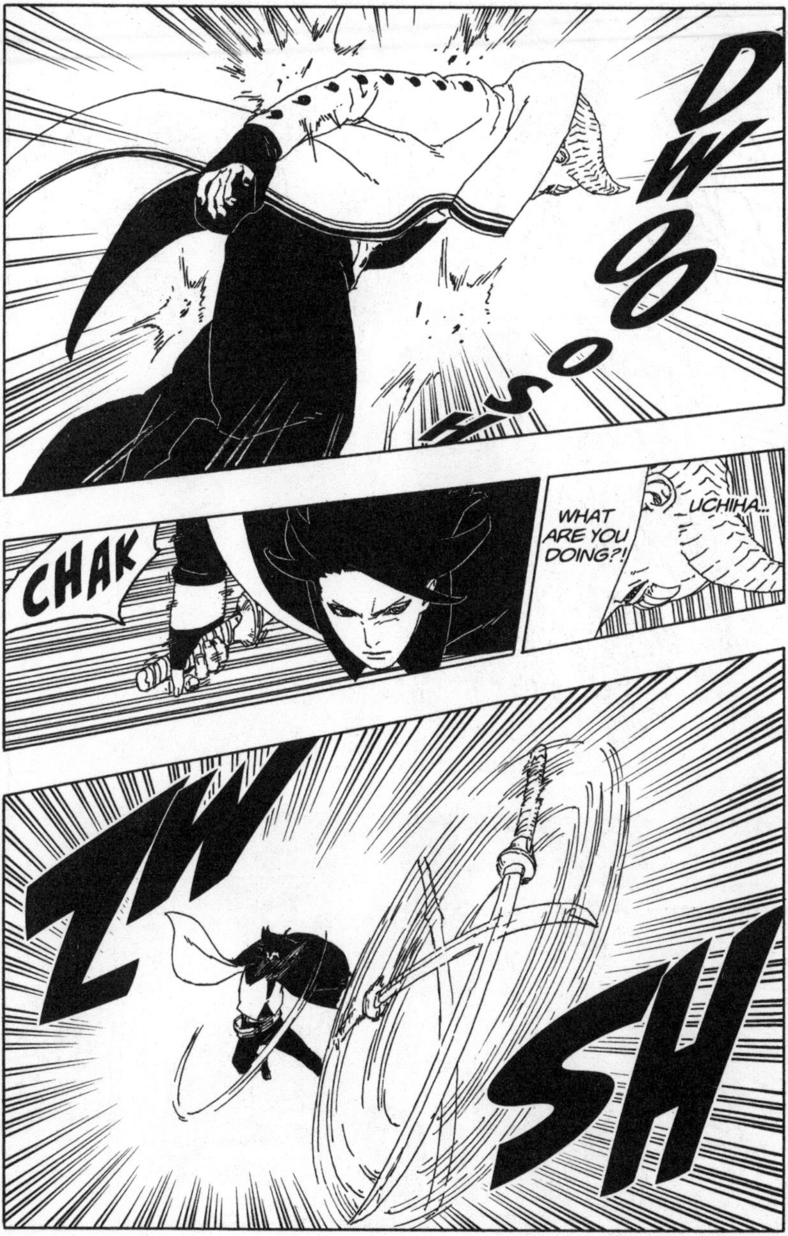
DWOOOSH
UCHIHA...
WHAT ARE YOU DOING?!
CHAK
ZWSH

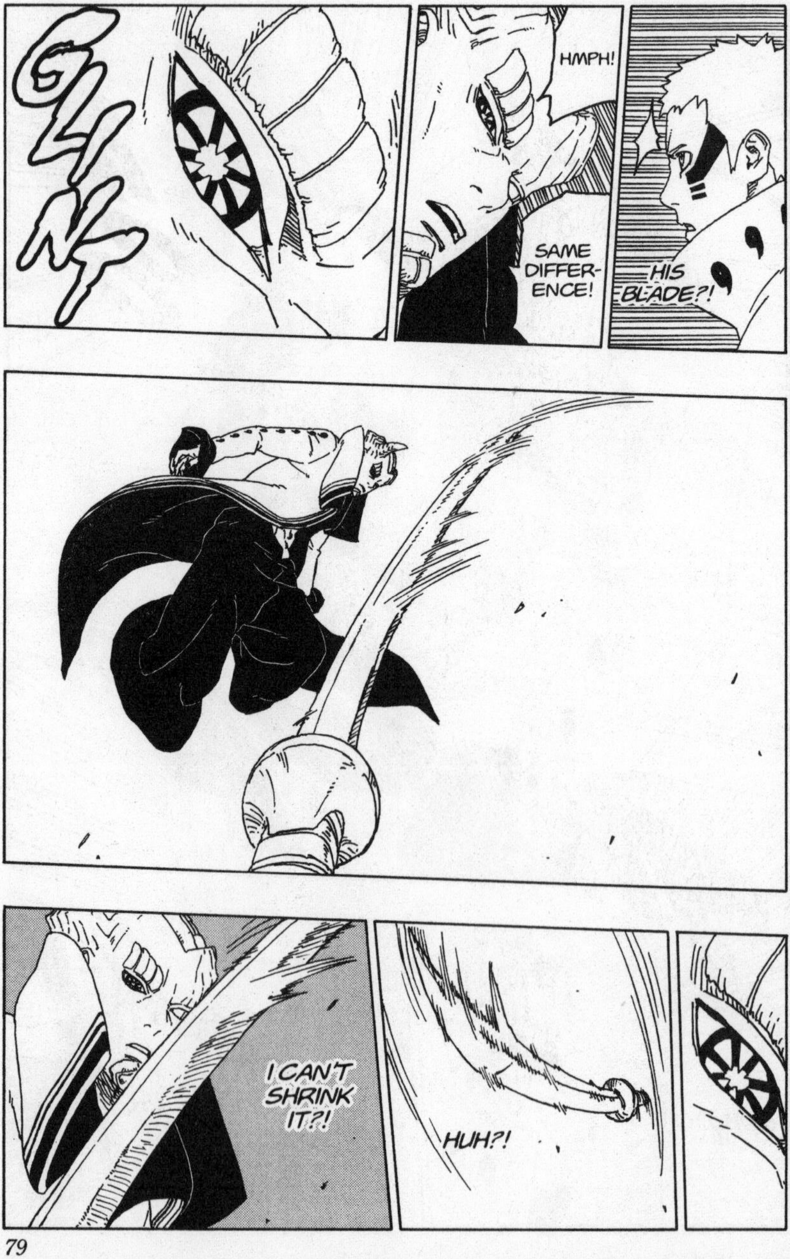
HIS BLADE?!
HMPH!
SAME DIFFERENCE!
GLINK
HUH?!
I CAN'T SHRINK IT?!

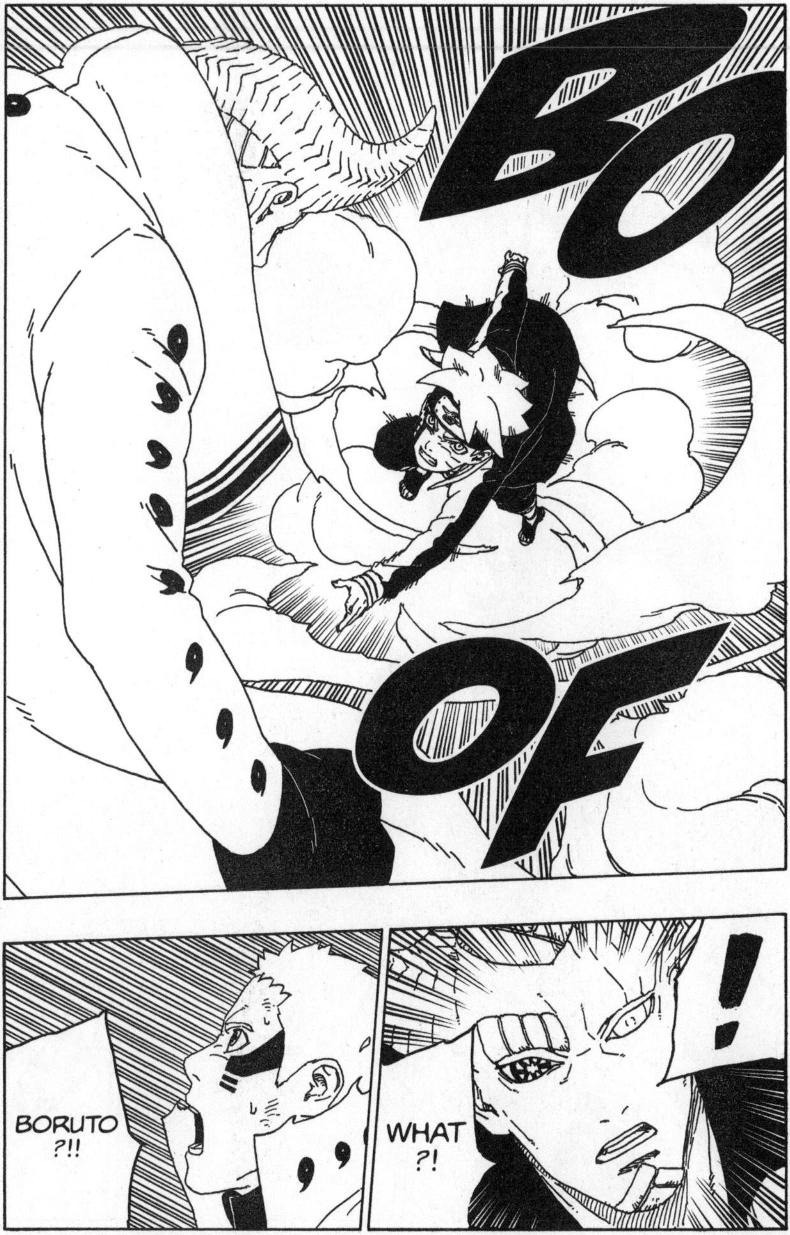
BO
OF
!
WHAT ?!
BORUTO ?!!

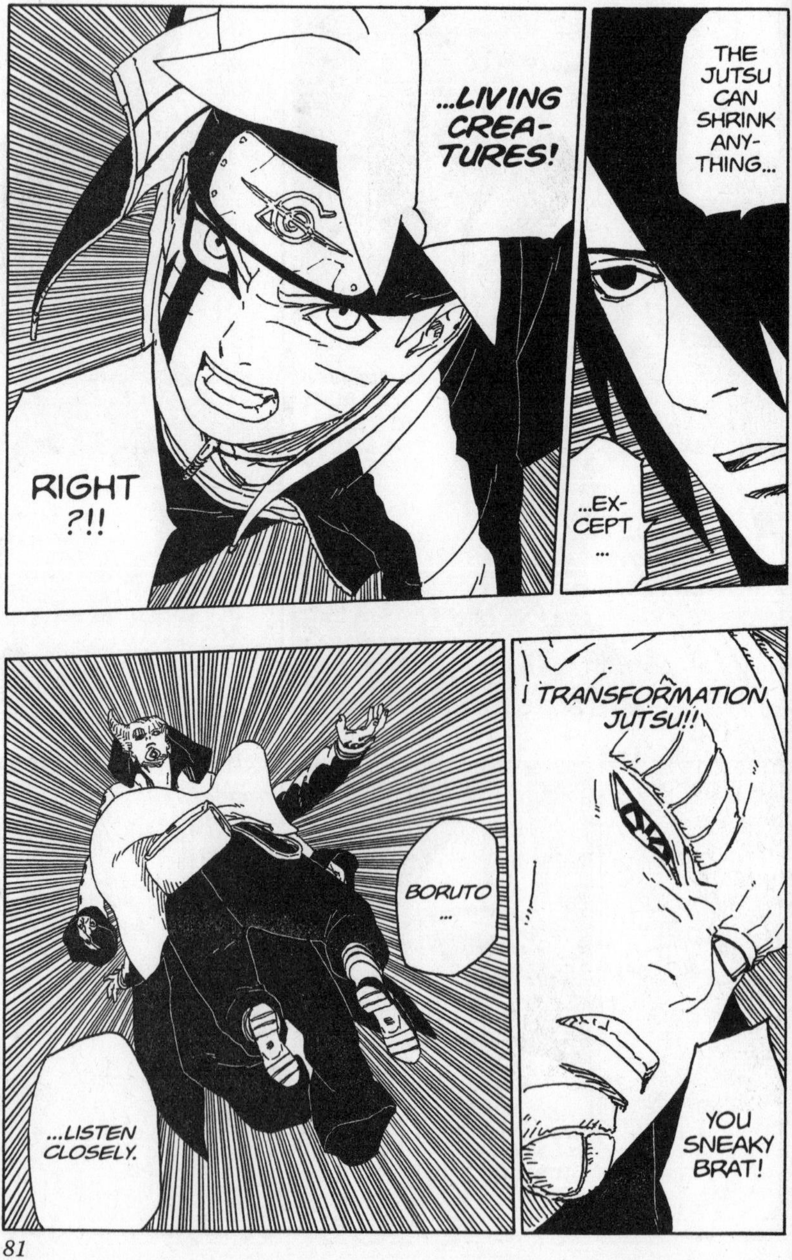
THE JUTSU CAN SHRINK ANYTHING...
...EXCEPT...
...LIVING CREATURES!
RIGHT?!!
TRANSFORMATION JUTSU!!
YOU SNEAKY BRAT!
BORUTO...
...LISTEN CLOSELY.

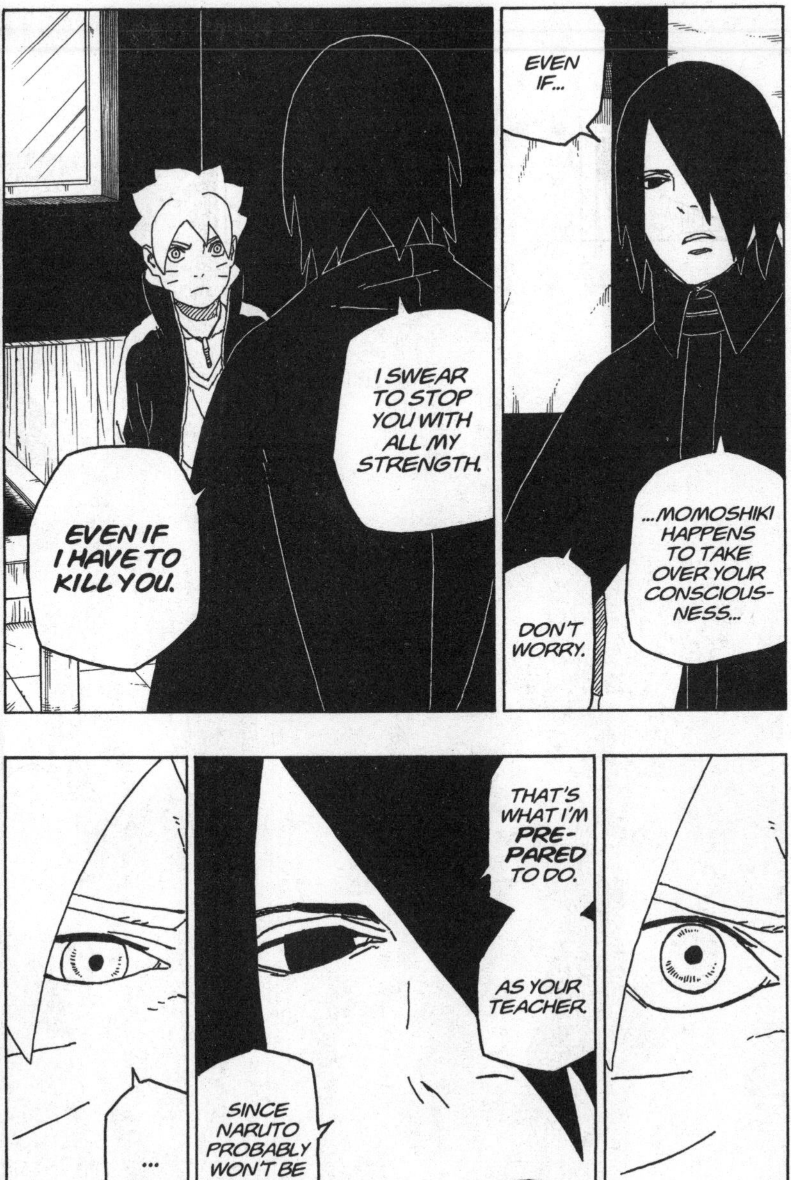
EVEN IF...
...MOMOSHIKI HAPPENS TO TAKE OVER YOUR CONSCIOUS-NESS...
DON'T WORRY.
I SWEAR TO STOP YOU WITH ALL MY STRENGTH.
EVEN IF I HAVE TO KILL YOU.
THAT'S WHAT I'M PRE-PARED TO DO.
AS YOUR TEACHER.
SINCE NARUTO PROBABLY WON'T BE ABLE TO.
...

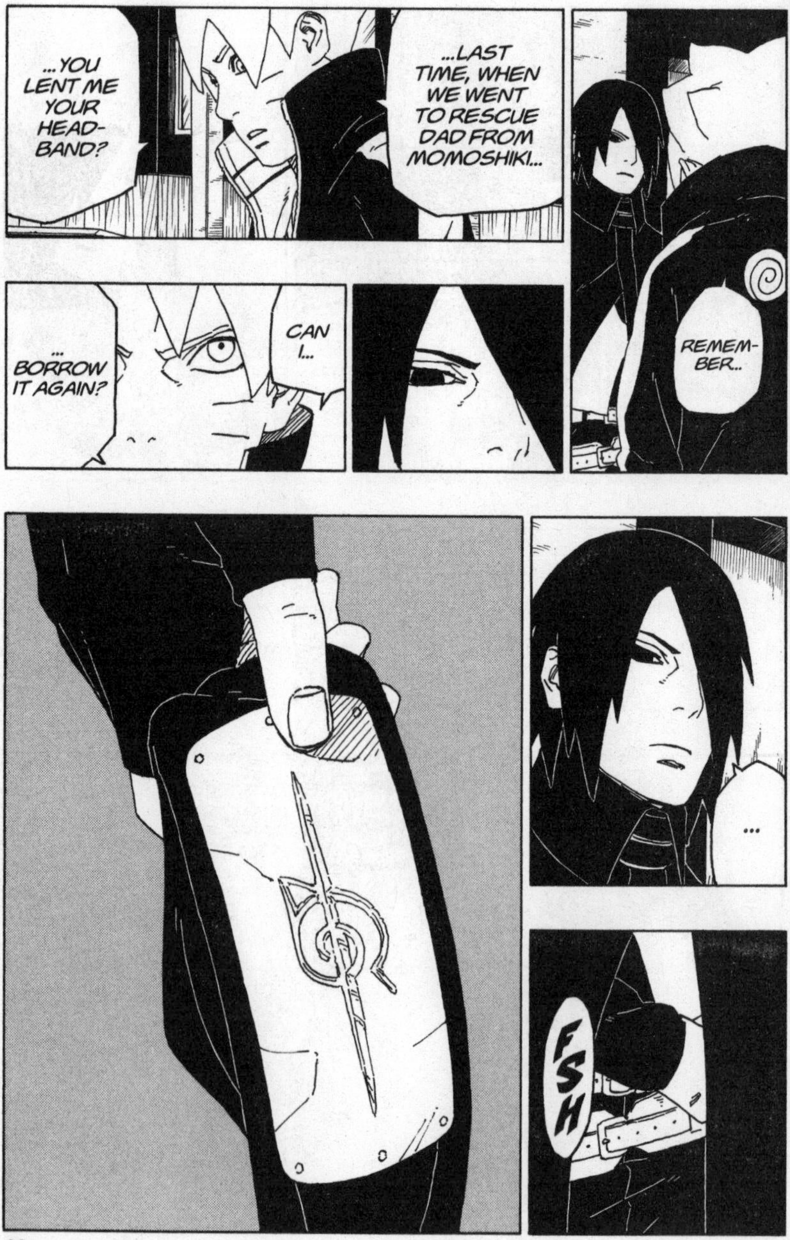
REMEM-
BER...
...LAST TIME, WHEN WE WENT TO RESCUE DAD FROM MOMOSHIKI...
...YOU LENT ME YOUR HEAD-BAND?
CAN I...
... BORROW IT AGAIN?
...
FSH

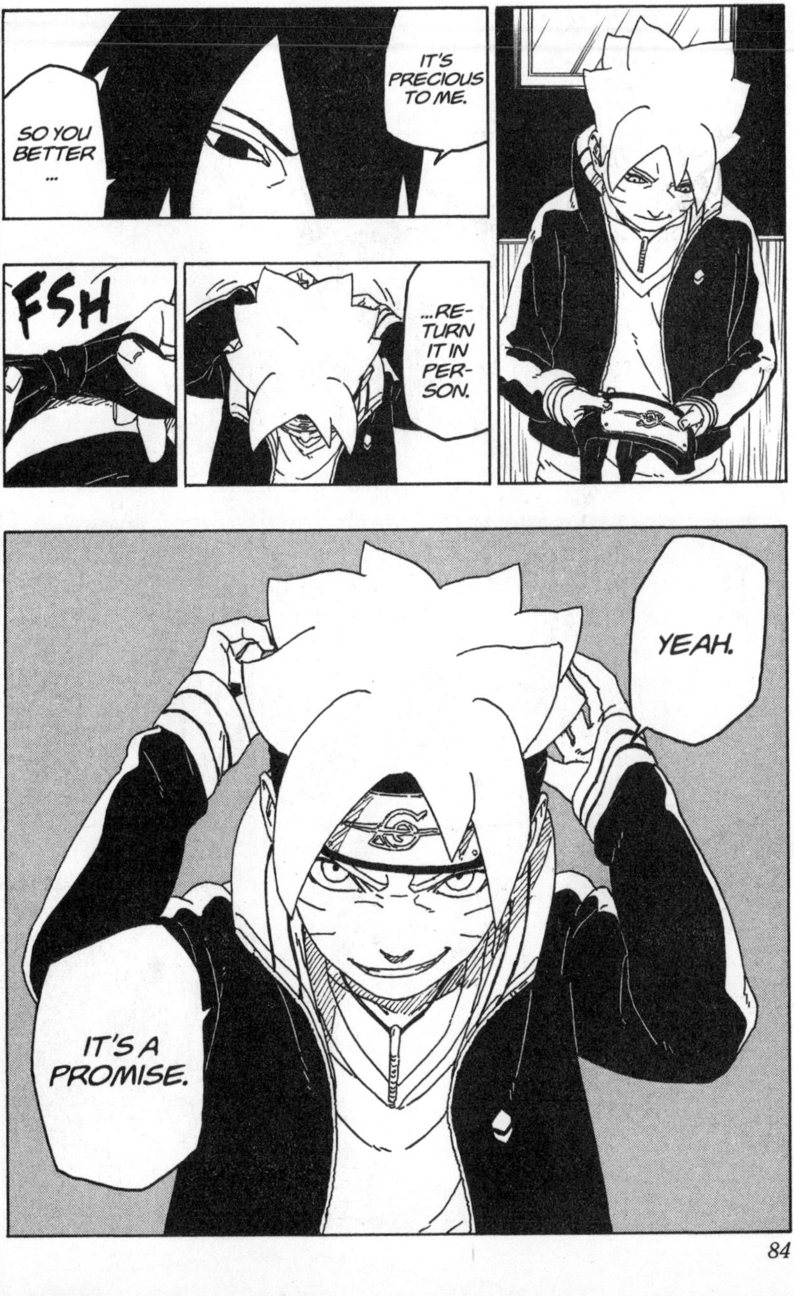
IT'S PRECIOUS TO ME.
SO YOU BETTER ...
...RE-TURN IT IN PER-SON.
FSH
YEAH.
IT'S A PROMISE.

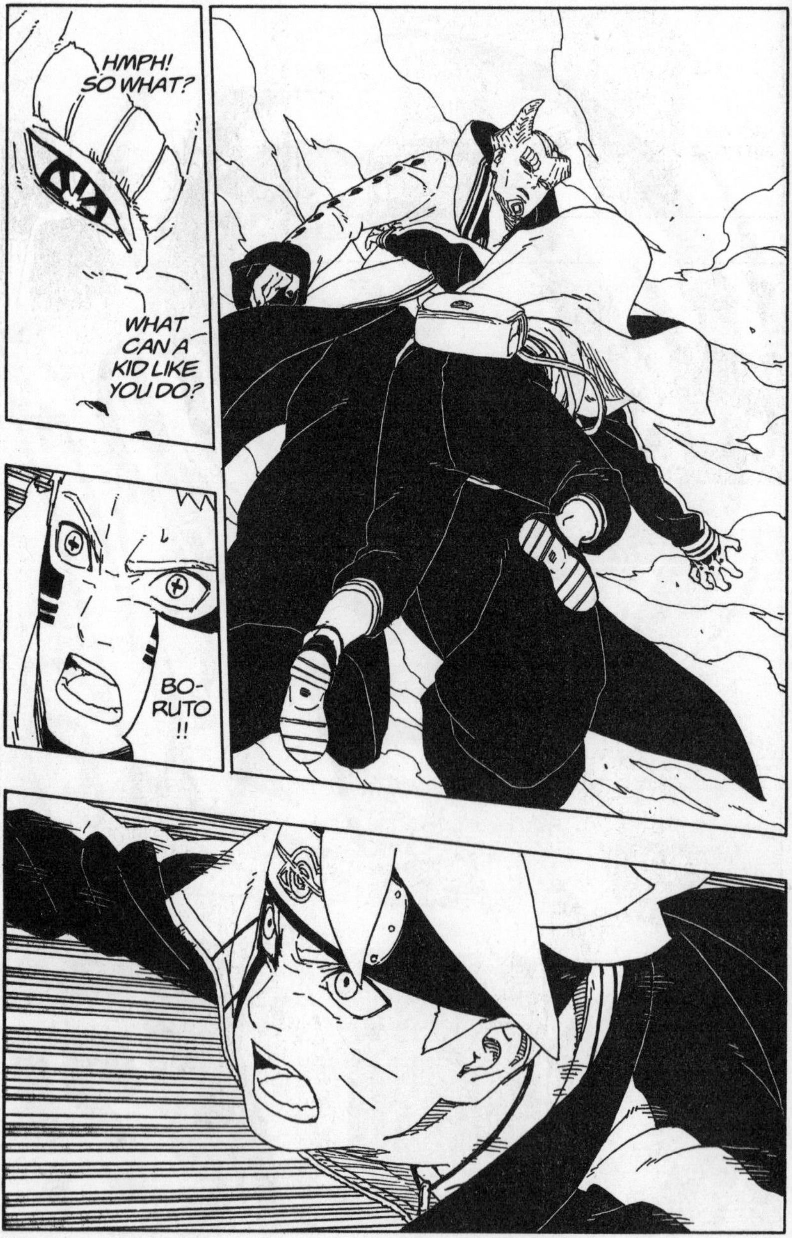
HMPH! SO WHAT?
WHAT CAN A KID LIKE YOU DO?
BO-RUTO !!

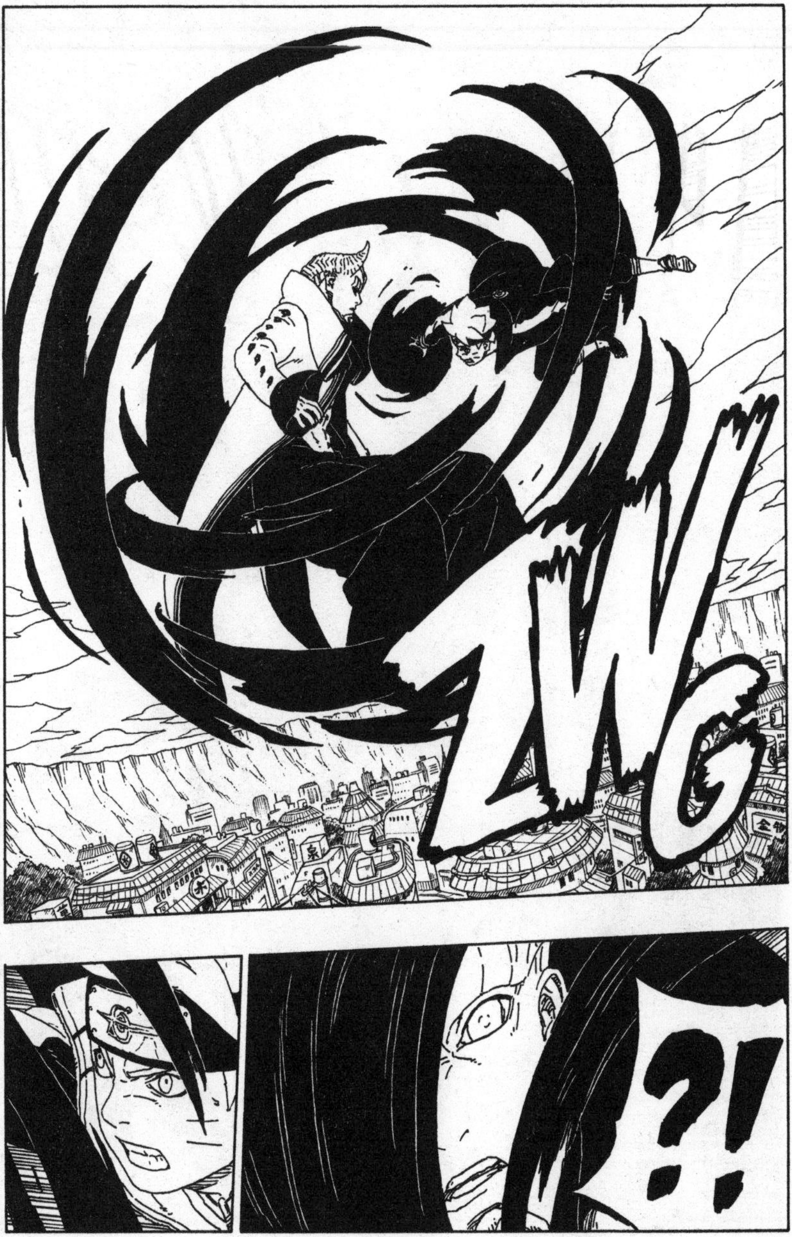
?!

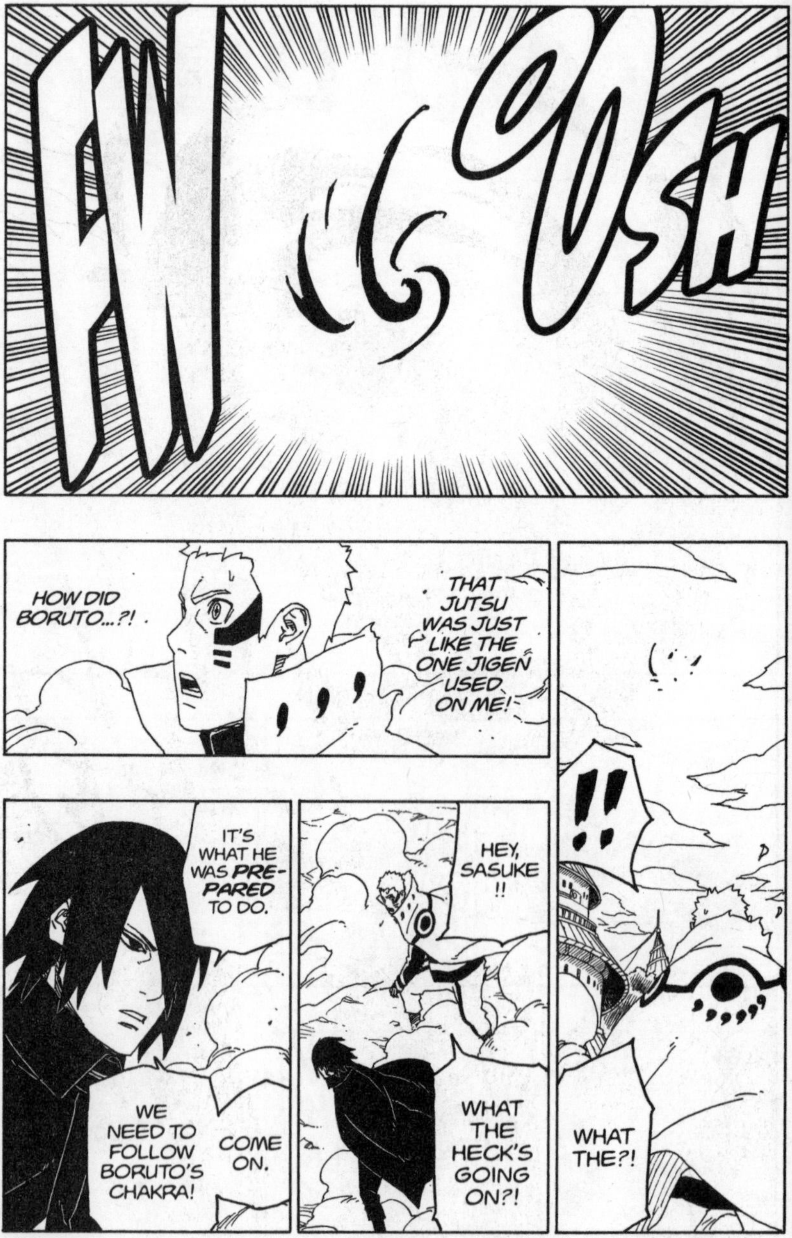
FWOOSH
!!
WHAT THE?!
THAT JUTSU WAS JUST LIKE THE ONE JIGEN USED ON ME!
HOW DID BORUTO...?!
HEY, SASUKE!!
WHAT THE HECK'S GOING ON?!
IT'S WHAT HE WAS PRE-PARED TO DO.
COME ON.
WE NEED TO FOLLOW BORUTO'S CHAKRA!

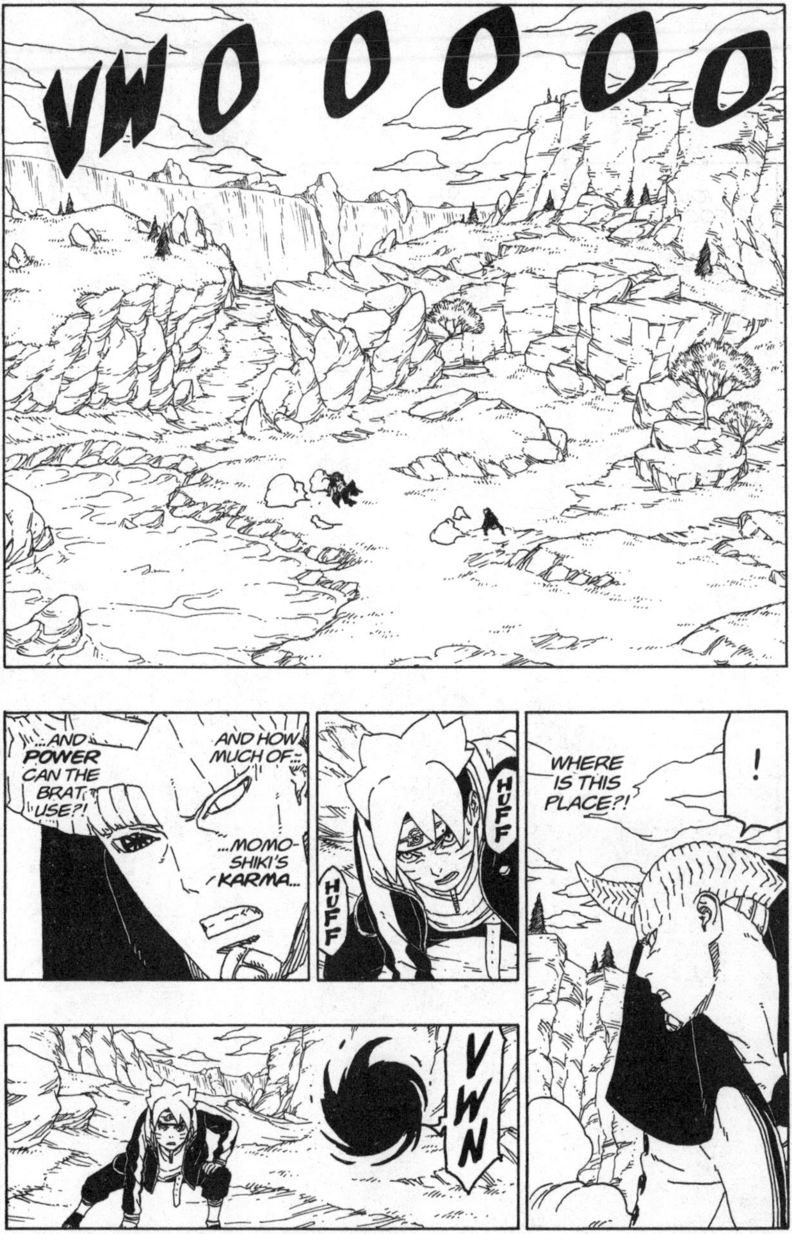
VWOOOOO
!
WHERE IS THIS PLACE?!
HUFF
HUFF
AND HOW MUCH OF...
...MOMOSHIKI'S KARMA...
...AND POWER CAN THE BRAT USE?!
VWN

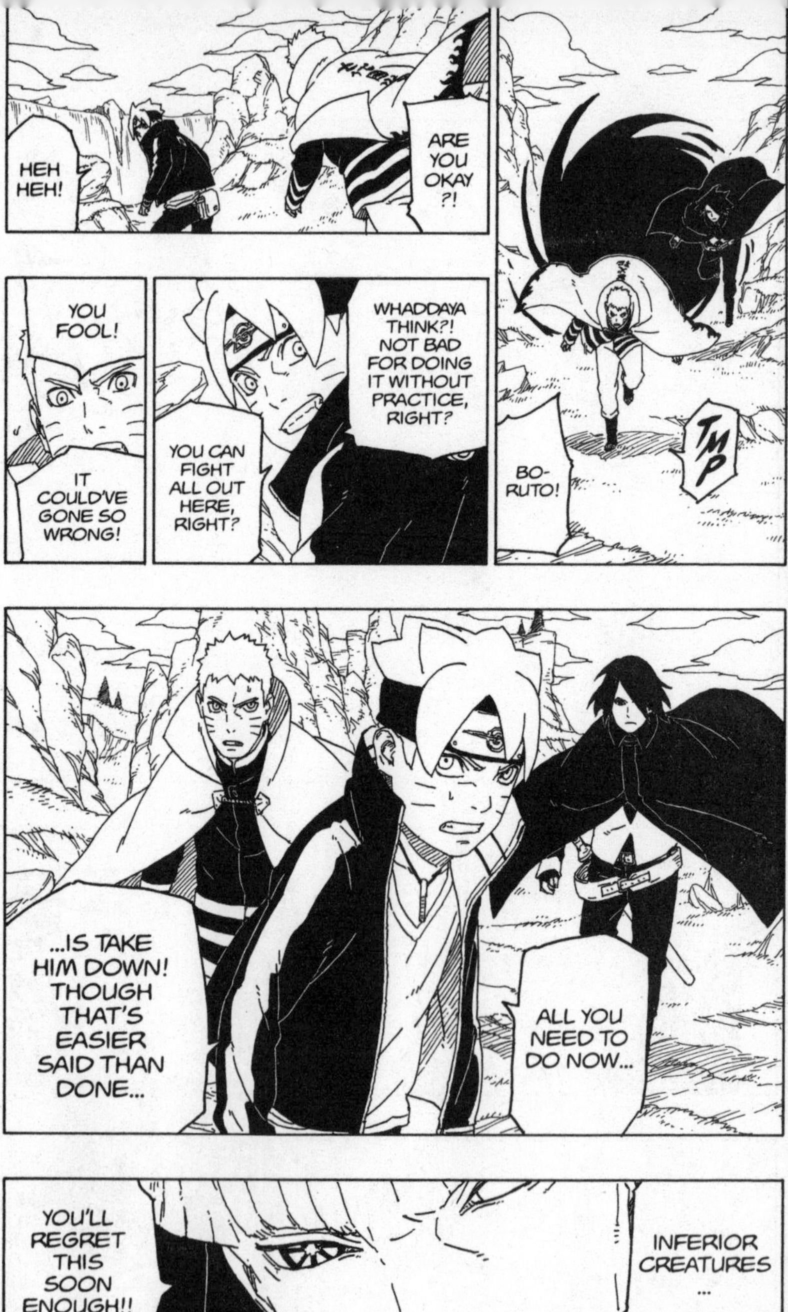
TMP
BO-RUTO!
ARE YOU OKAY ?!
HEH HEH!
WHADDAYA THINK?! NOT BAD FOR DOING IT WITHOUT PRACTICE, RIGHT?
YOU CAN FIGHT ALL OUT HERE, RIGHT?
YOU FOOL!
IT COULD'VE GONE SO WRONG!
ALL YOU NEED TO DO NOW...
...IS TAKE HIM DOWN! THOUGH THAT'S EASIER SAID THAN DONE...
INFERIOR CREATURES ...
YOU'LL REGRET THIS SOON ENOUGH!!

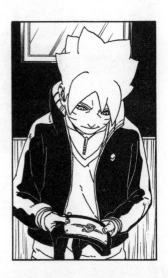

Number 50: Potential Value

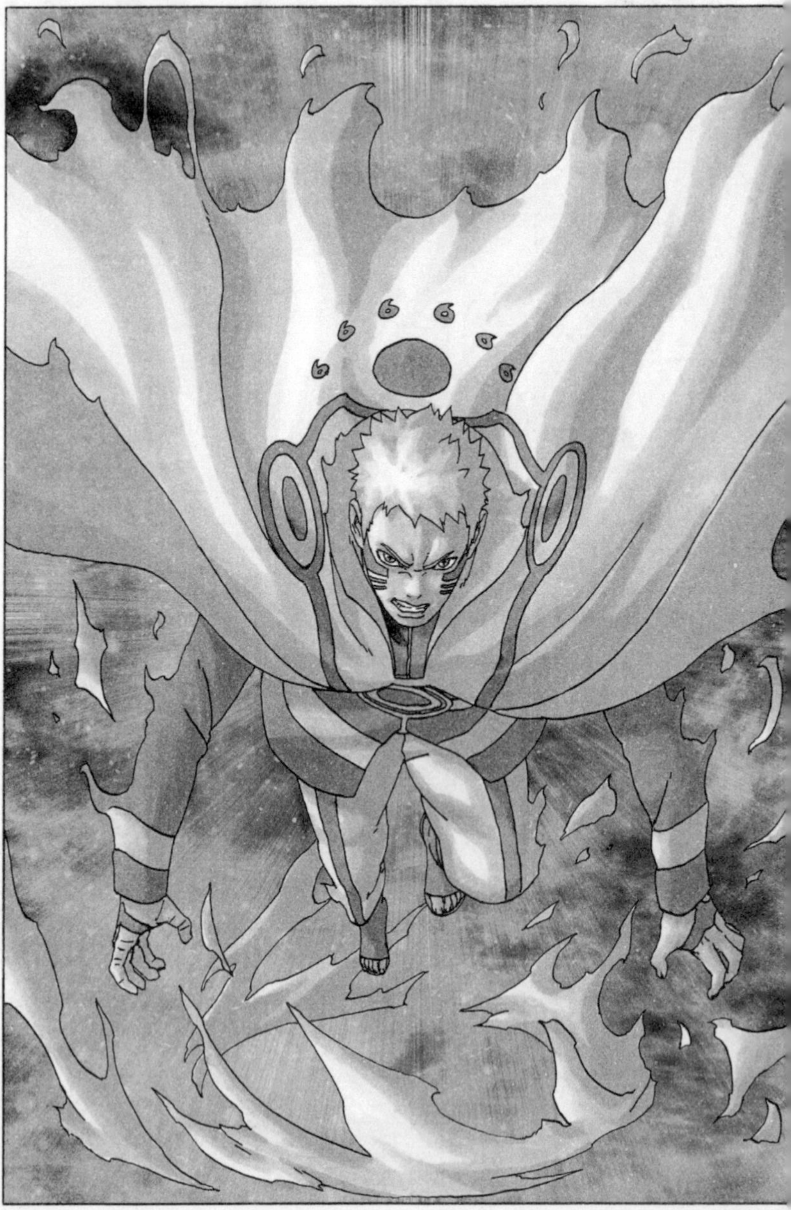

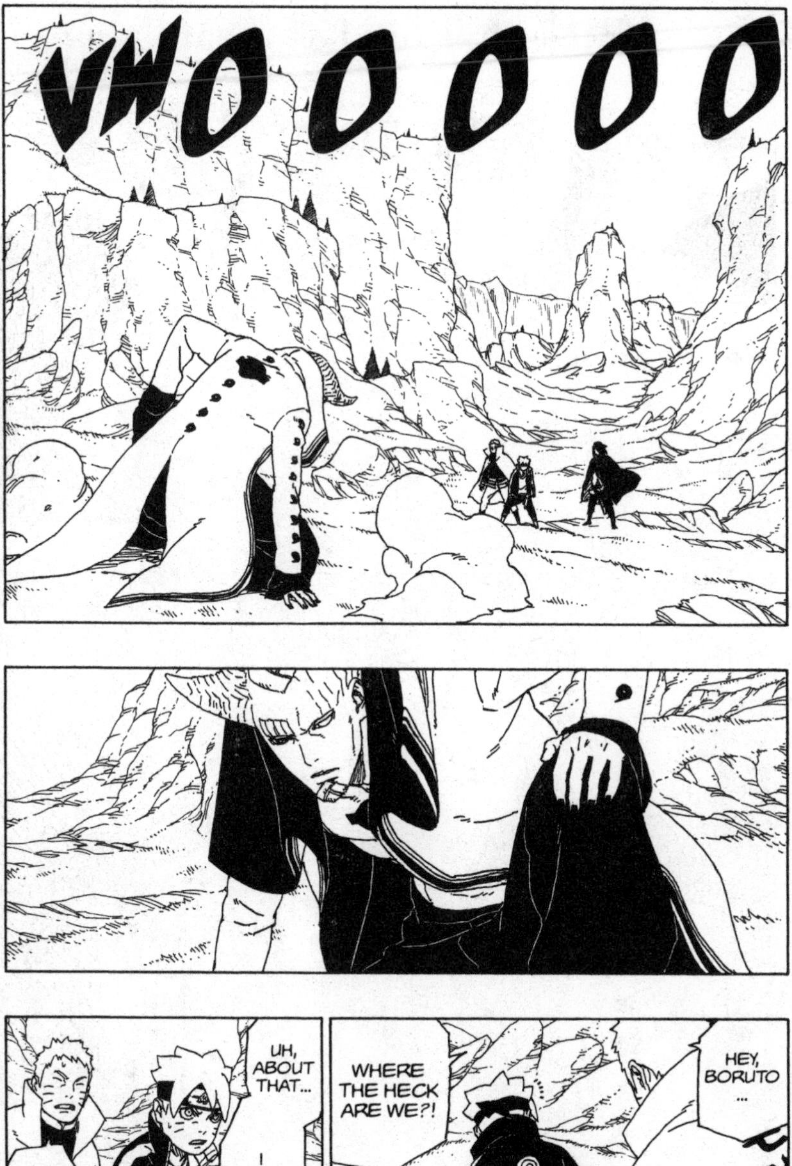
VWOOOOO
HEY, BORUTO ...
WHERE THE HECK ARE WE?!
UH, ABOUT THAT...
I DUNNO!
WHAT ?!

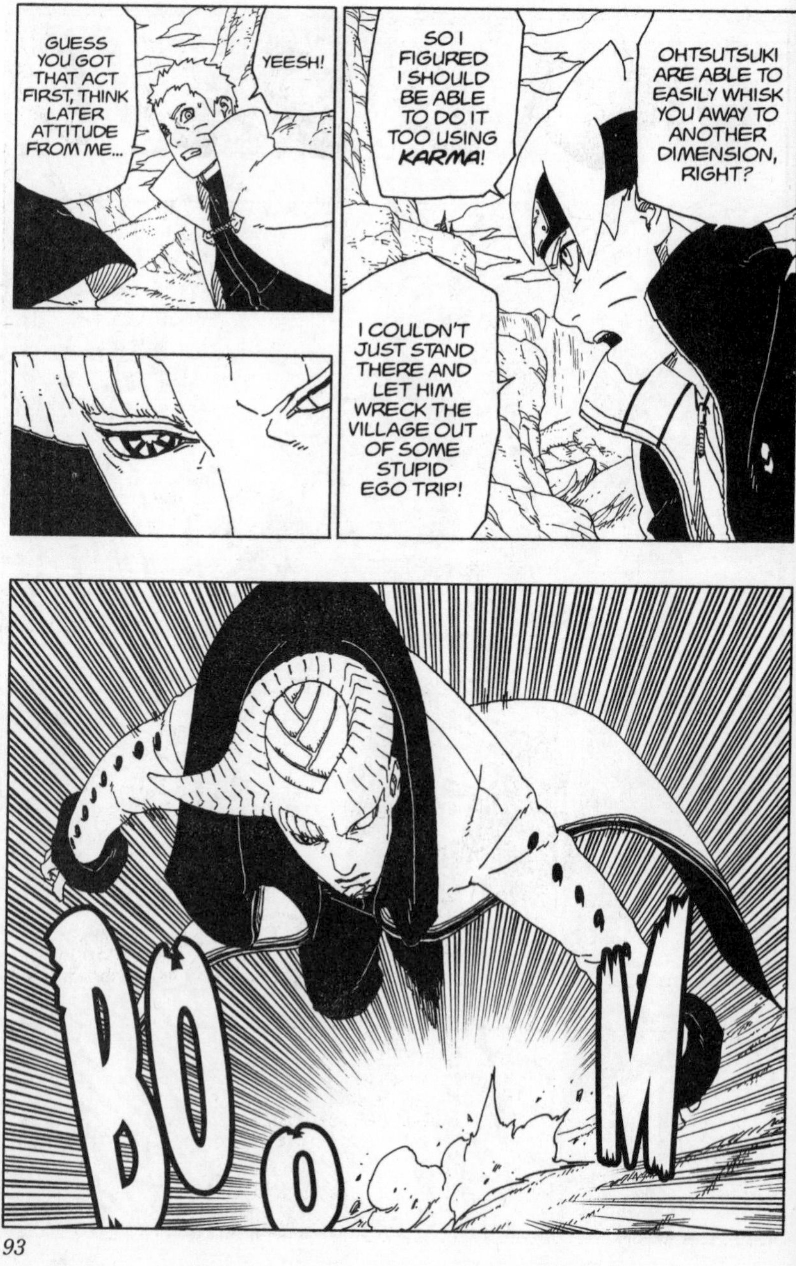
OHTSUTSUKI ARE ABLE TO EASILY WHISK YOU AWAY TO ANOTHER DIMENSION, RIGHT?
SO I FIGURED I SHOULD BE ABLE TO DO IT TOO USING *KARMA*!
I COULDN'T JUST STAND THERE AND LET HIM WRECK THE VILLAGE OUT OF SOME STUPID EGO TRIP!
YEESH!
GUESS YOU GOT THAT ACT FIRST, THINK LATER ATTITUDE FROM ME...
BOOOM

!!
BORUTO!!
!
TAK
SHF
!
NARUTO! ABOVE US!!

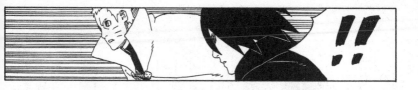

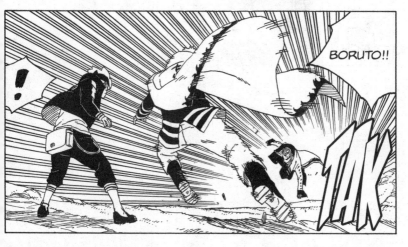

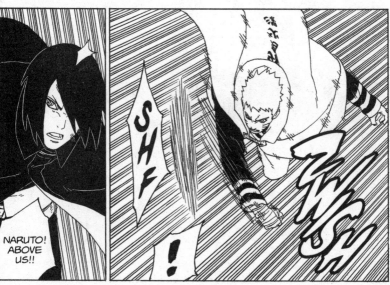

!!
VWOOOOOOO
GGH ...
G-GAH ...
YOU BASTARD !!
UZUMAKI BORUTO. MOMOSHIKI'S VESSEL.
YOUR OHTSUTSUKIFICATION HAS PROGRESSED FURTHER THAN I EXPECTED.
IT'S ALREADY 70--MAYBE EVEN 80 PERCENT COMPLETE.
...
HOW MUCH POWER HIDES WITHIN YOU?
SHOW ME.

!
VWP
GOFF
GOFF
BORUTO!

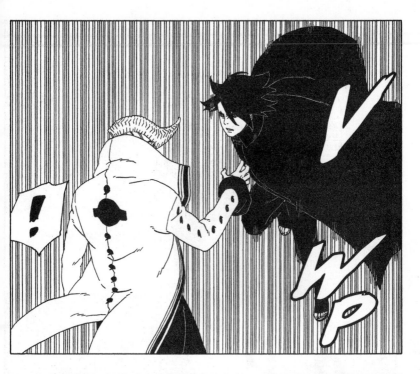

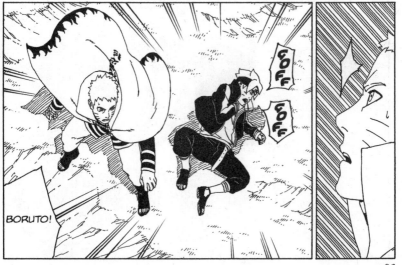

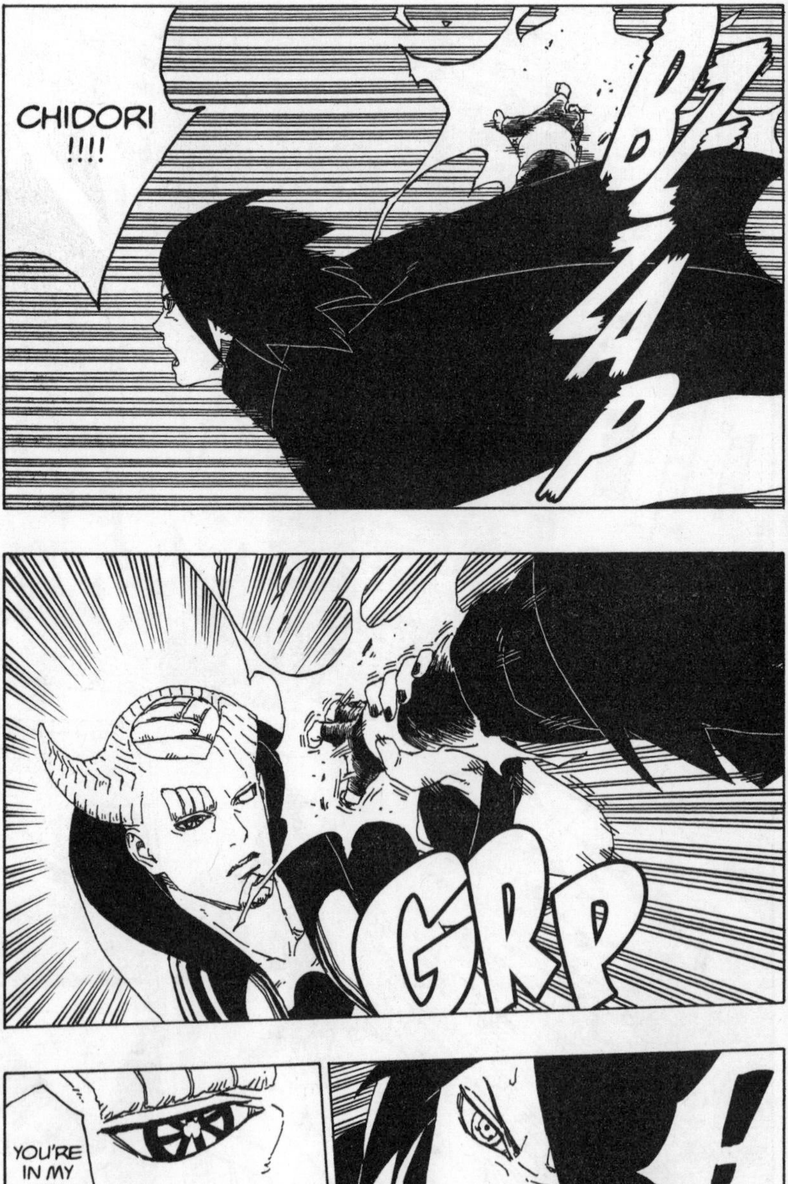
CHIDORI !!!!
BZZAP
GRP
!
YOU'RE IN MY WAY.

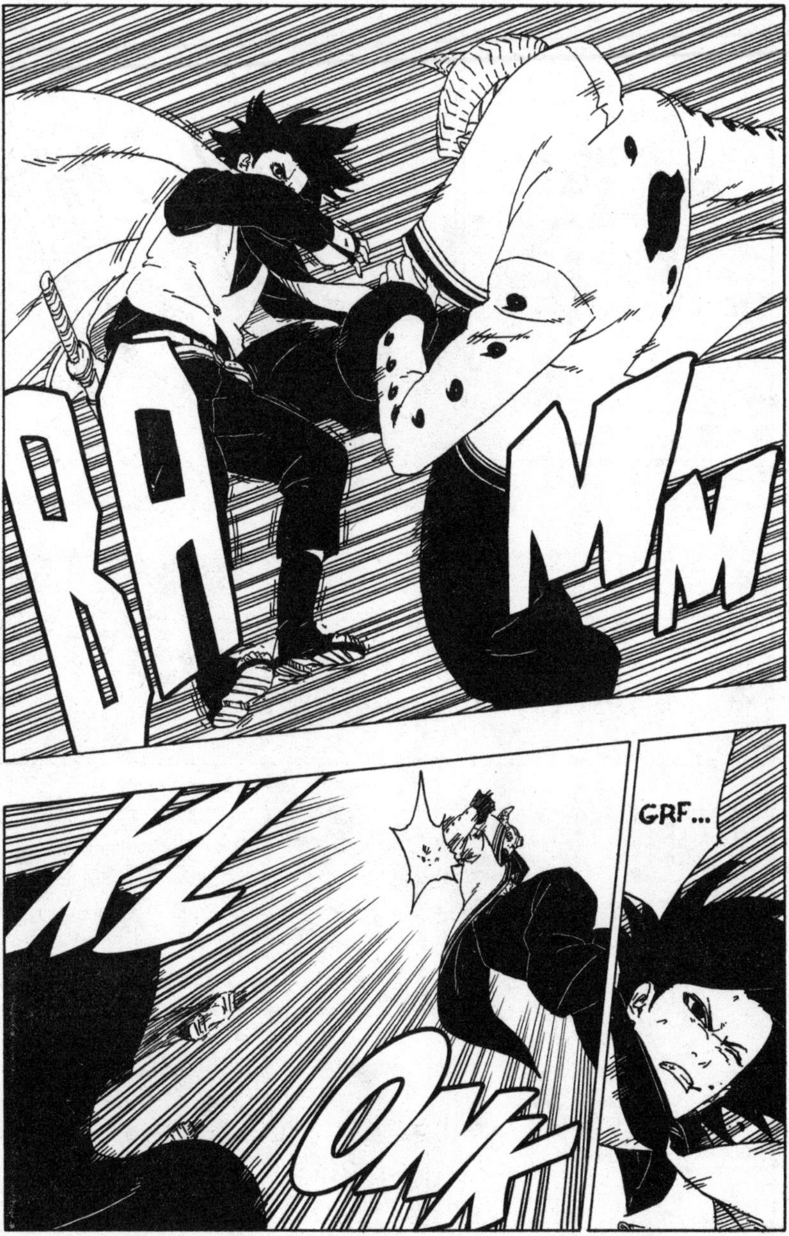
GRF...

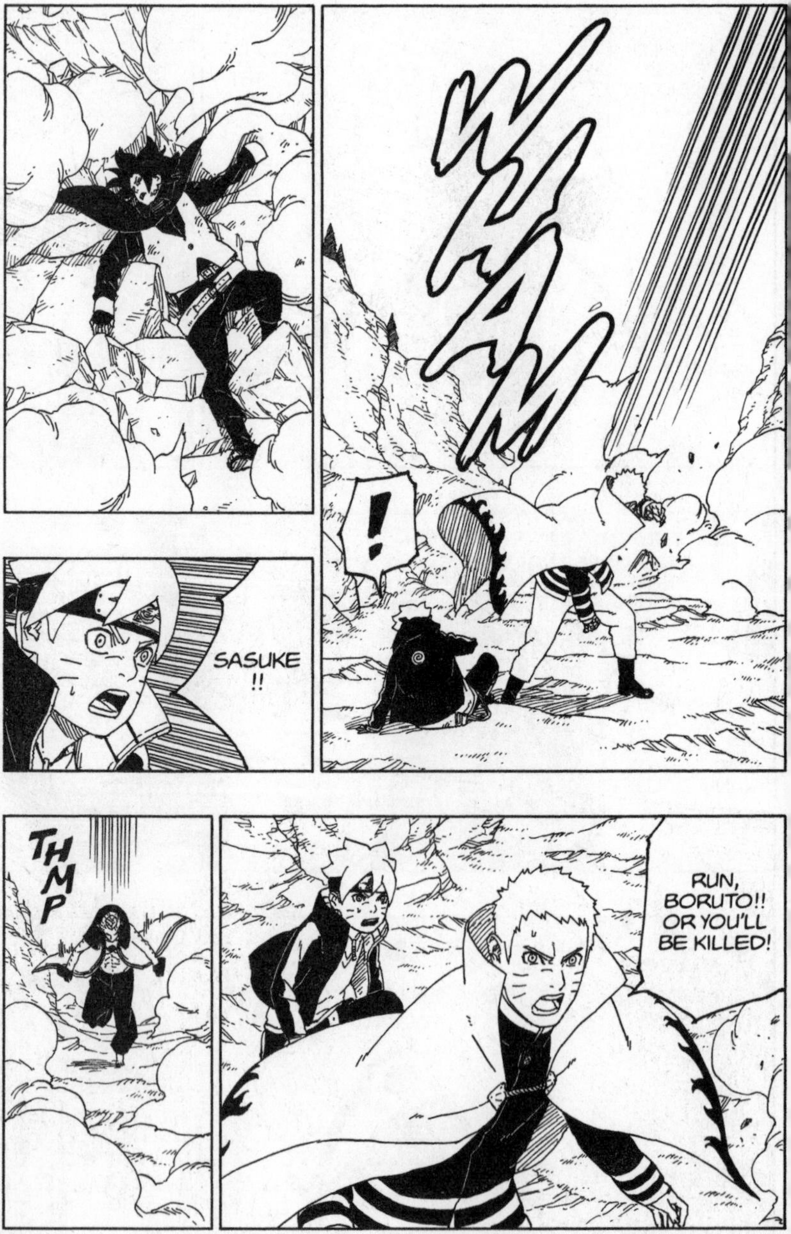
WHAM
!
SASUKE !!
RUN, BORUTO!! OR YOU'LL BE KILLED!
THMP

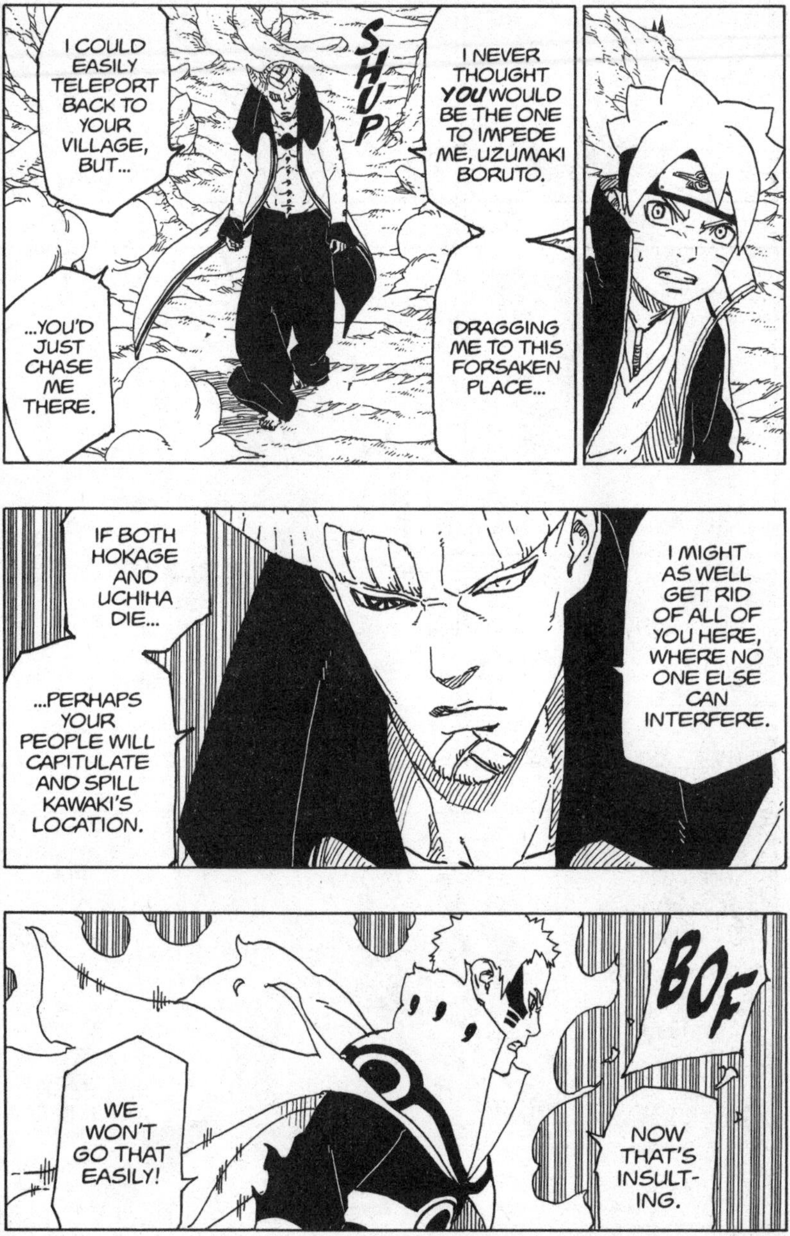
I NEVER THOUGHT YOU WOULD BE THE ONE TO IMPEDE ME, UZUMAKI BORUTO.
DRAGGING ME TO THIS FORSAKEN PLACE...
SHUP
I COULD EASILY TELEPORT BACK TO YOUR VILLAGE, BUT...
...YOU'D JUST CHASE ME THERE.
I MIGHT AS WELL GET RID OF ALL OF YOU HERE, WHERE NO ONE ELSE CAN INTERFERE.
IF BOTH HOKAGE AND UCHIHA DIE...
...PERHAPS YOUR PEOPLE WILL CAPITULATE AND SPILL KAWAKI'S LOCATION.
BOF
NOW THAT'S INSULT-ING.
WE WON'T GO THAT EASILY!

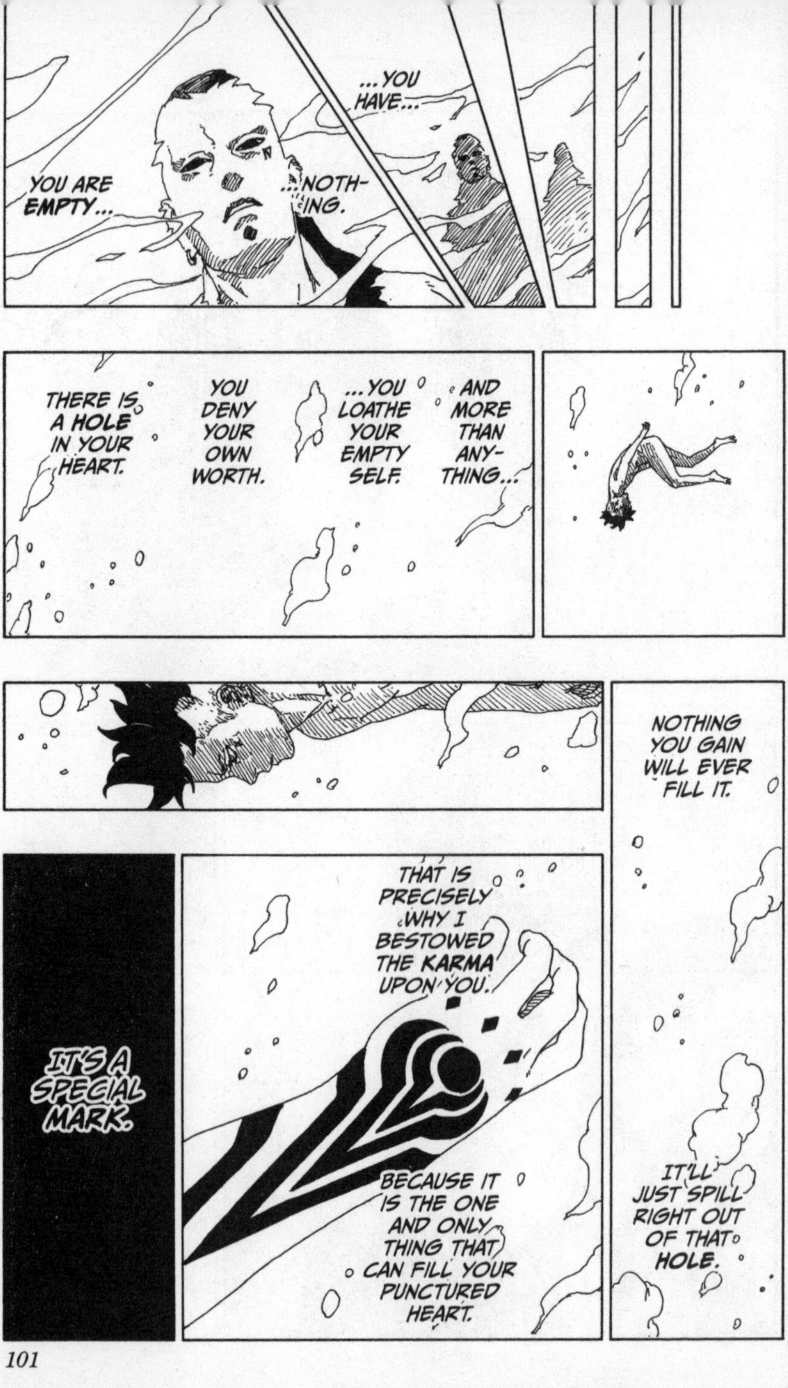
...YOU HAVE...
...NOTHING.
YOU ARE EMPTY...
AND MORE THAN ANYTHING...
...YOU LOATHE YOUR EMPTY SELF.
YOU DENY YOUR OWN WORTH.
THERE IS A HOLE IN YOUR HEART.
NOTHING YOU GAIN WILL EVER FILL IT.
IT'LL JUST SPILL RIGHT OUT OF THAT HOLE.
THAT IS PRECISELY WHY I BESTOWED THE KARMA UPON YOU.
BECAUSE IT IS THE ONE AND ONLY THING THAT CAN FILL YOUR PUNCTURED HEART.
IT'S A SPECIAL MARK.

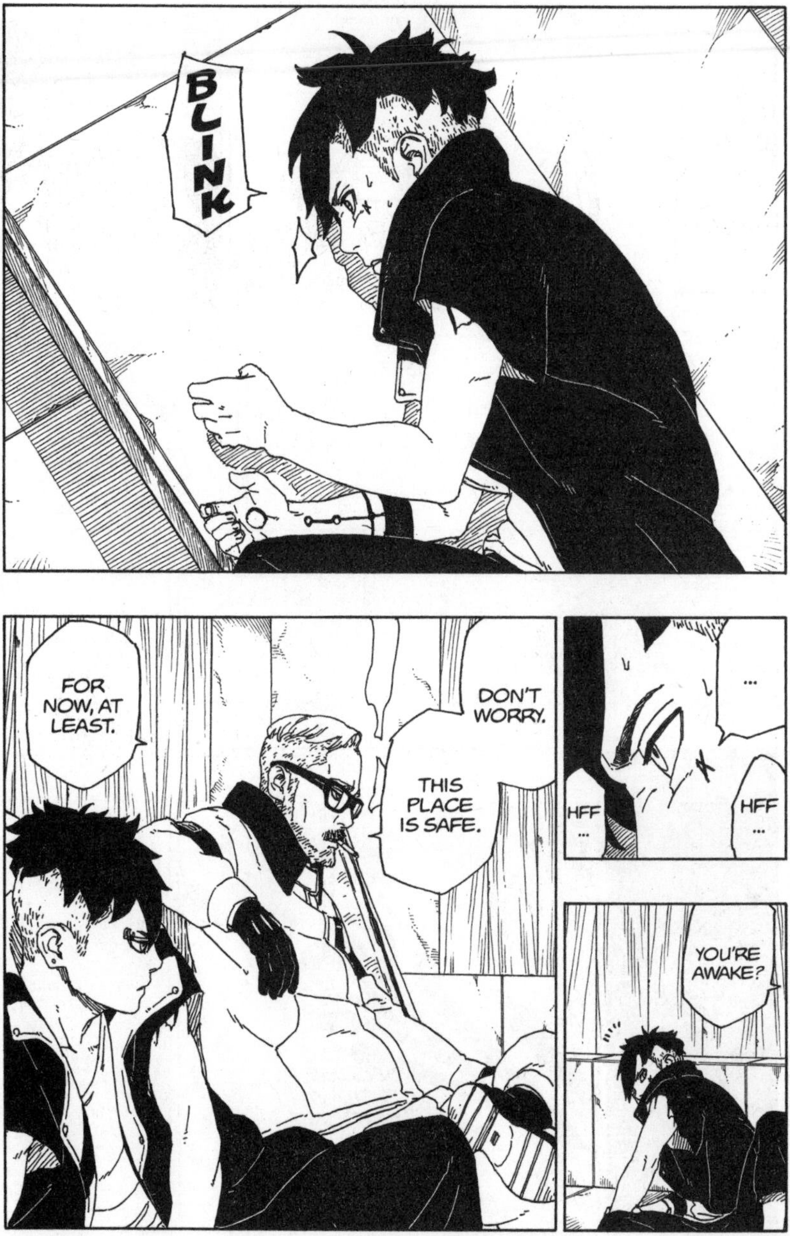
BLINK
...
HFF ...
HFF ...
YOU'RE AWAKE?
DON'T WORRY.
THIS PLACE IS SAFE.
FOR NOW, AT LEAST.

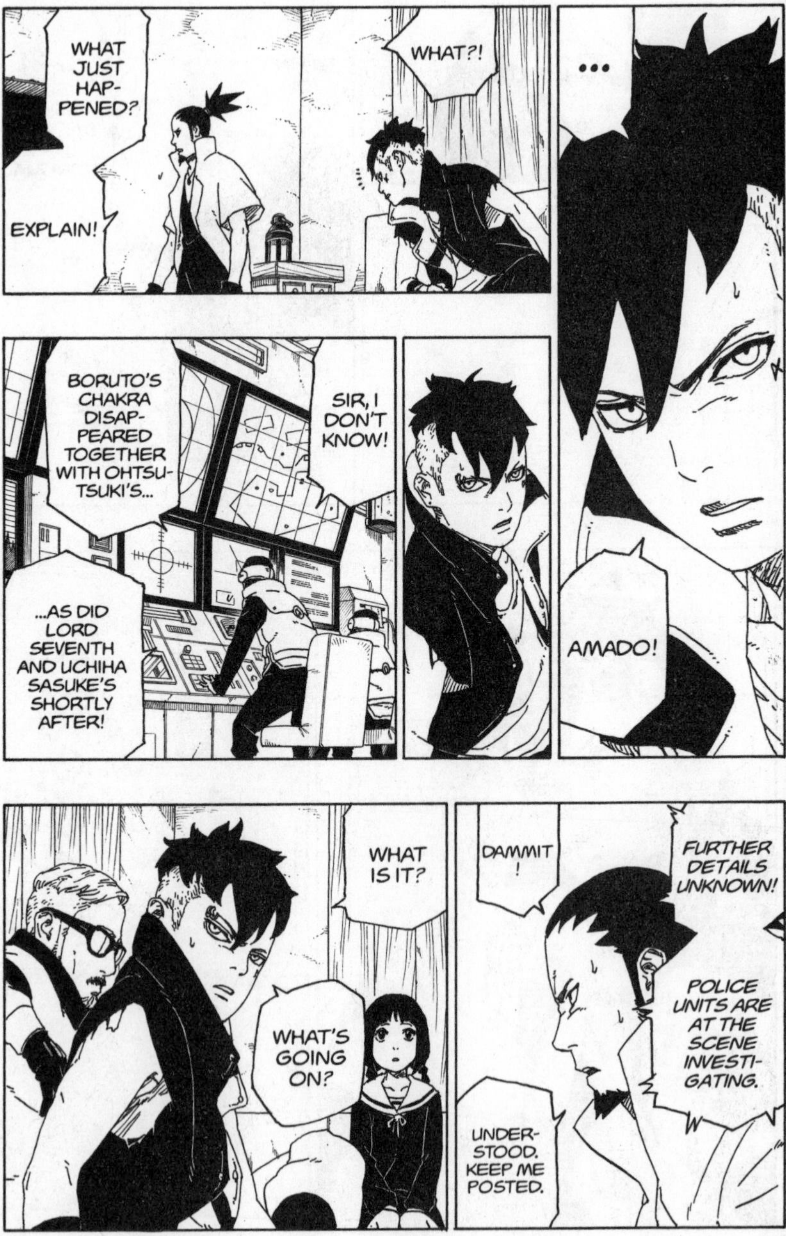
...
AMADO!
WHAT?!
WHAT JUST HAPPENED?
EXPLAIN!
SIR, I DON'T KNOW!
BORUTO'S CHAKRA DISAPPEARED TOGETHER WITH OHTSUTSUKI'S...
...AS DID LORD SEVENTH AND UCHIHA SASUKE'S SHORTLY AFTER!
FURTHER DETAILS UNKNOWN!
DAMMIT!
POLICE UNITS ARE AT THE SCENE INVESTIGATING.
UNDERSTOOD. KEEP ME POSTED.
WHAT IS IT?
WHAT'S GOING ON?

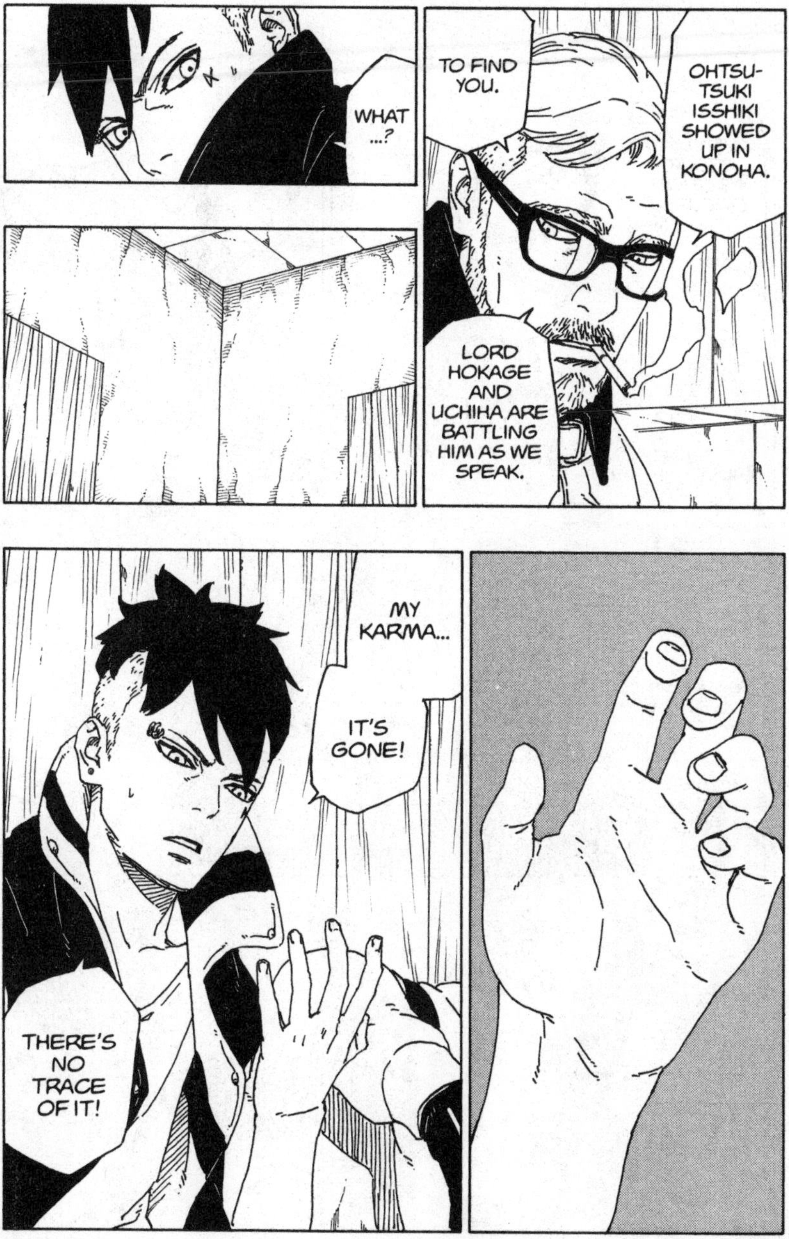
OHTSUTSUKI ISSHIKI SHOWED UP IN KONOHA.
TO FIND YOU.
LORD HOKAGE AND UCHIHA ARE BATTLING HIM AS WE SPEAK.
WHAT ...?
MY KARMA...
IT'S GONE!
THERE'S NO TRACE OF IT!

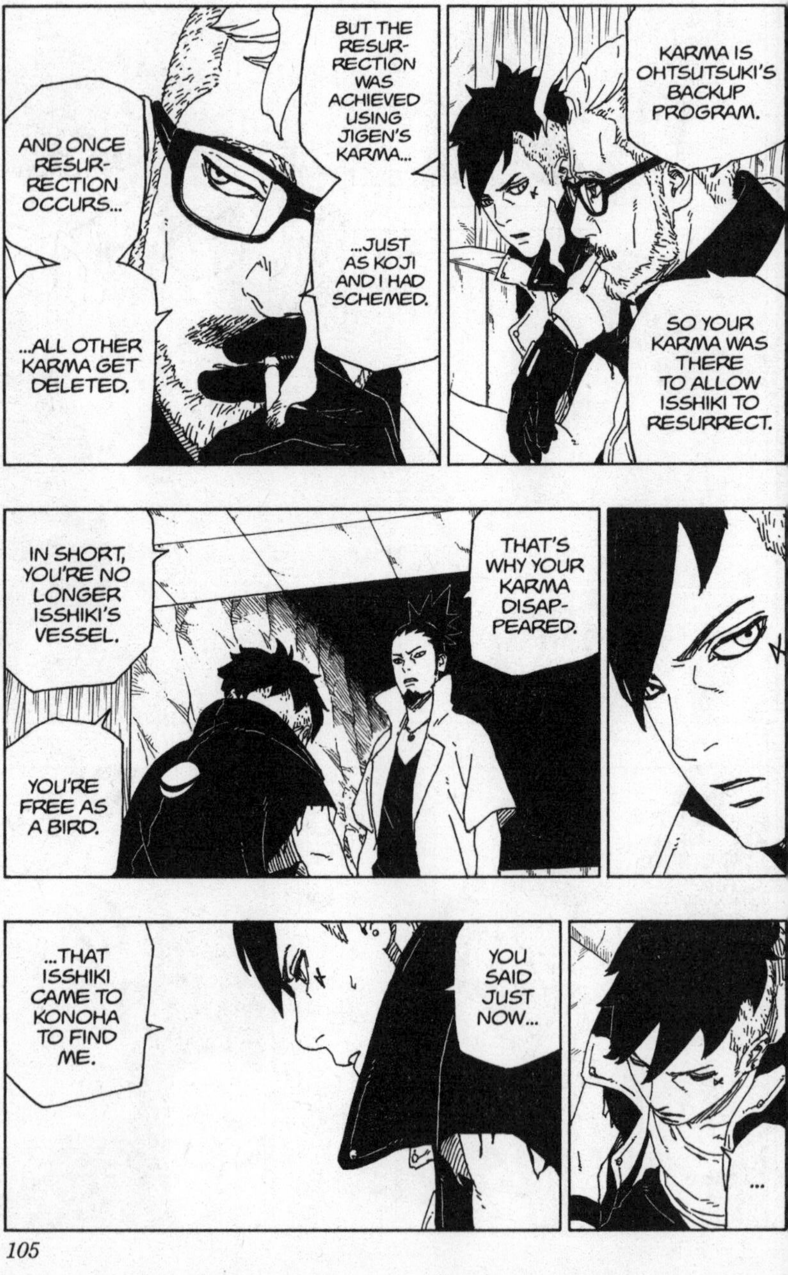
KARMA IS OHTSUTSUKI'S BACKUP PROGRAM.
SO YOUR KARMA WAS THERE TO ALLOW ISSHIKI TO RESURRECT.
BUT THE RESURRECTION WAS ACHIEVED USING JIGEN'S KARMA...
...JUST AS KOJI AND I HAD SCHEMED.
AND ONCE RESURRECTION OCCURS...
...ALL OTHER KARMA GET DELETED.
THAT'S WHY YOUR KARMA DISAPPEARED.
IN SHORT, YOU'RE NO LONGER ISSHIKI'S VESSEL.
YOU'RE FREE AS A BIRD.
...
YOU SAID JUST NOW...
...THAT ISSHIKI CAME TO KONOHA TO FIND ME.

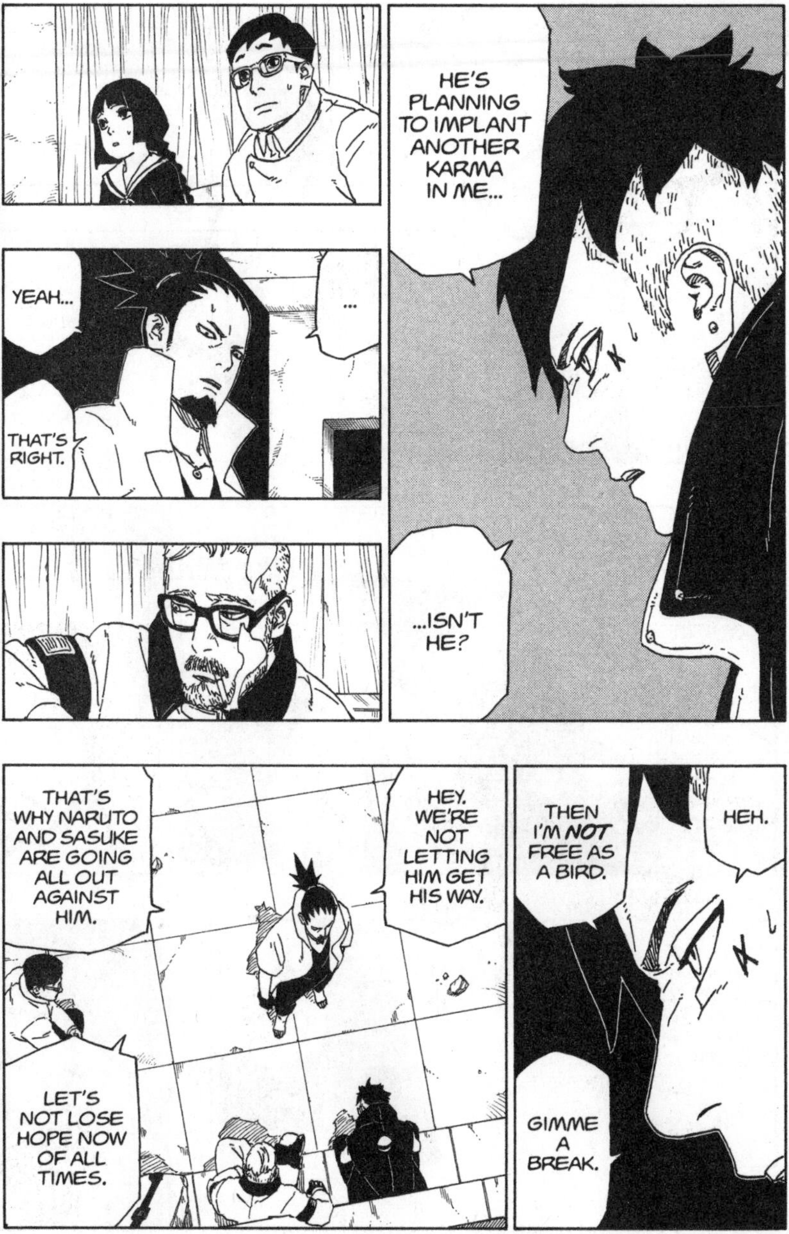
HE'S PLANNING TO IMPLANT ANOTHER KARMA IN ME...
...ISN'T HE?
...
YEAH...
THAT'S RIGHT.
HEH.
THEN I'M ***NOT*** FREE AS A BIRD.
GIMME A BREAK.
HEY. WE'RE NOT LETTING HIM GET HIS WAY.
THAT'S WHY NARUTO AND SASUKE ARE GOING ALL OUT AGAINST HIM.
LET'S NOT LOSE HOPE NOW OF ALL TIMES.

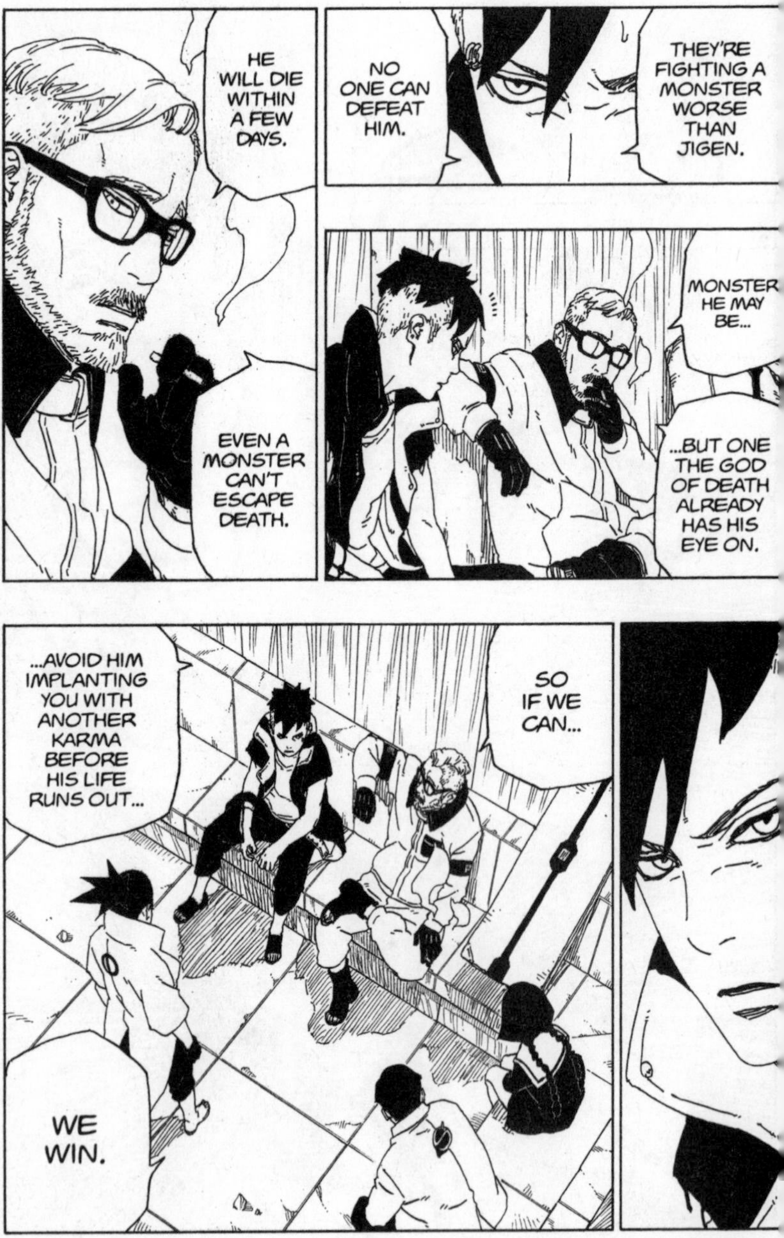
THEY'RE FIGHTING A MONSTER WORSE THAN JIGEN.
NO ONE CAN DEFEAT HIM.
MONSTER HE MAY BE...
...BUT ONE THE GOD OF DEATH ALREADY HAS HIS EYE ON.
HE WILL DIE WITHIN A FEW DAYS.
EVEN A MONSTER CAN'T ESCAPE DEATH.
SO IF WE CAN...
...AVOID HIM IMPLANTING YOU WITH ANOTHER KARMA BEFORE HIS LIFE RUNS OUT...
WE WIN.

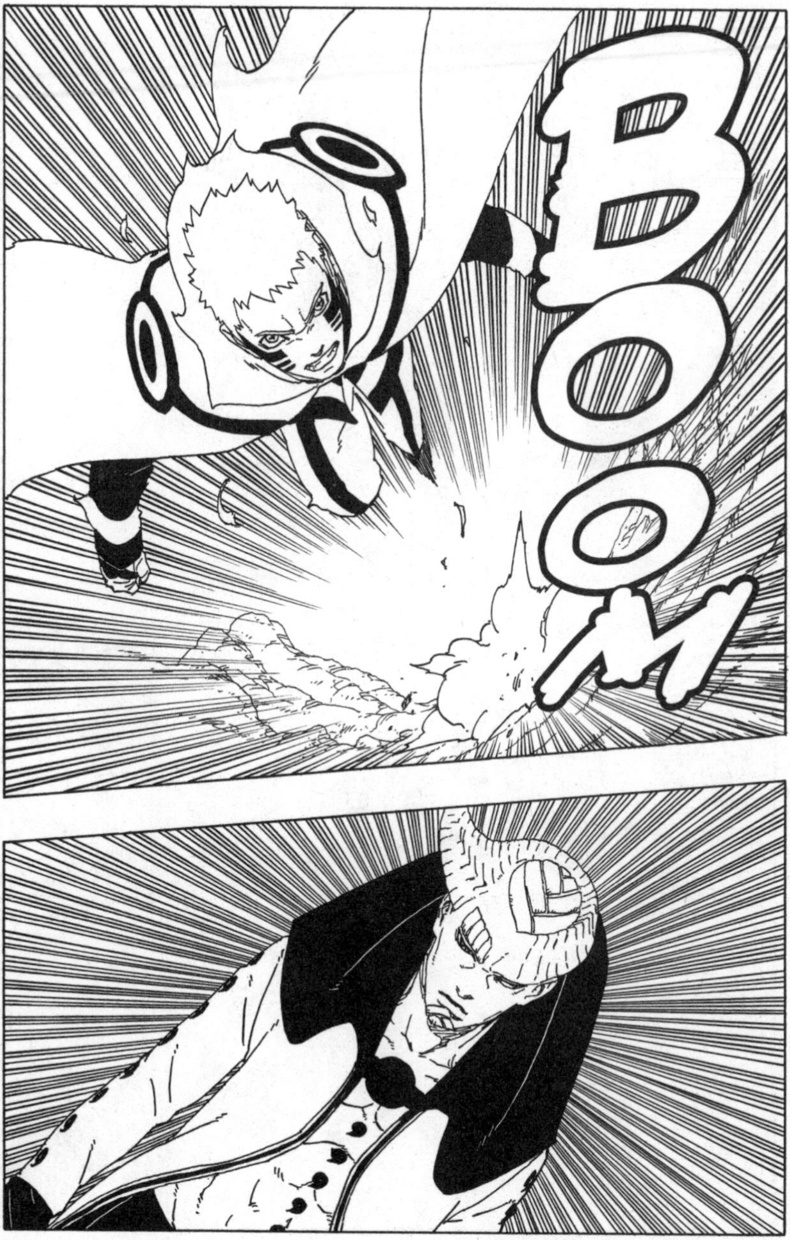
BOOOM

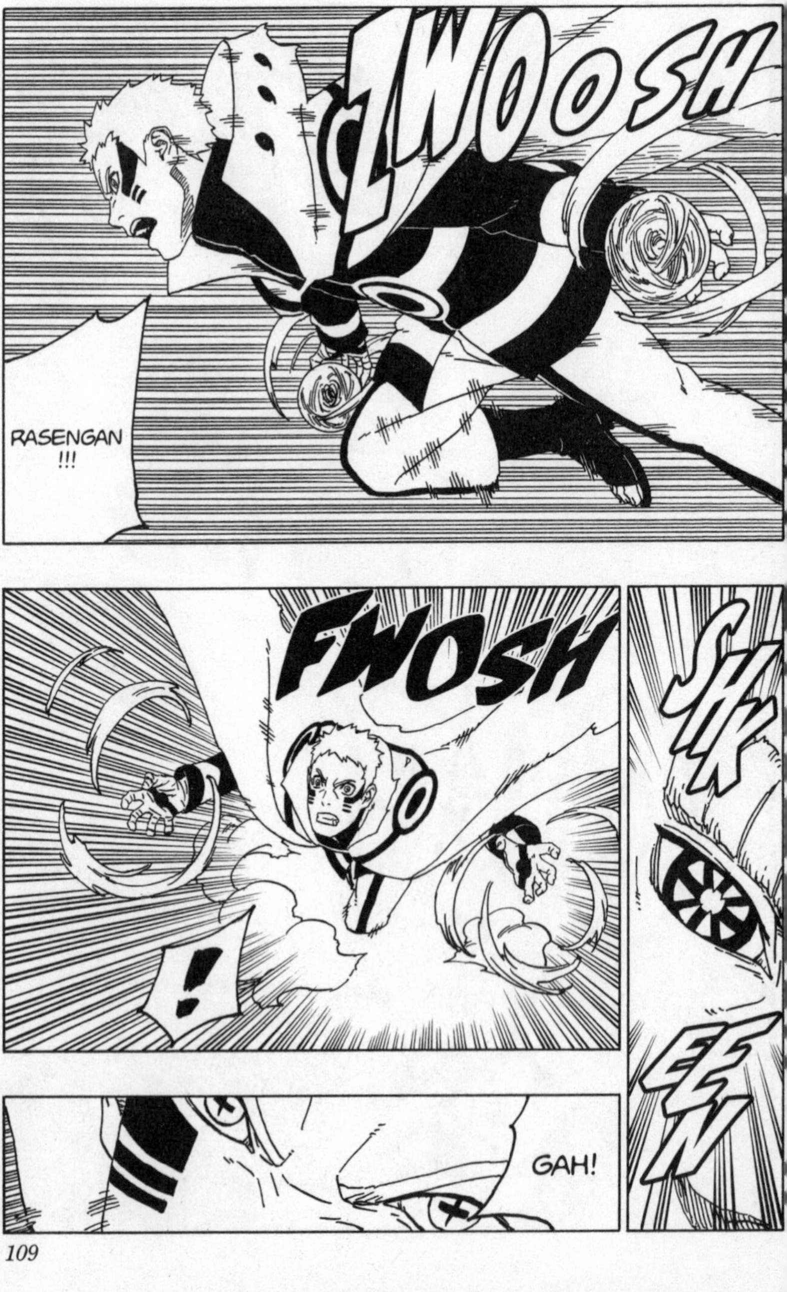
ZWOOSH
RASENGAN!!!
SHK
EEN
FWOSH
!
GAH!

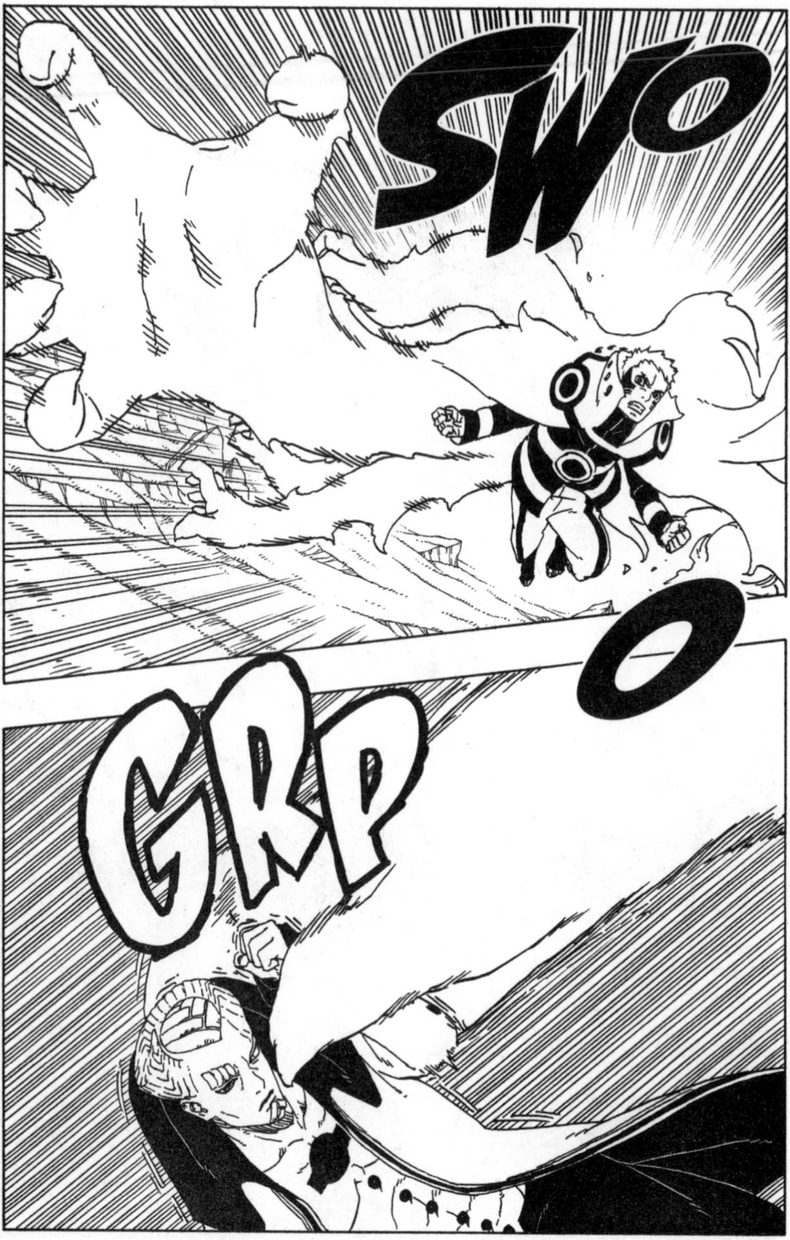
SWOO
GRP

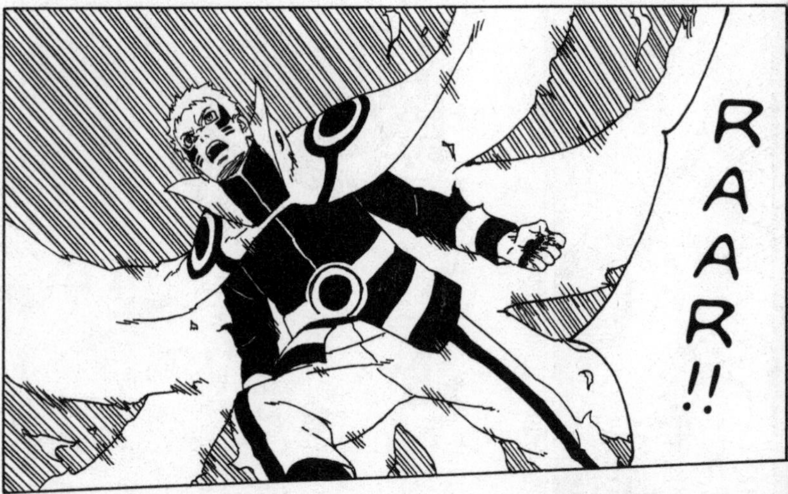
RAAR!!

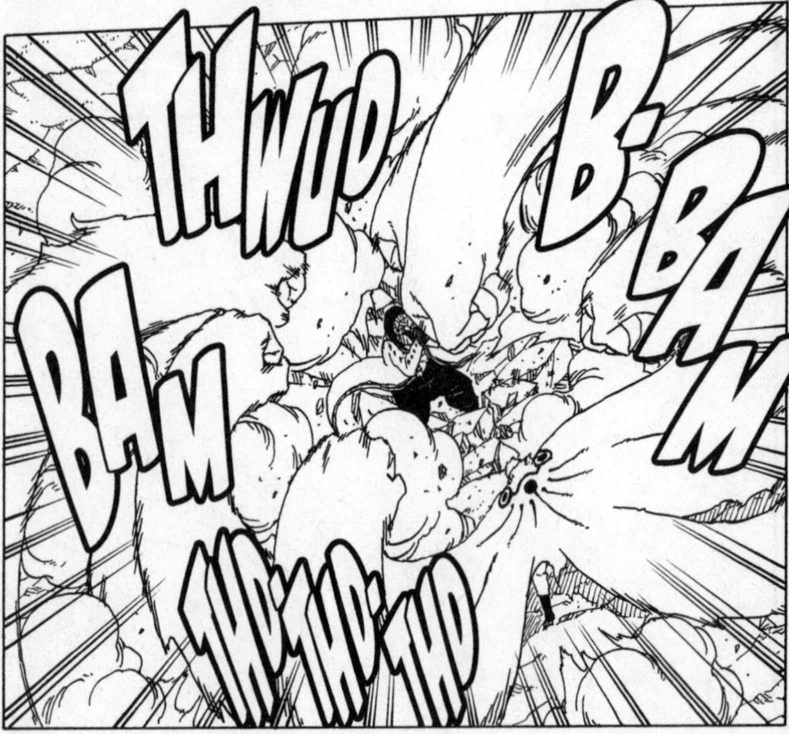
B-BAM
THWUD
BAM
THD-THD-THD

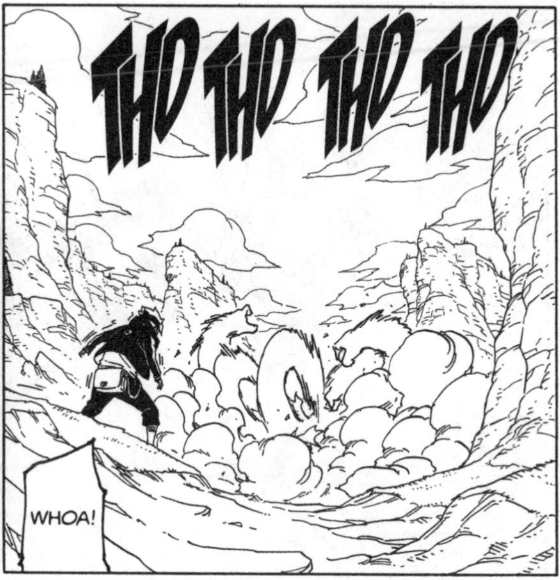
THD THD THD THD
WHOA!

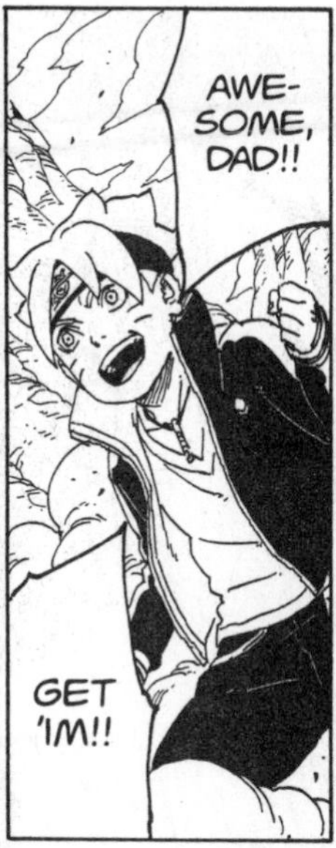
AWE-SOME, DAD!!
GET 'IM!!

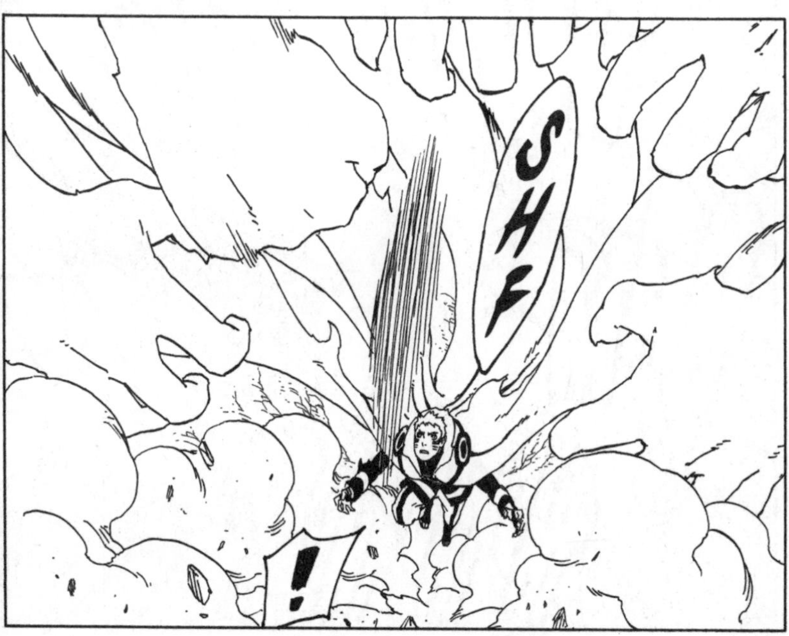
SHF
!

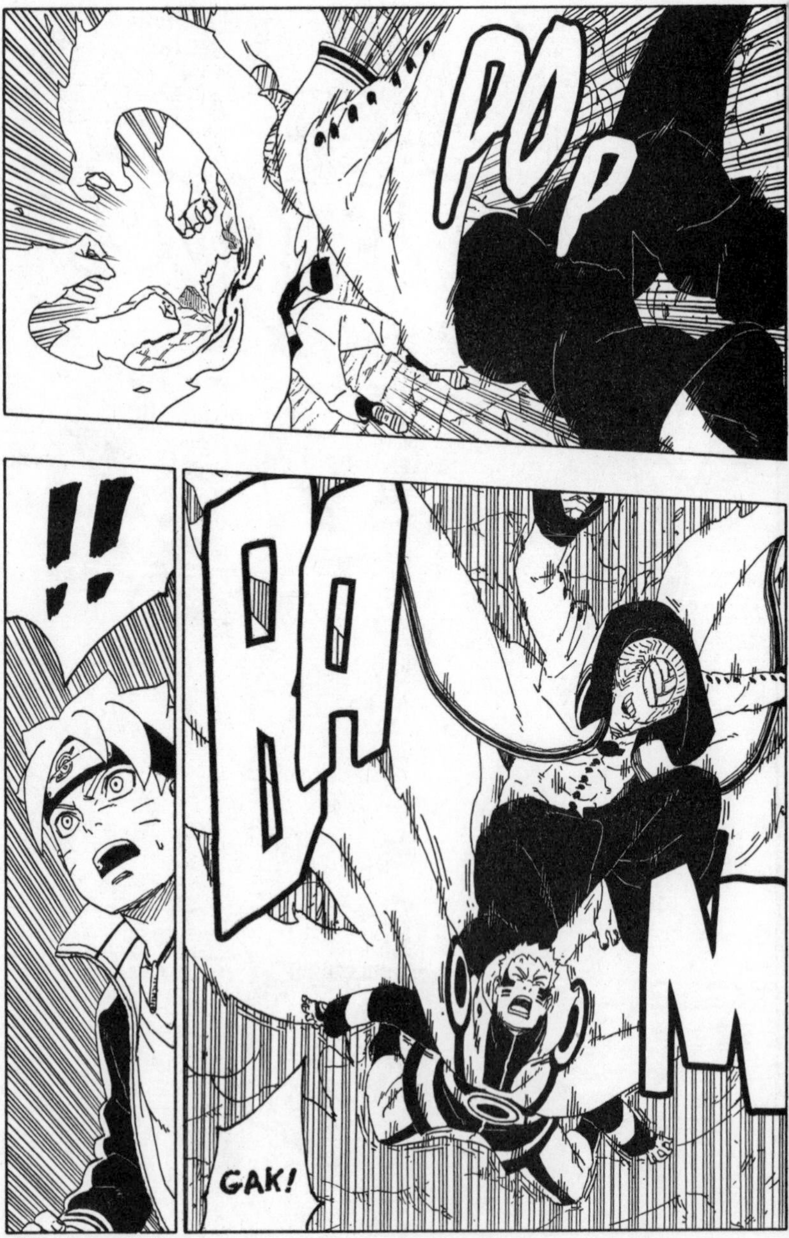
POP
BAM
GAK!
!!

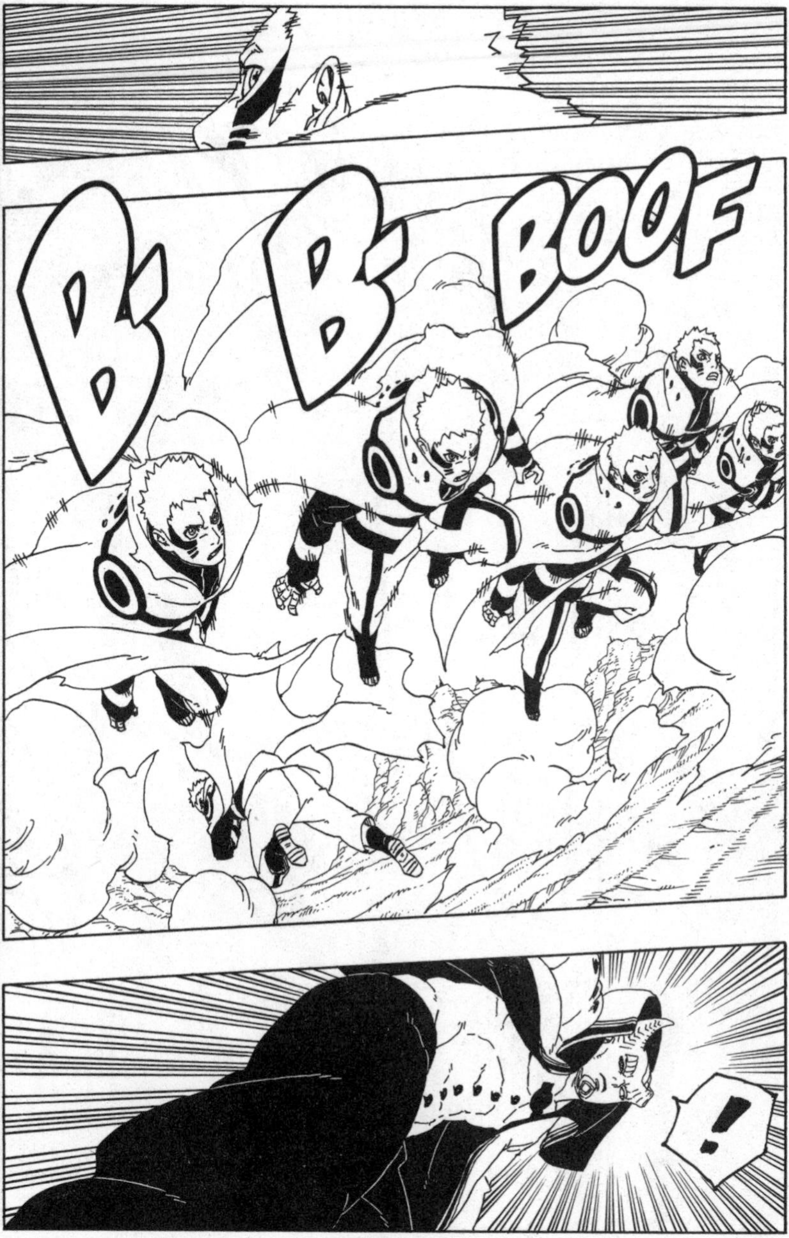
B- B- BOOF
!

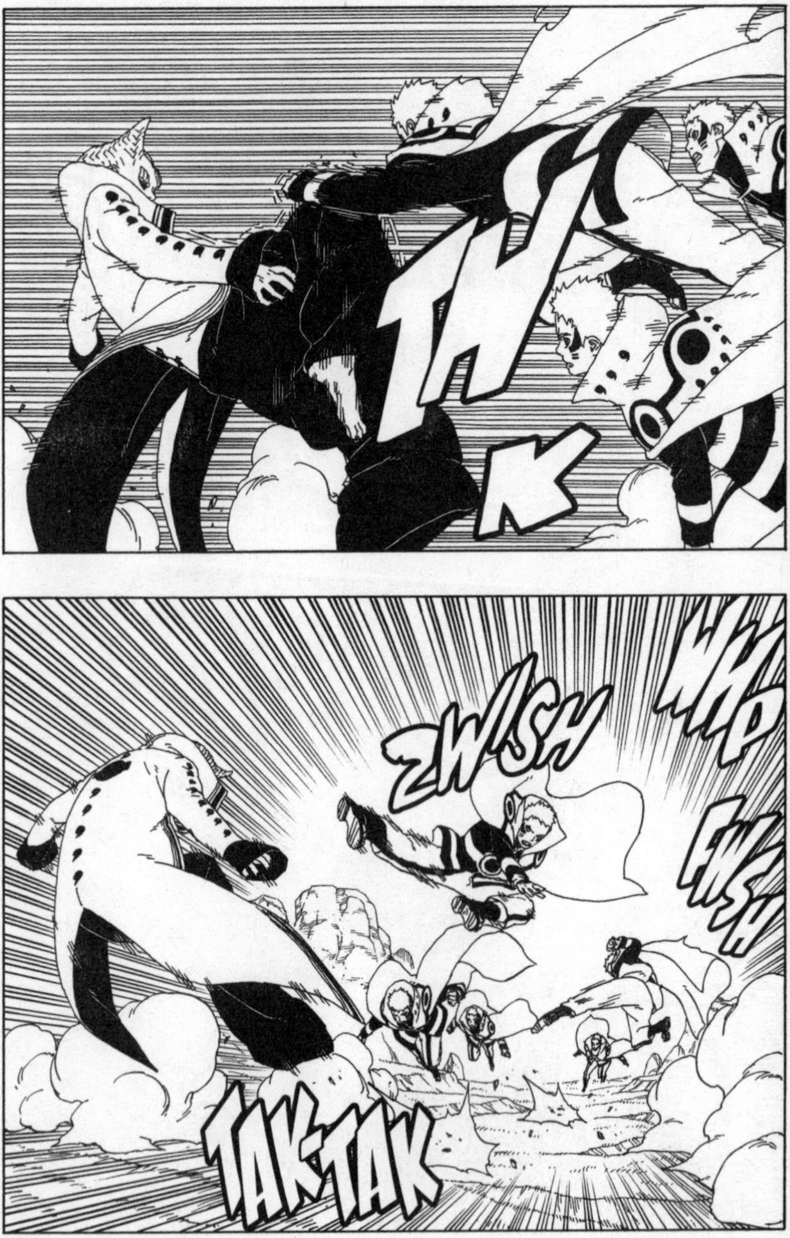
THK
WHP
FWSH
ZWISH
TAK-TAK

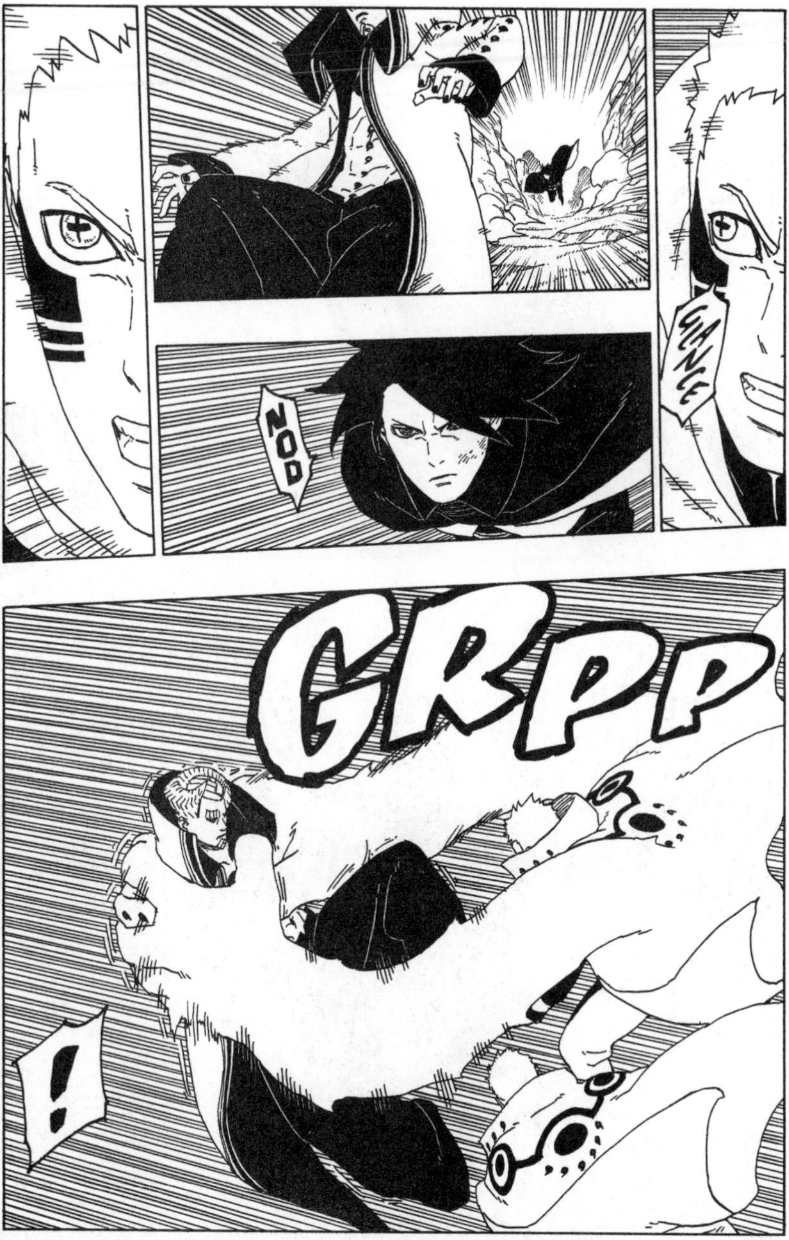
GLANCE
NOD
GRPP
!

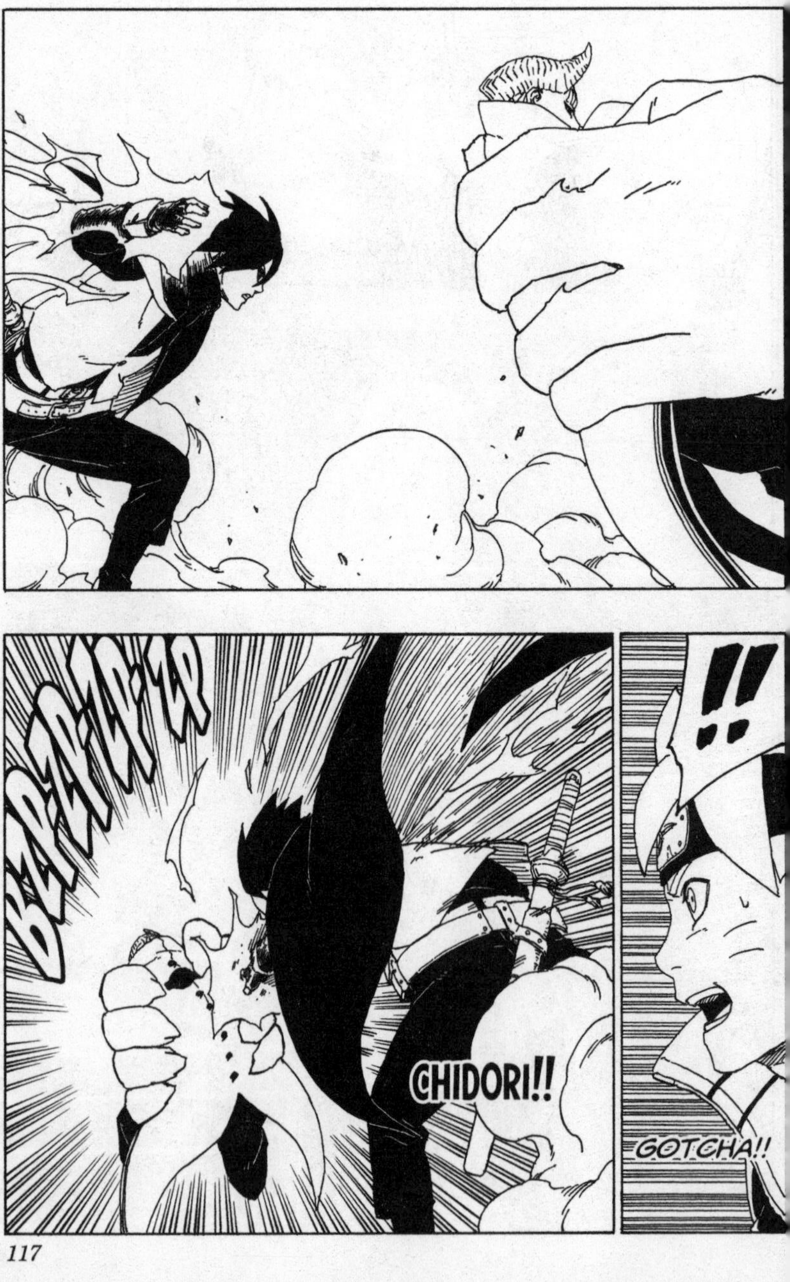
!!
GOTCHA!!
CHIDORI!!

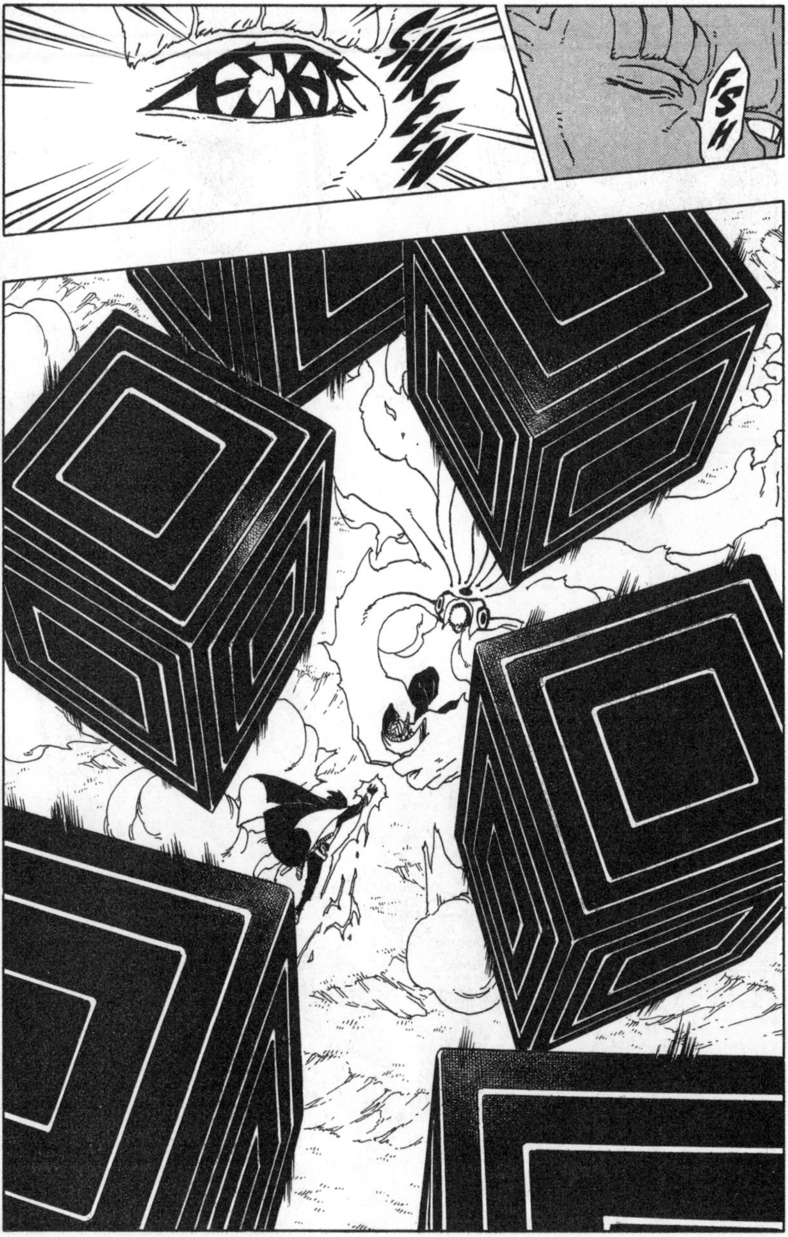
FSH
SHKEEN

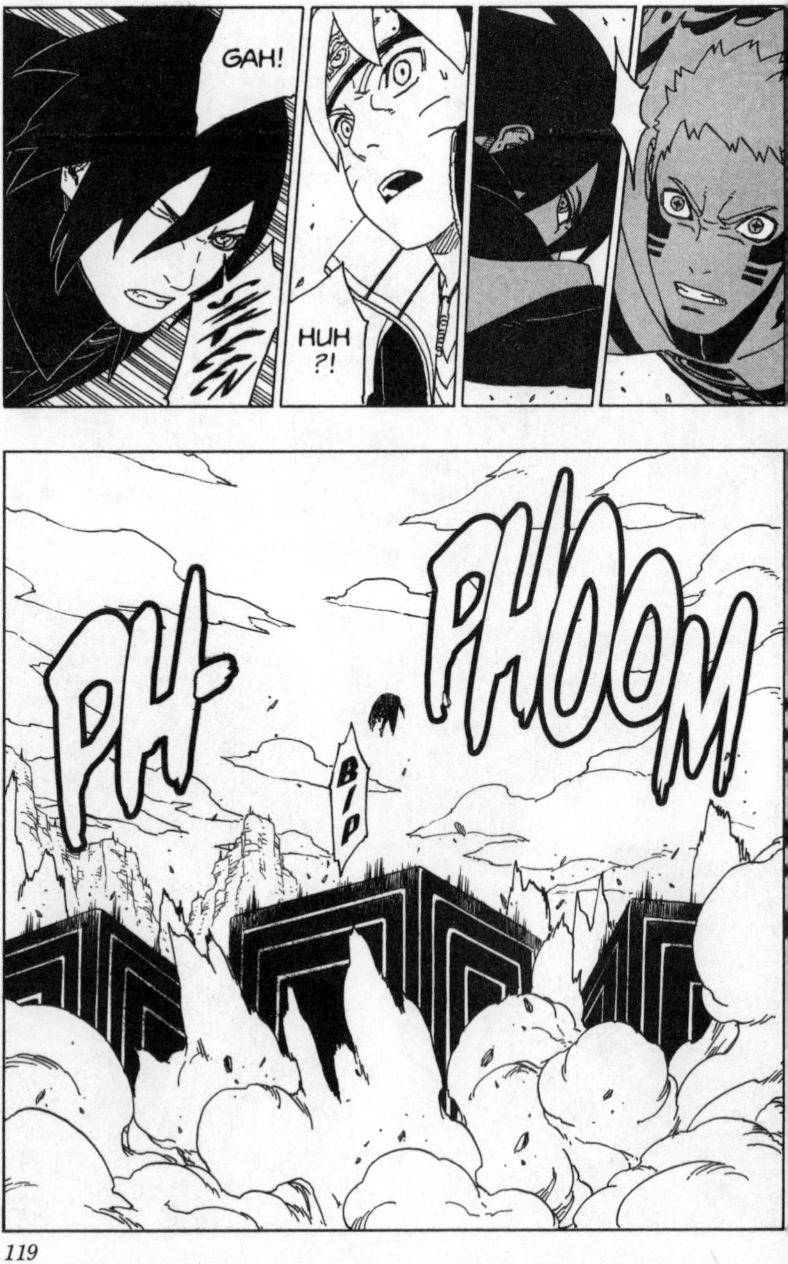
HUH ?!
GAH!
SHKEEN
PH PHOOM
BIP

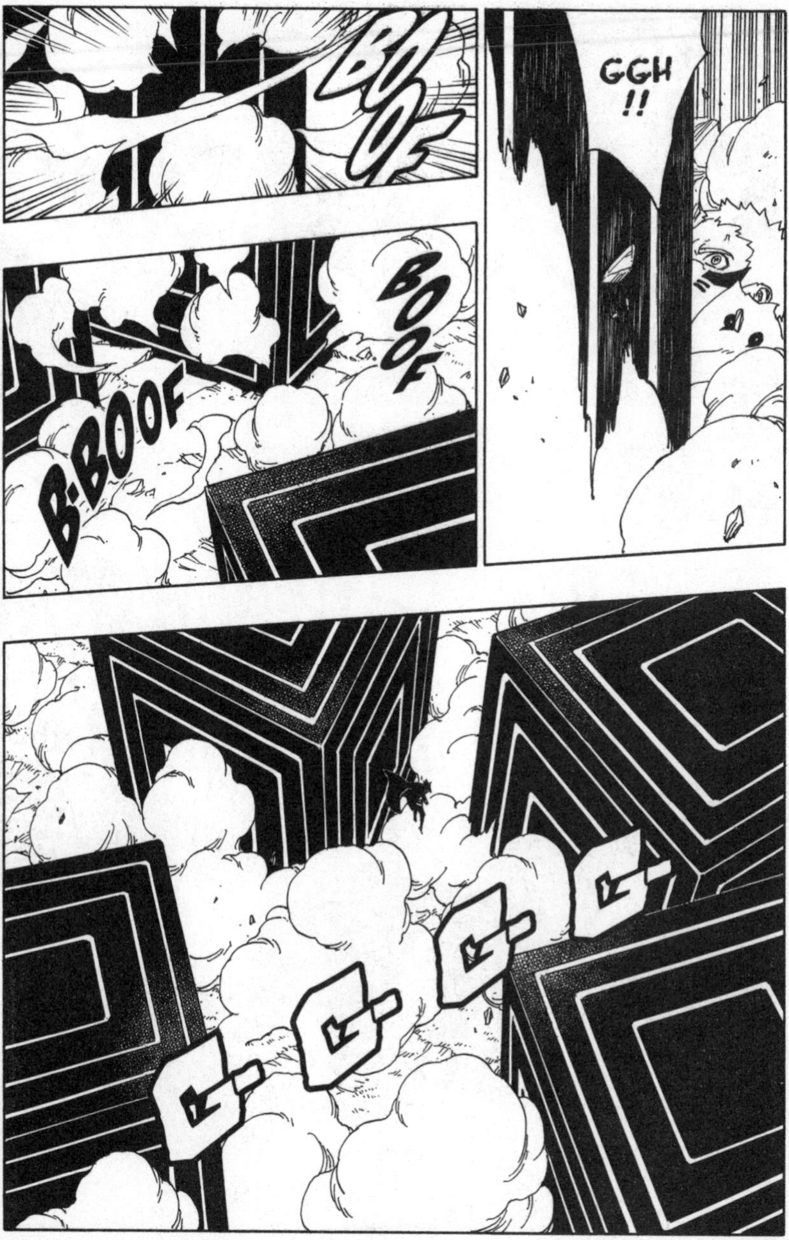
GGH !!
BOOF
BOOF
B-BOOF

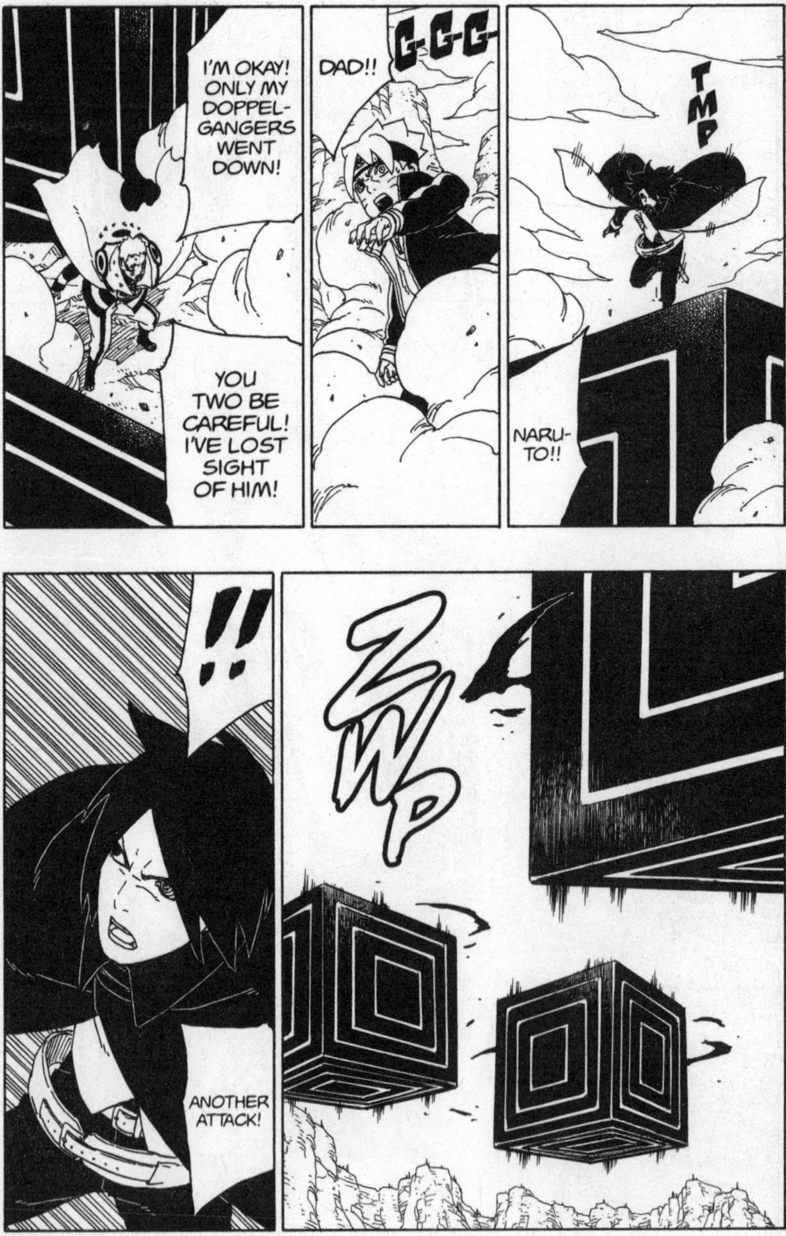
TMP
NARU-TO!!
G-G-G-
DAD!!
I'M OKAY! ONLY MY DOPPEL-GANGERS WENT DOWN!
YOU TWO BE CAREFUL! I'VE LOST SIGHT OF HIM!
ZWP
!!
ANOTHER ATTACK!

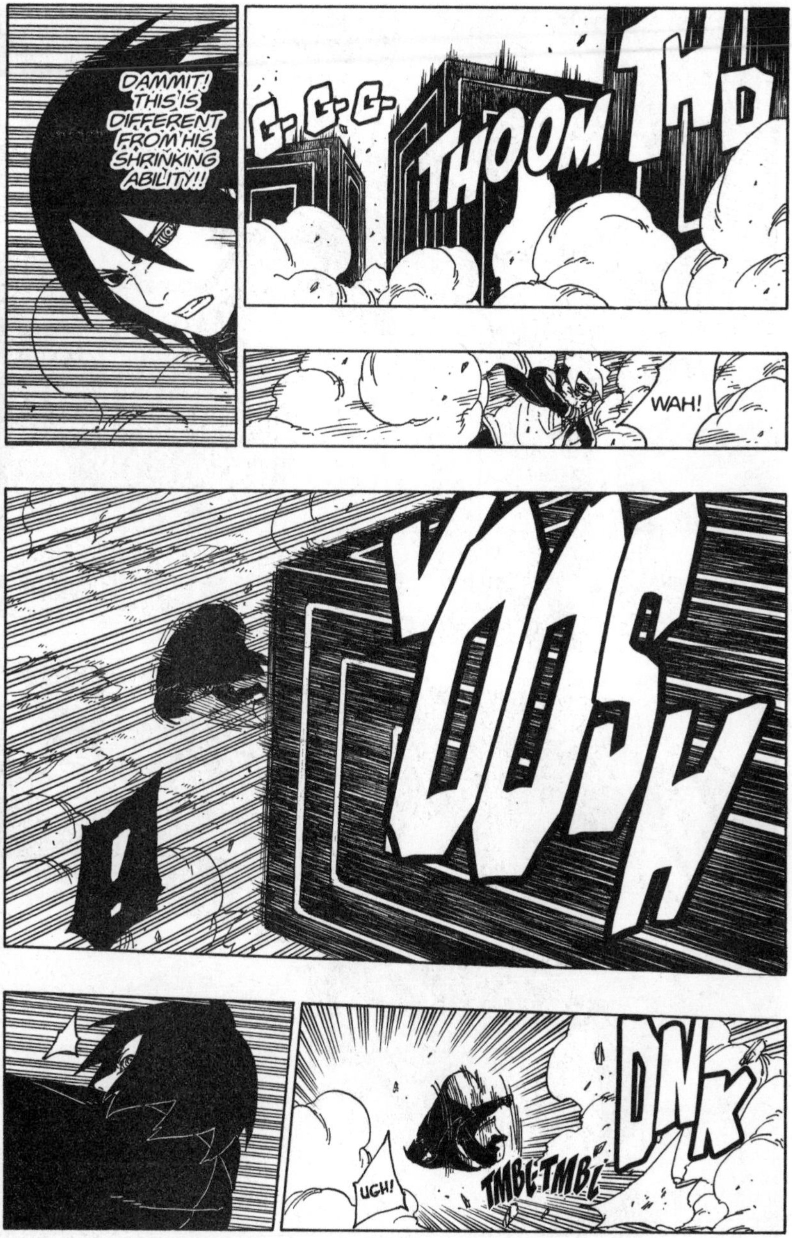

G-G-G-
THOOM
THD
WAH!
DAMMIT! THIS IS DIFFERENT FROM HIS SHRINKING ABILITY!!
YOOSH
DNK
TMBL TMBL
UGH!

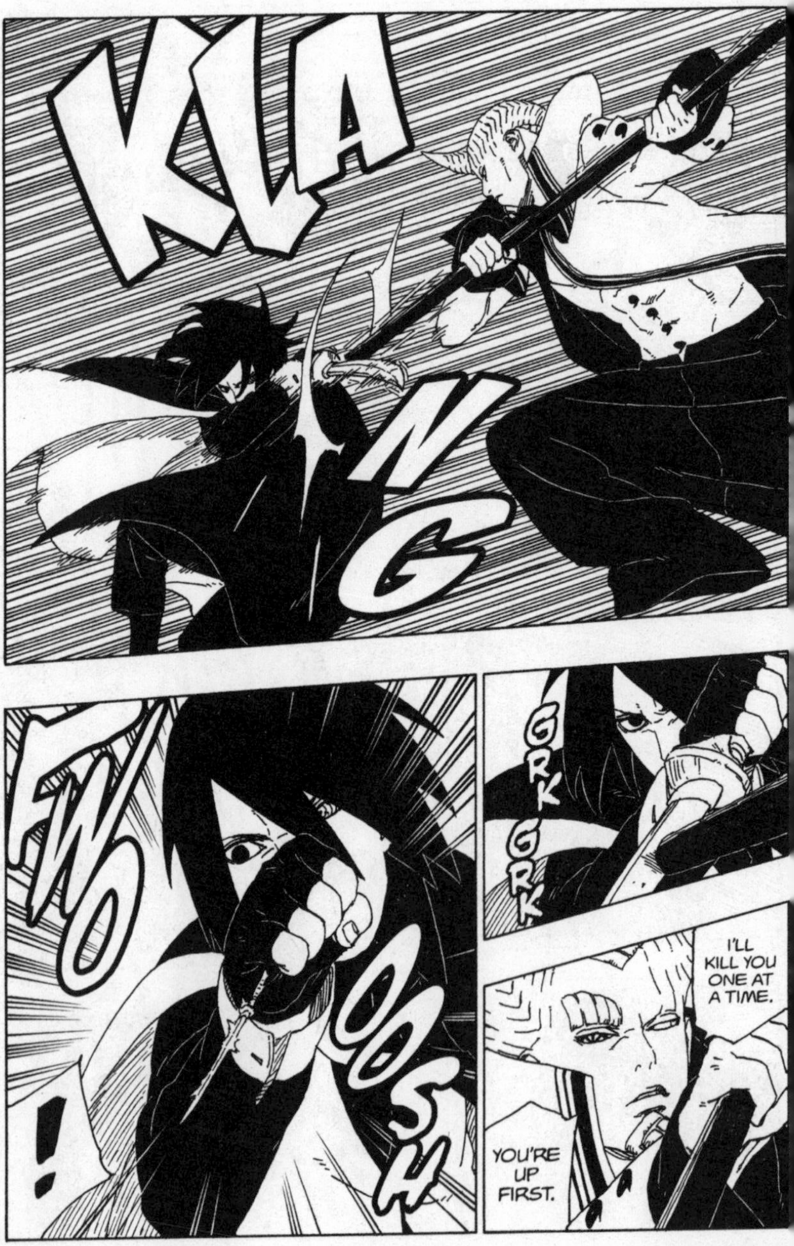
KLANG
GRK GRK
I'LL KILL YOU ONE AT A TIME.
YOU'RE UP FIRST.
FWOOOSH
!

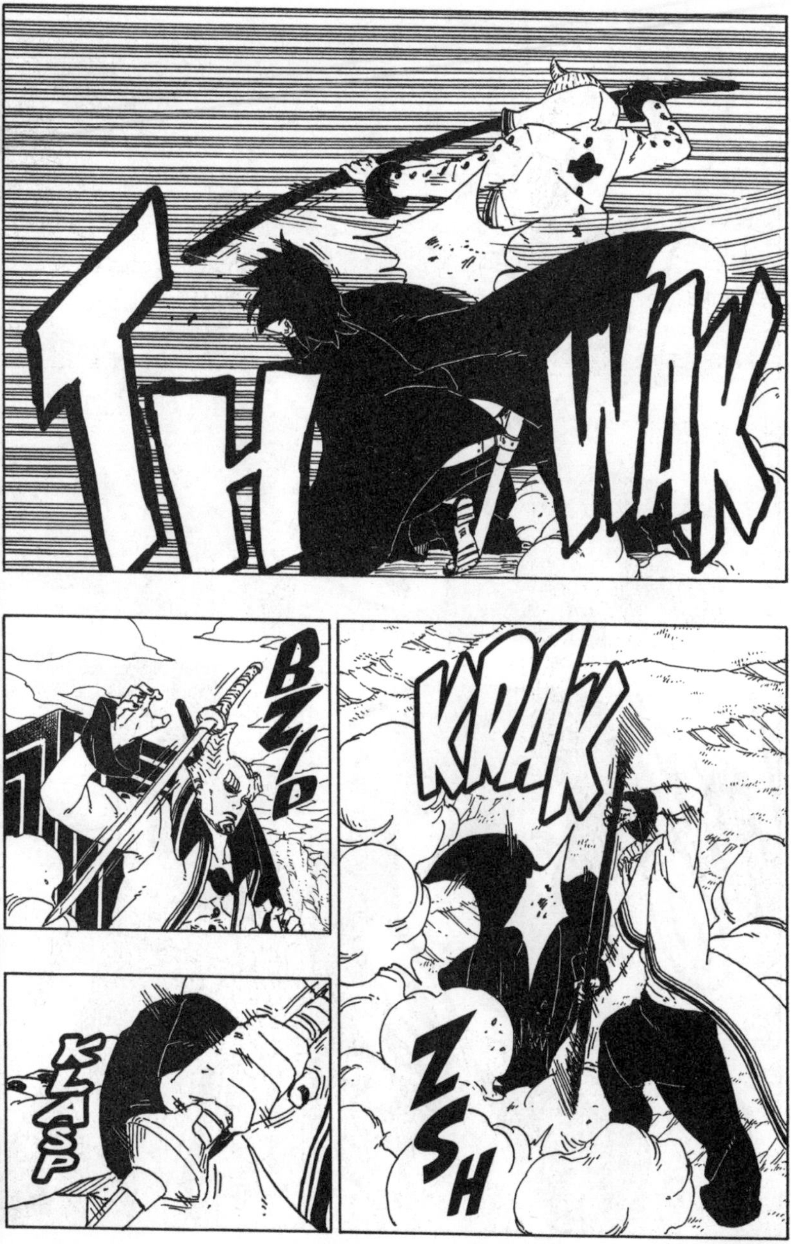
THWAK
KRAK
ZSH
BZIP
KLASP

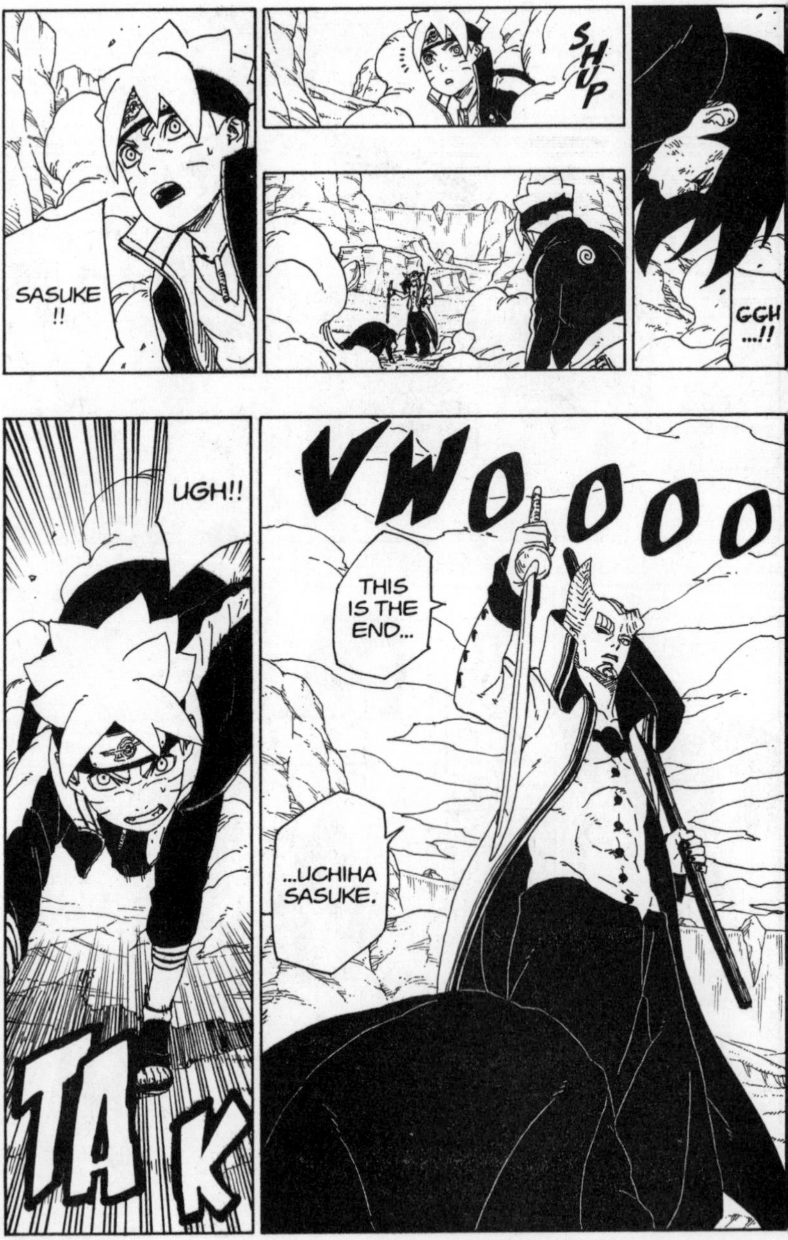
GGH ...!!
SHUP
SASUKE !!
VWOOOO
THIS IS THE END...
...UCHIHA SASUKE.
UGH!!
TAK

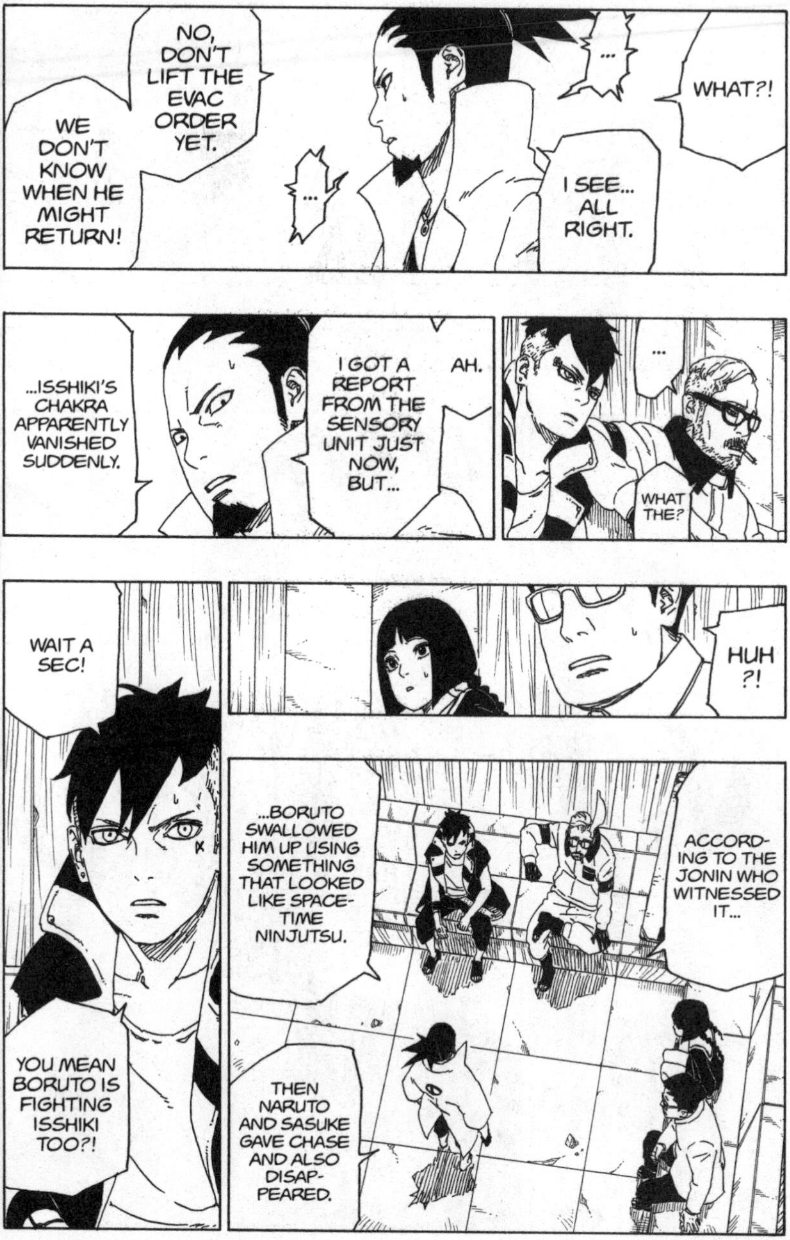
WHAT?!
...
I SEE... ALL RIGHT.
NO, DON'T LIFT THE EVAC ORDER YET.
...
WE DON'T KNOW WHEN HE MIGHT RETURN!
...
WHAT THE?
AH.
I GOT A REPORT FROM THE SENSORY UNIT JUST NOW, BUT...
...ISSHIKI'S CHAKRA APPARENTLY VANISHED SUDDENLY.
HUH?!
ACCORDING TO THE JONIN WHO WITNESSED IT...
...BORUTO SWALLOWED HIM UP USING SOMETHING THAT LOOKED LIKE SPACE-TIME NINJUTSU.
THEN NARUTO AND SASUKE GAVE CHASE AND ALSO DISAPPEARED.
WAIT A SEC!
YOU MEAN BORUTO IS FIGHTING ISSHIKI TOO?!

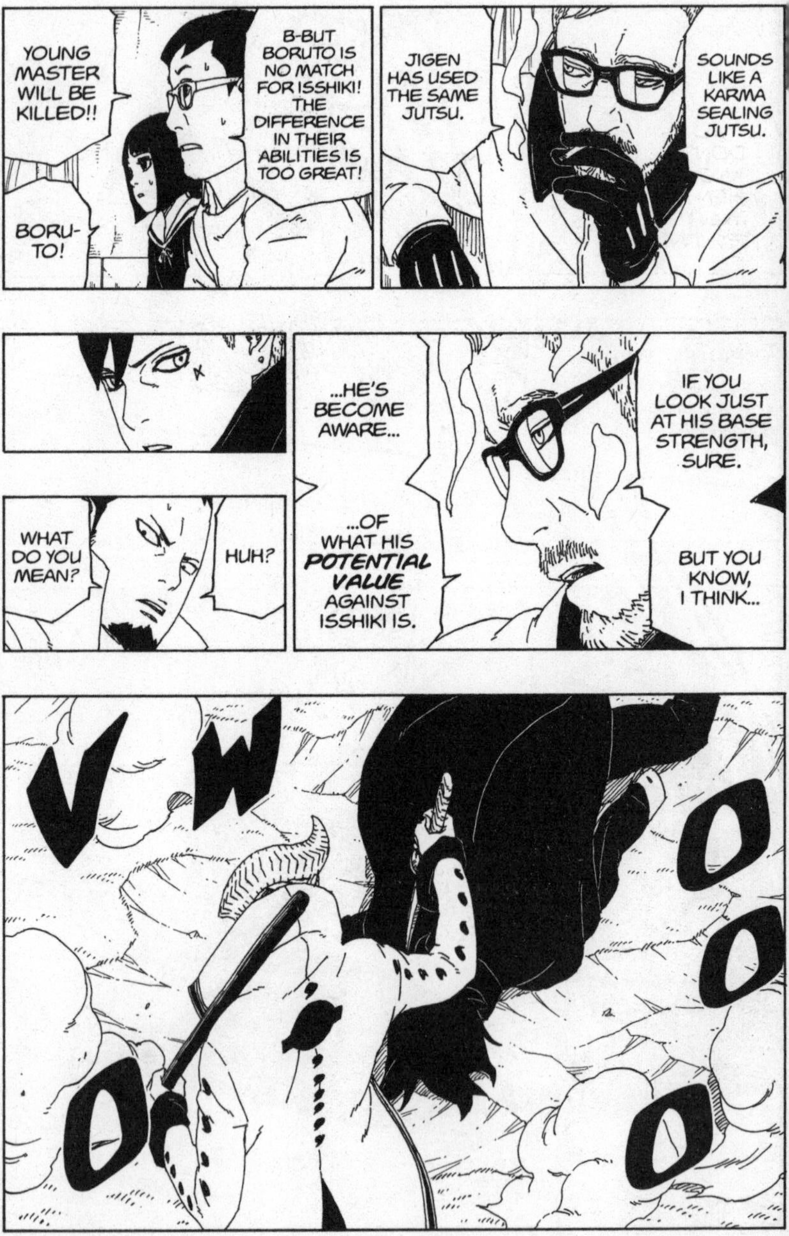
SOUNDS LIKE A KARMA SEALING JUTSU.
JIGEN HAS USED THE SAME JUTSU.
B-BUT BORUTO IS NO MATCH FOR ISSHIKI! THE DIFFERENCE IN THEIR ABILITIES IS TOO GREAT!
YOUNG MASTER WILL BE KILLED!!
BORU-TO!
IF YOU LOOK JUST AT HIS BASE STRENGTH, SURE.
BUT YOU KNOW, I THINK...
...HE'S BECOME AWARE...
...OF WHAT HIS **POTENTIAL VALUE** AGAINST ISSHIKI IS.
HUH?
WHAT DO YOU MEAN?
VWOOOO

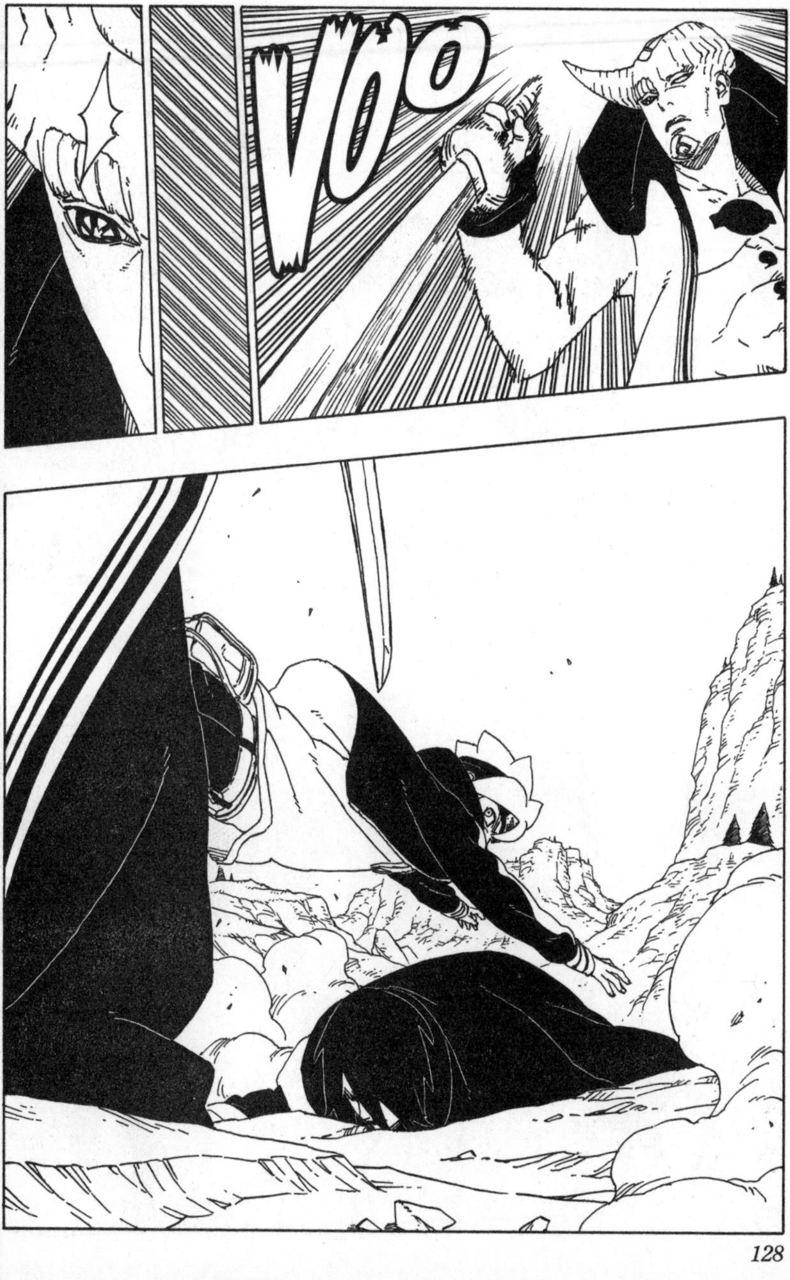
VOO

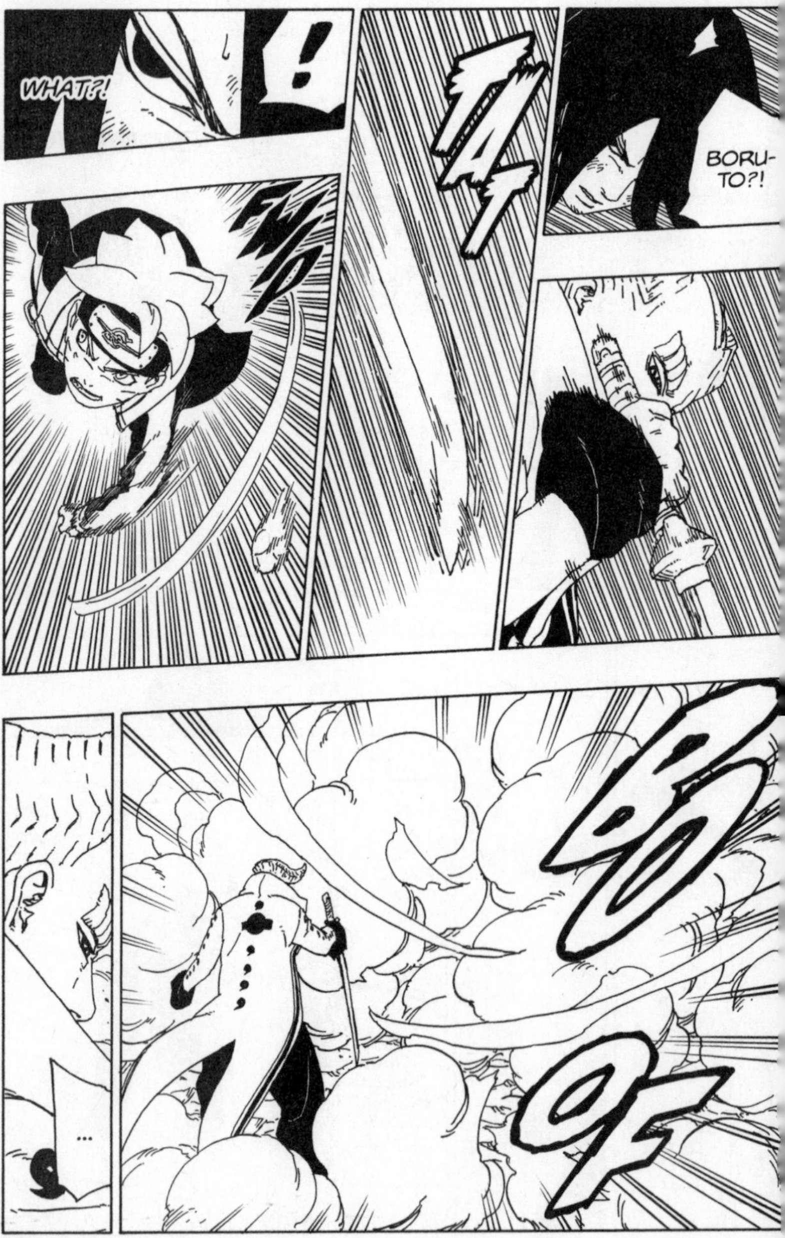
BORU-TO?!
WHAT?!
...

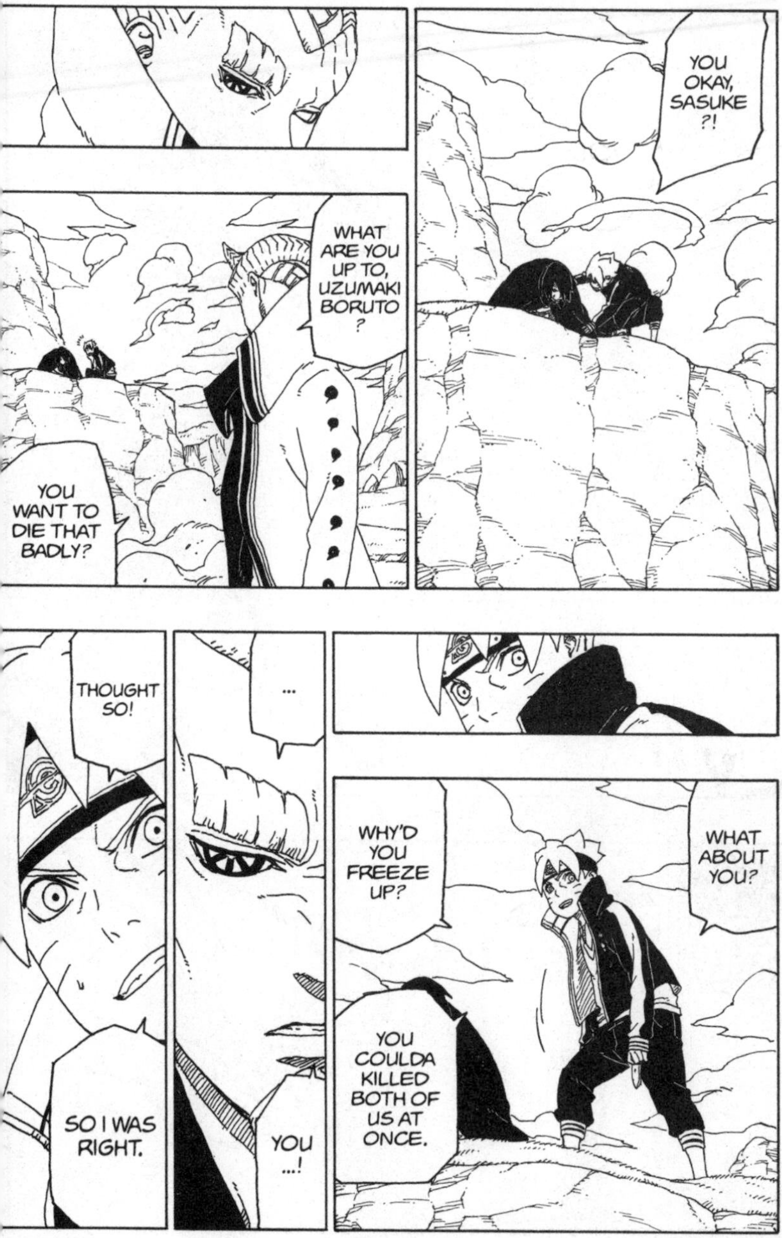
YOU OKAY, SASUKE?!
WHAT ARE YOU UP TO, UZUMAKI BORUTO?
YOU WANT TO DIE THAT BADLY?
WHAT ABOUT YOU?
WHY'D YOU FREEZE UP?
YOU COULDA KILLED BOTH OF US AT ONCE.
...
YOU ...!
THOUGHT SO!
SO I WAS RIGHT.

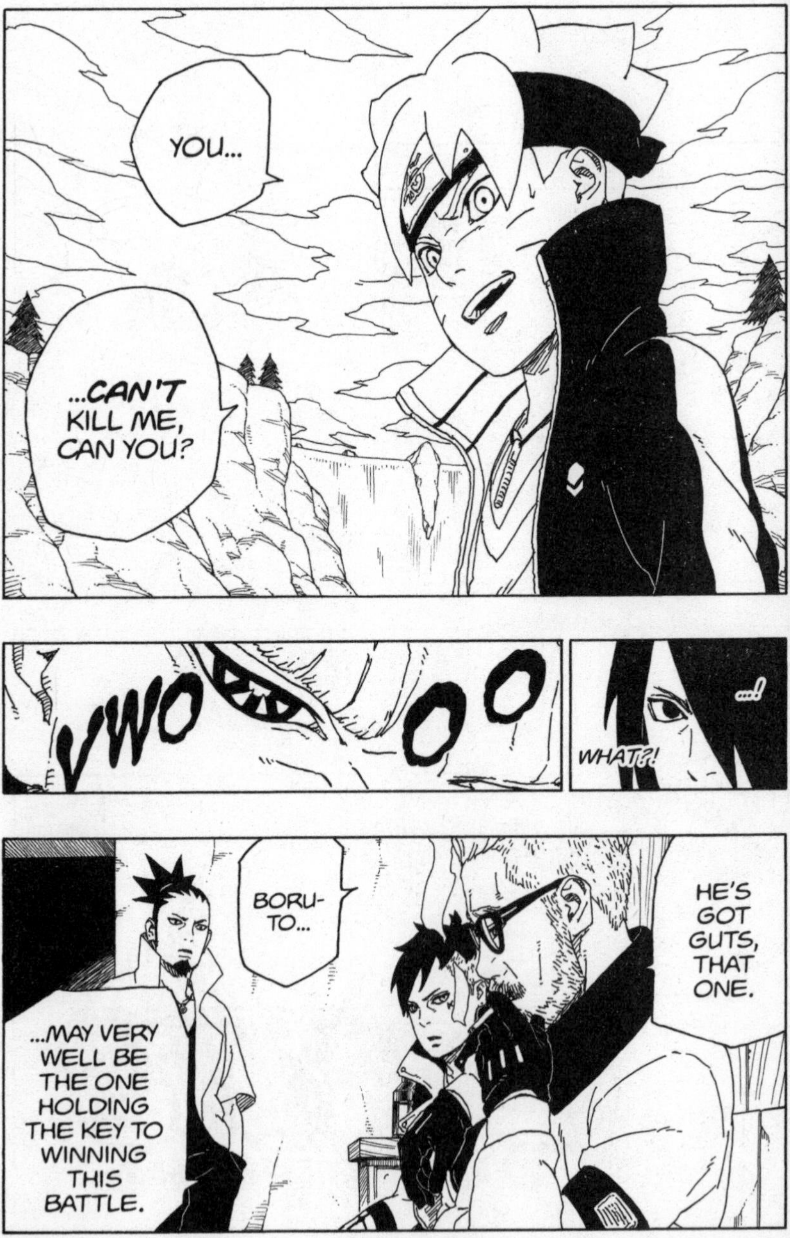
YOU...
...CAN'T KILL ME, CAN YOU?
...!
WHAT?!
VWOOO
HE'S GOT GUTS, THAT ONE.
BORU-TO...
...MAY VERY WELL BE THE ONE HOLDING THE KEY TO WINNING THIS BATTLE.

BORUTO

-NARUTO NEXT GENERATIONS-

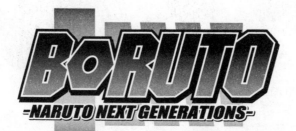

Number 51: Sacrifice

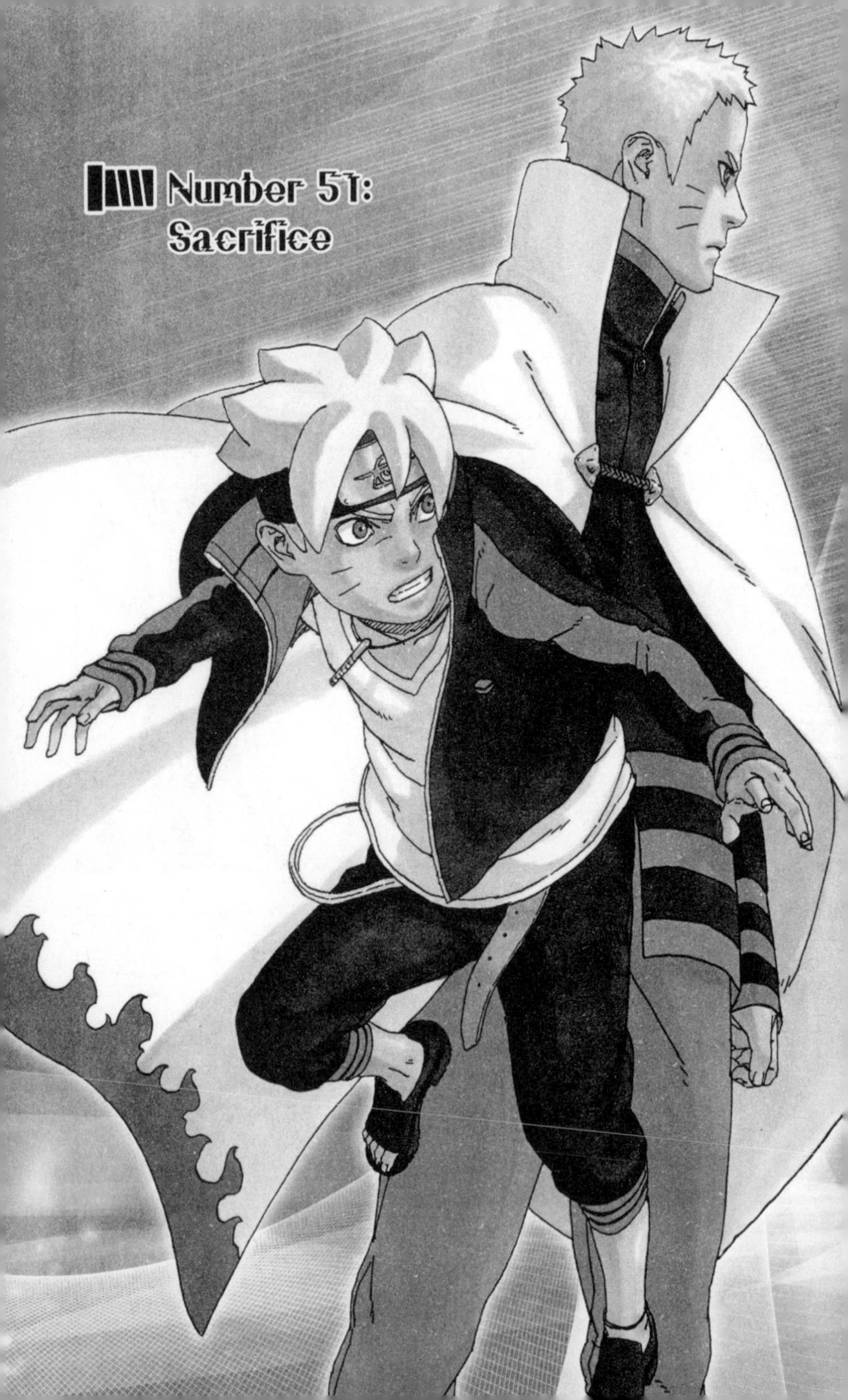

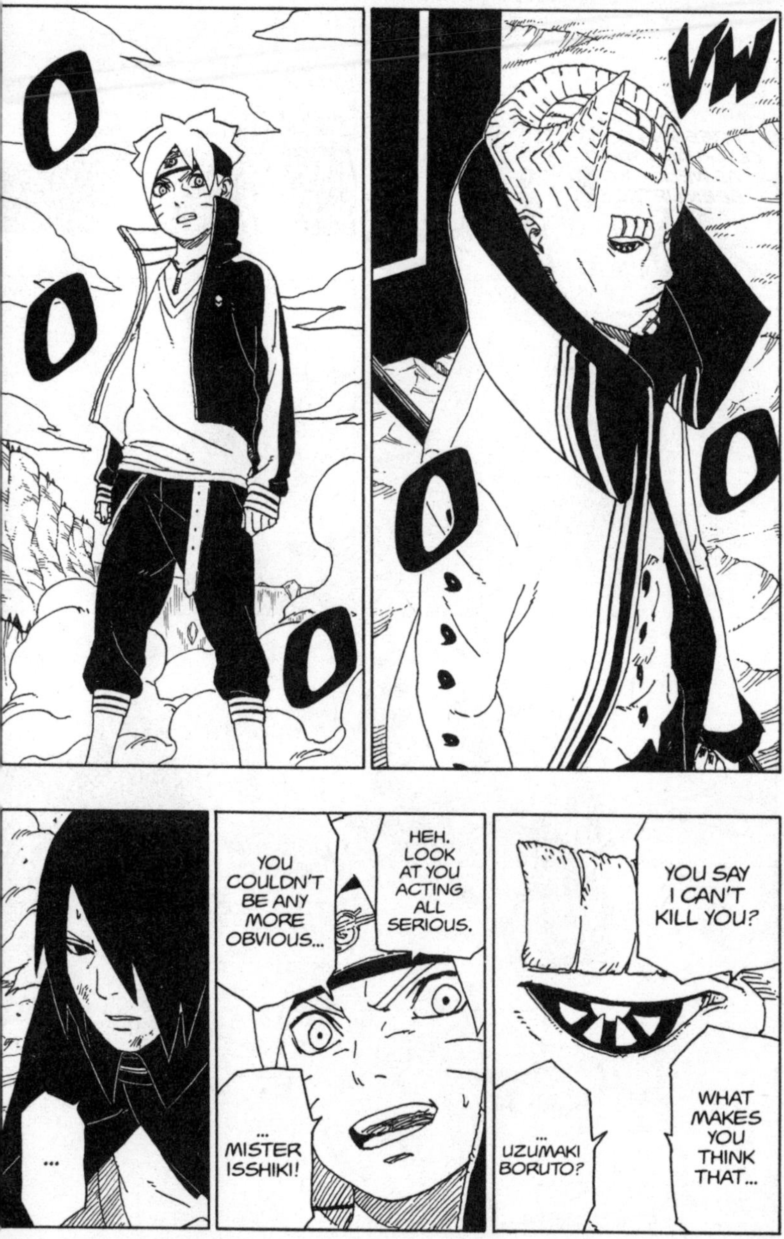
VW
O
O
O
O
O
YOU SAY I CAN'T KILL YOU?
WHAT MAKES YOU THINK THAT...
... UZUMAKI BORUTO?
HEH. LOOK AT YOU ACTING ALL SERIOUS.
YOU COULDN'T BE ANY MORE OBVIOUS...
... MISTER ISSHIKI!
...

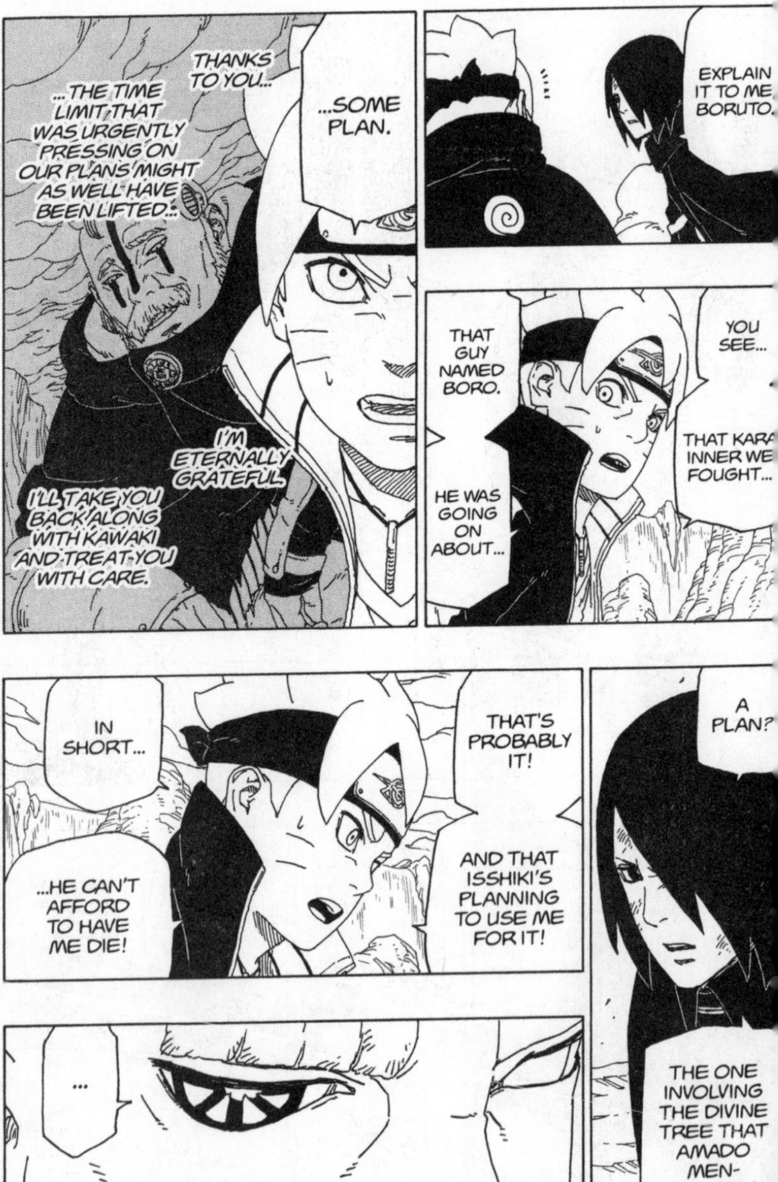
!!
EXPLAIN IT TO ME, BORUTO.
YOU SEE...
THAT KARA INNER WE FOUGHT...
THAT GUY NAMED BORO.
HE WAS GOING ON ABOUT...
...SOME PLAN.
THANKS TO YOU...
...THE TIME LIMIT THAT WAS URGENTLY PRESSING ON OUR PLANS MIGHT AS WELL HAVE BEEN LIFTED...
I'M ETERNALLY GRATEFUL.
I'LL TAKE YOU BACK ALONG WITH KAWAKI AND TREAT YOU WITH CARE.
A PLAN?
THE ONE INVOLVING THE DIVINE TREE THAT AMADO MENTIONED?
THAT'S PROBABLY IT!
AND THAT ISSHIKI'S PLANNING TO USE ME FOR IT!
IN SHORT...
...HE CAN'T AFFORD TO HAVE ME DIE!
...

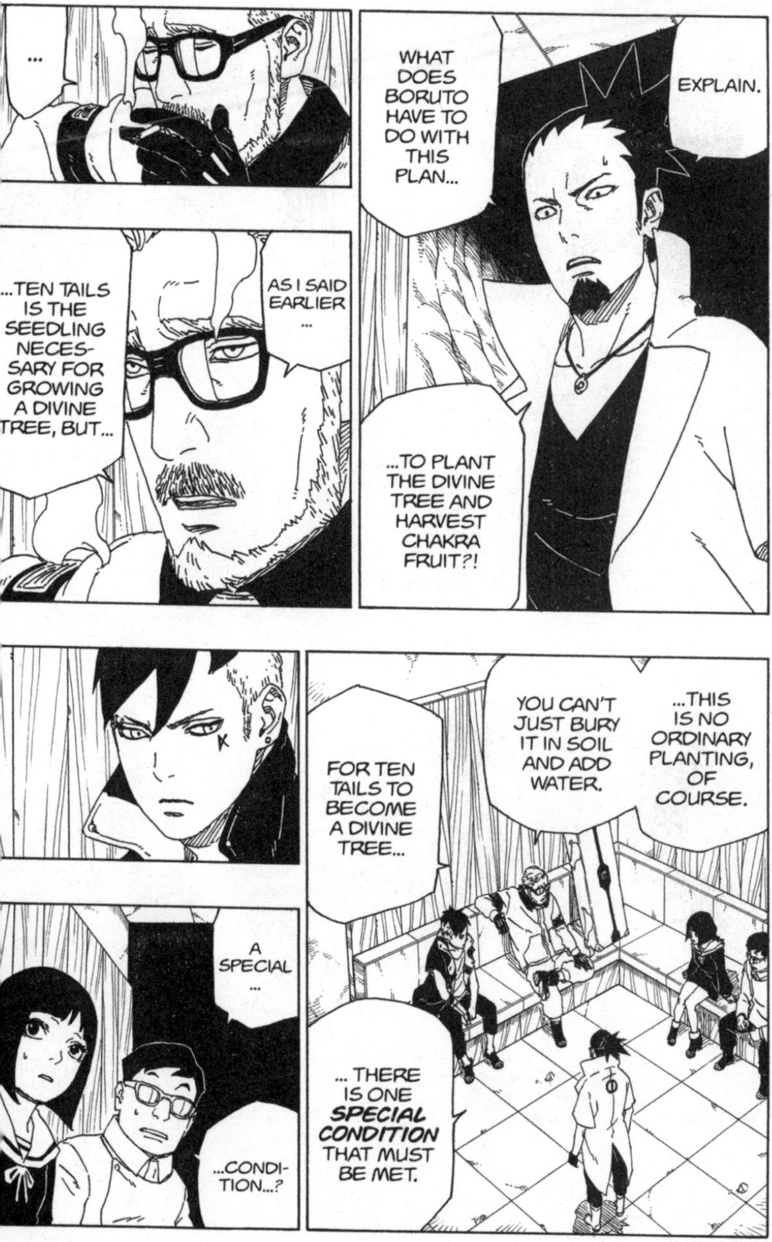
WHAT DOES BORUTO HAVE TO DO WITH THIS PLAN...
...TO PLANT THE DIVINE TREE AND HARVEST CHAKRA FRUIT?!
EXPLAIN.
...
AS I SAID EARLIER ...
...TEN TAILS IS THE SEEDLING NECES-SARY FOR GROWING A DIVINE TREE, BUT...
...THIS IS NO ORDINARY PLANTING, OF COURSE.
YOU CAN'T JUST BURY IT IN SOIL AND ADD WATER.
FOR TEN TAILS TO BECOME A DIVINE TREE...
... THERE IS ONE ***SPECIAL CONDITION*** THAT MUST BE MET.
A SPECIAL ...
...CONDI-TION...?

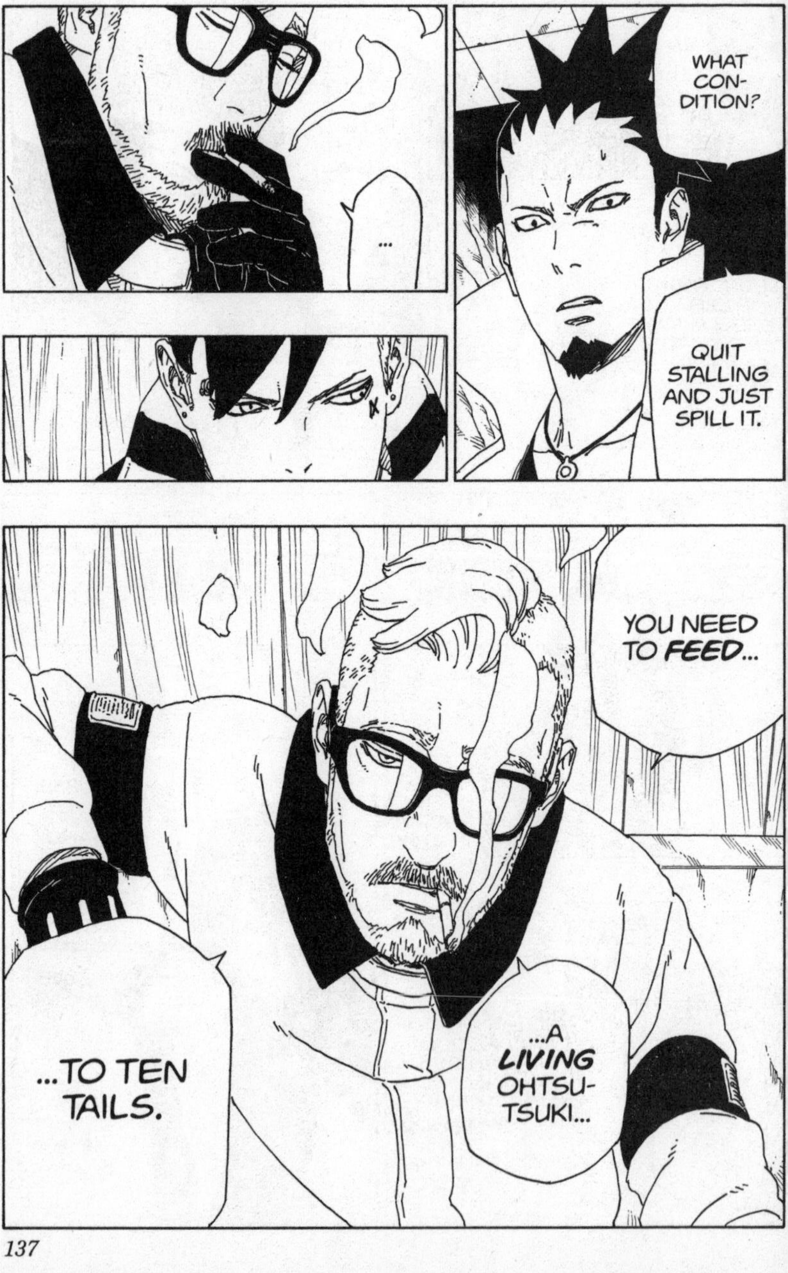
WHAT CON-DITION?
QUIT STALLING AND JUST SPILL IT.
...
YOU NEED TO **FEED**...
...A ***LIVING*** OHTSU-TSUKI...
...TO TEN TAILS.

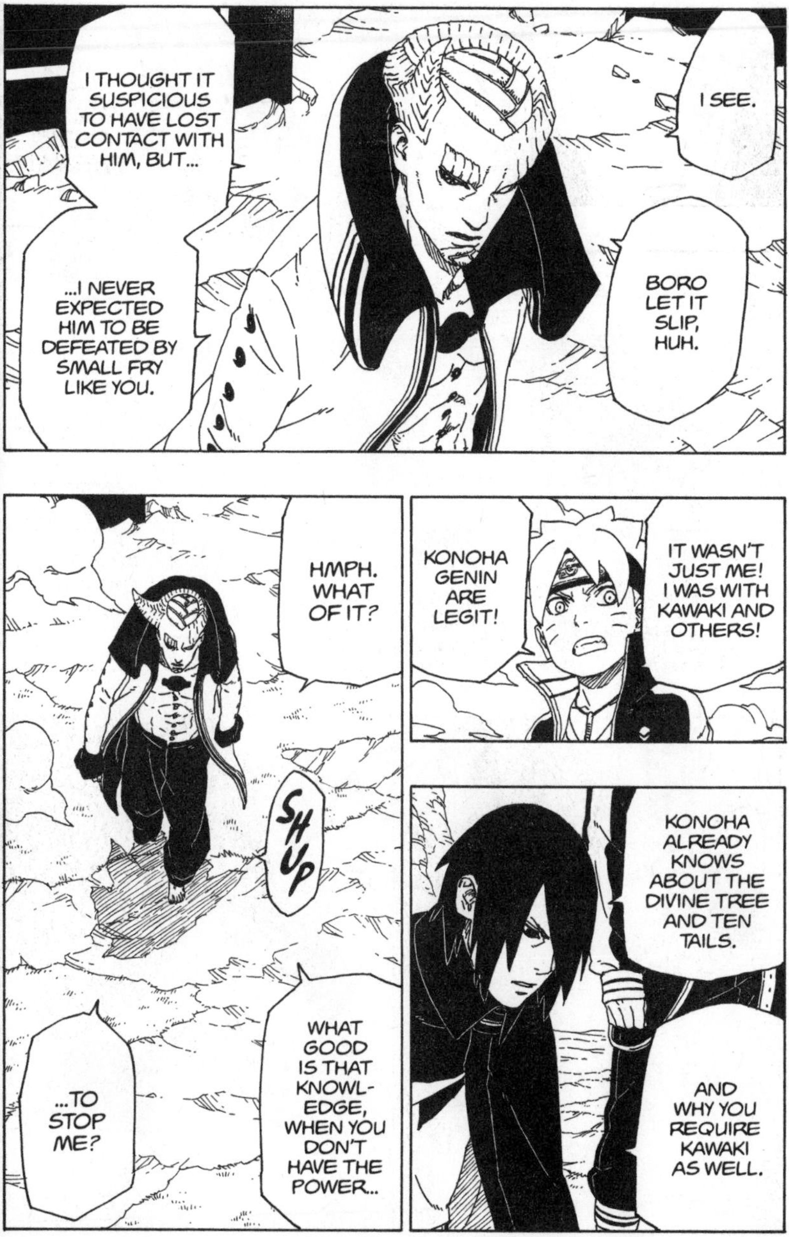
I SEE.
BORO LET IT SLIP, HUH.
I THOUGHT IT SUSPICIOUS TO HAVE LOST CONTACT WITH HIM, BUT...
...I NEVER EXPECTED HIM TO BE DEFEATED BY SMALL FRY LIKE YOU.
IT WASN'T JUST ME! I WAS WITH KAWAKI AND OTHERS!
KONOHA GENIN ARE LEGIT!
KONOHA ALREADY KNOWS ABOUT THE DIVINE TREE AND TEN TAILS.
AND WHY YOU REQUIRE KAWAKI AS WELL.
HMPH. WHAT OF IT?
SHUP
WHAT GOOD IS THAT KNOWL-EDGE, WHEN YOU DON'T HAVE THE POWER..
...TO STOP ME?

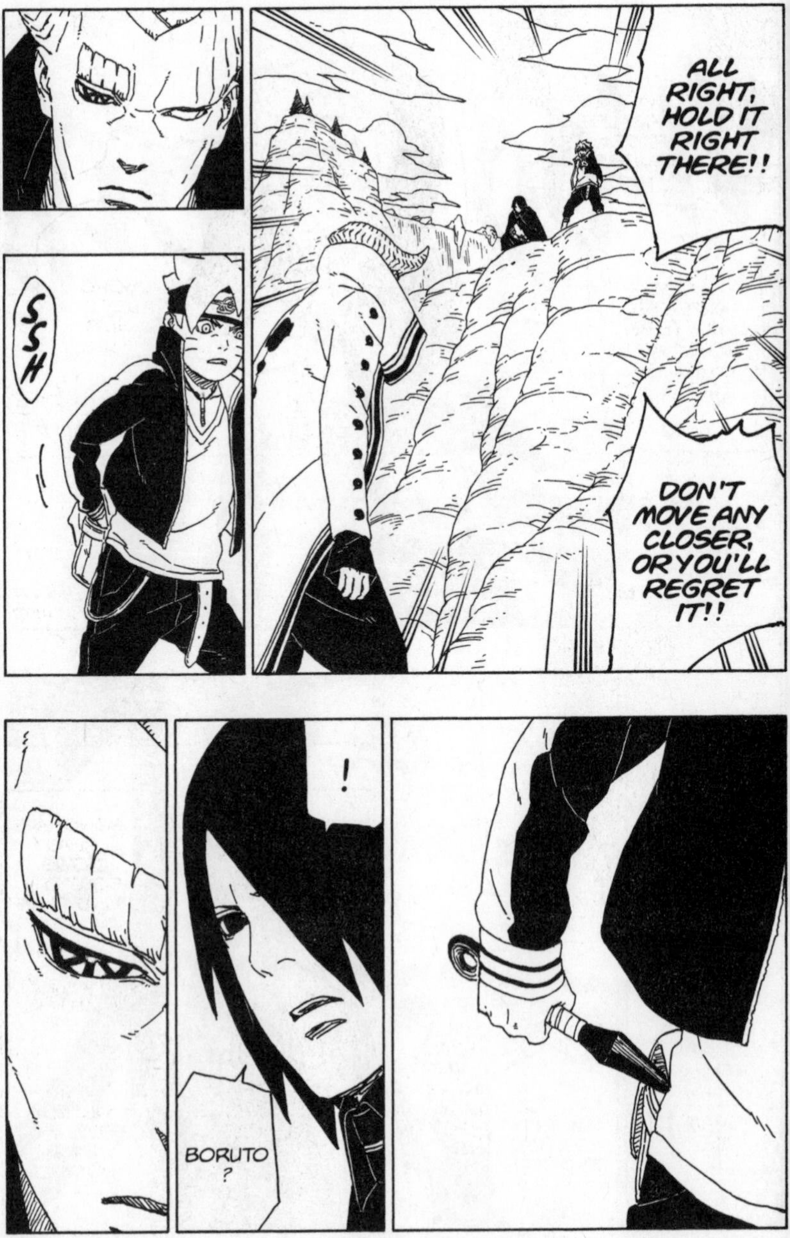
ALL RIGHT, HOLD IT RIGHT THERE!!
DON'T MOVE ANY CLOSER, OR YOU'LL REGRET IT!!
SSH
!
BORUTO?

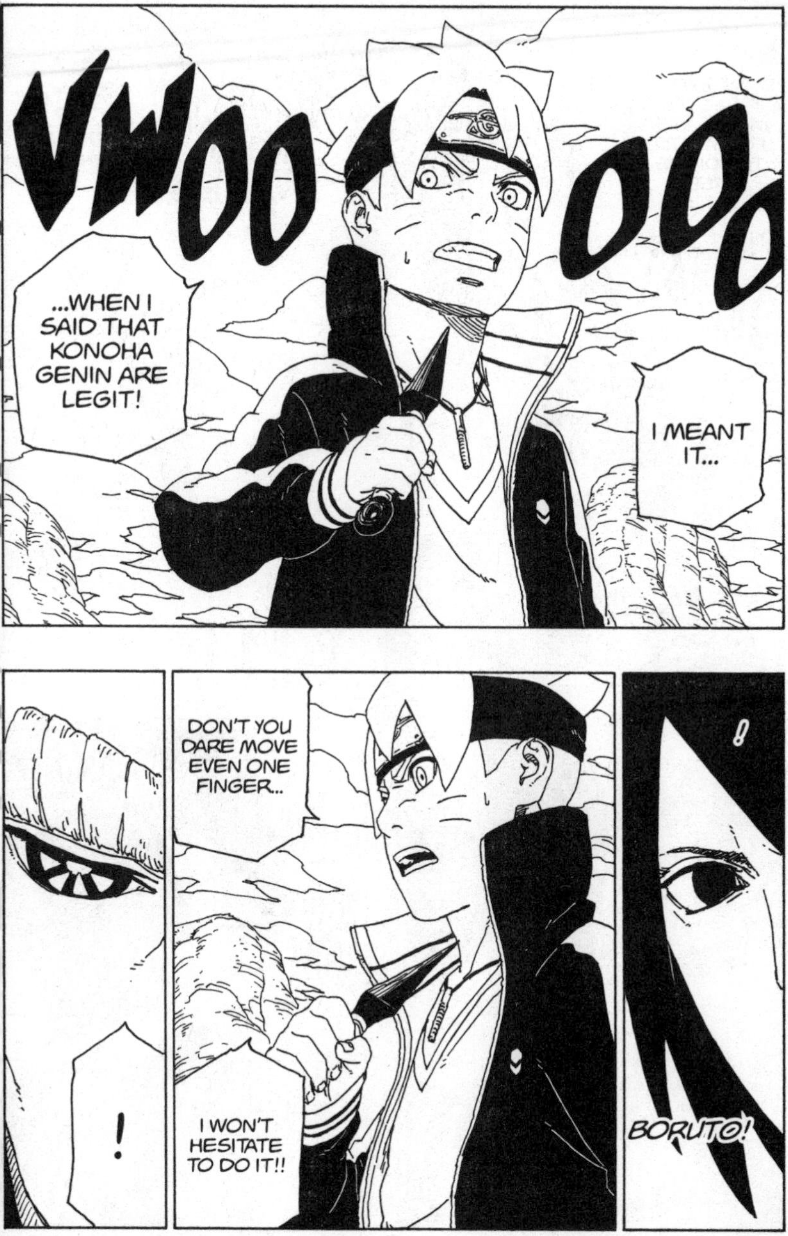
VWOOOOO
I MEANT IT...
...WHEN I SAID THAT KONOHA GENIN ARE LEGIT!
!
BORUTO!
DON'T YOU DARE MOVE EVEN ONE FINGER...
I WON'T HESITATE TO DO IT!!
!

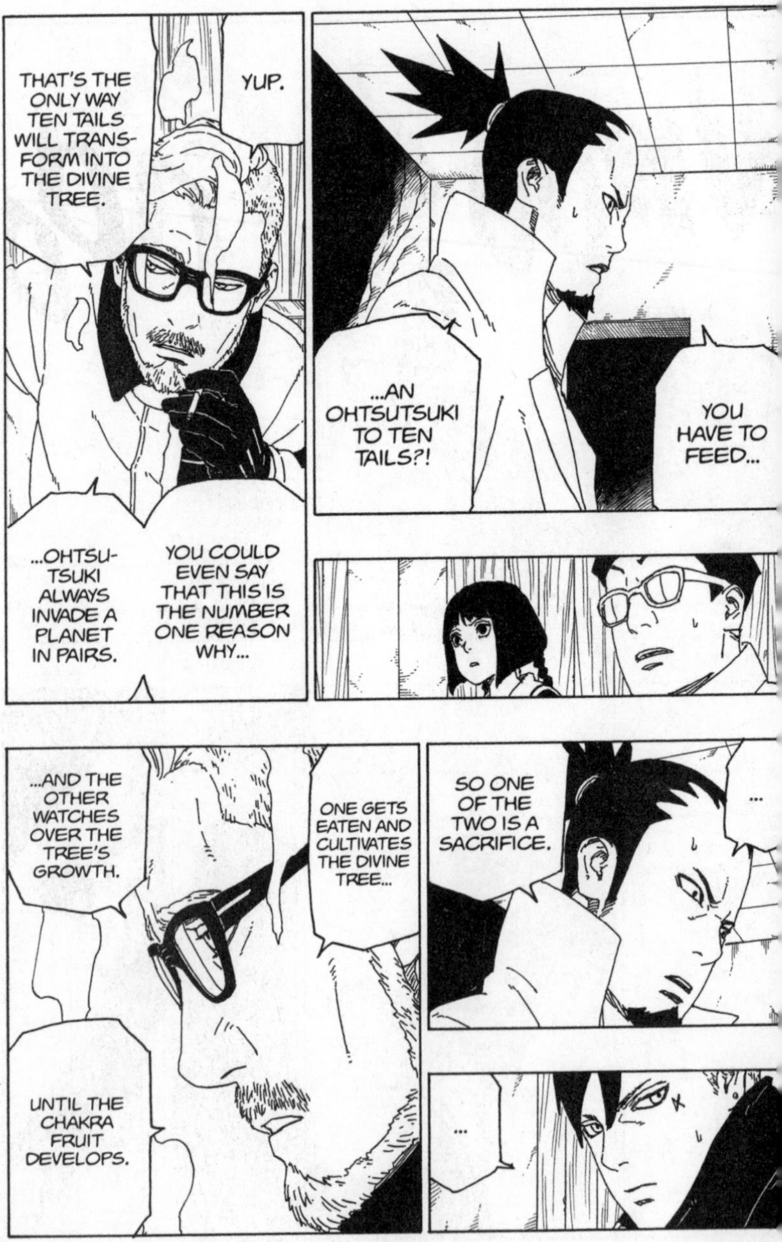
YOU HAVE TO FEED...
...AN OHTSUTSUKI TO TEN TAILS?!
YUP.
THAT'S THE ONLY WAY TEN TAILS WILL TRANSFORM INTO THE DIVINE TREE.
YOU COULD EVEN SAY THAT THIS IS THE NUMBER ONE REASON WHY...
...OHTSUTSUKI ALWAYS INVADE A PLANET IN PAIRS.
...
SO ONE OF THE TWO IS A SACRIFICE.
...
ONE GETS EATEN AND CULTIVATES THE DIVINE TREE...
...AND THE OTHER WATCHES OVER THE TREE'S GROWTH.
UNTIL THE CHAKRA FRUIT DEVELOPS.

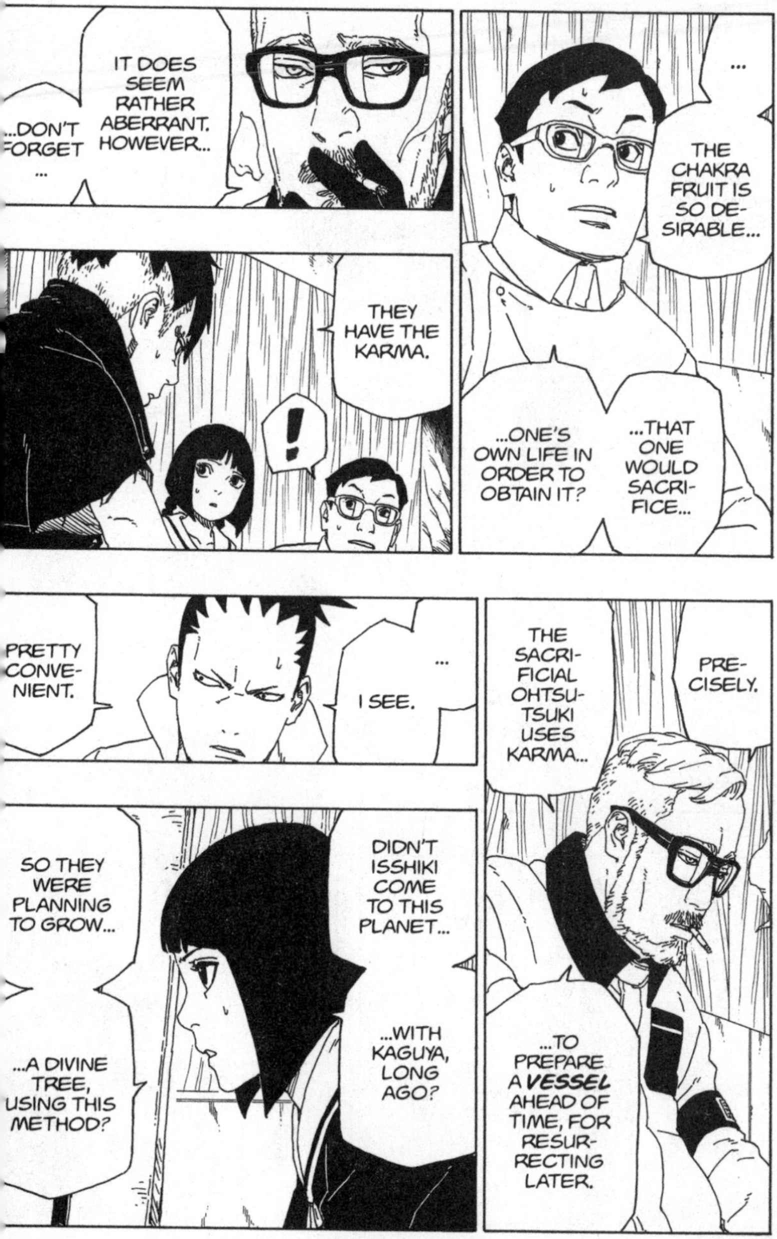
...
THE CHAKRA FRUIT IS SO DESIRABLE...
...THAT ONE WOULD SACRIFICE...
...ONE'S OWN LIFE IN ORDER TO OBTAIN IT?
IT DOES SEEM RATHER ABERRANT. HOWEVER...
...DON'T FORGET ...
THEY HAVE THE KARMA.
!
PRECISELY.
THE SACRIFICIAL OHTSUTSUKI USES KARMA...
...TO PREPARE A ***VESSEL*** AHEAD OF TIME, FOR RESURRECTING LATER.
... I SEE.
PRETTY CONVENIENT.
DIDN'T ISSHIKI COME TO THIS PLANET...
...WITH KAGUYA, LONG AGO?
SO THEY WERE PLANNING TO GROW...
...A DIVINE TREE, USING THIS METHOD?

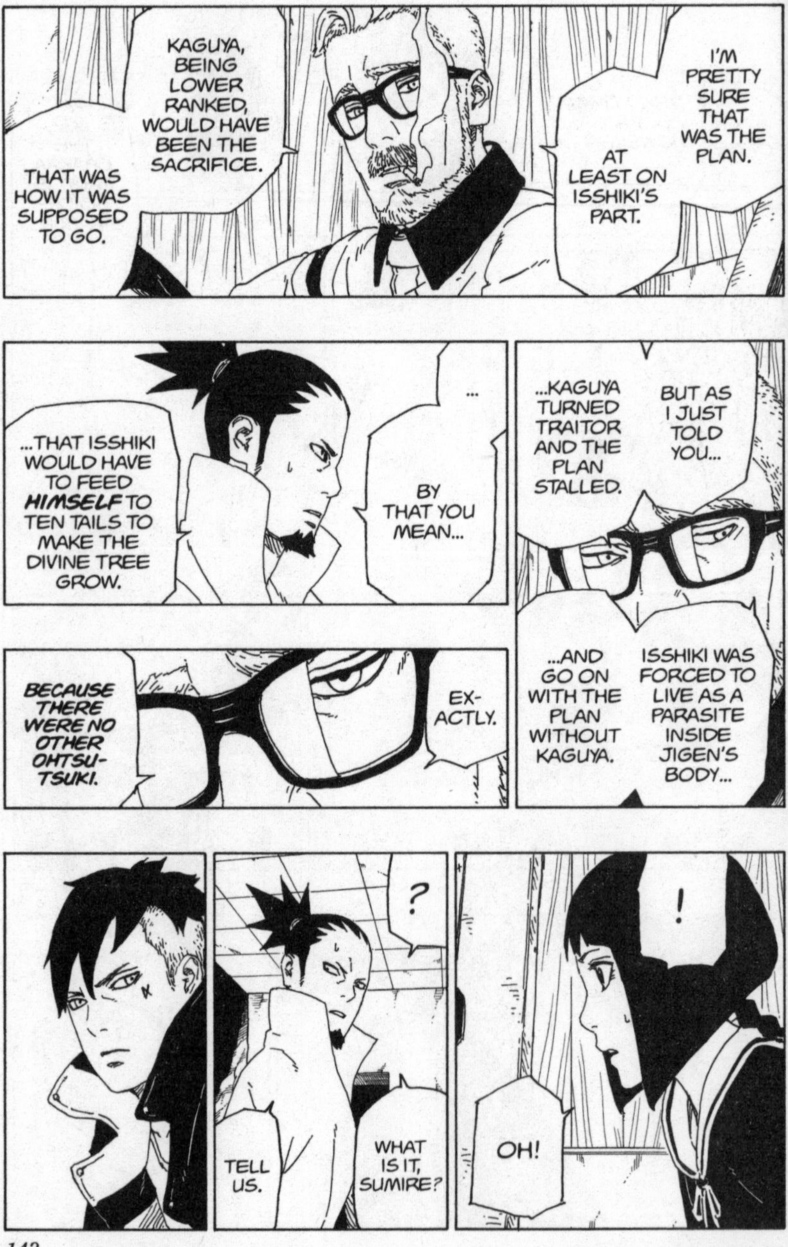
I'M PRETTY SURE THAT WAS THE PLAN.
AT LEAST ON ISSHIKI'S PART.
KAGUYA, BEING LOWER RANKED, WOULD HAVE BEEN THE SACRIFICE.
THAT WAS HOW IT WAS SUPPOSED TO GO.
BUT AS I JUST TOLD YOU...
...KAGUYA TURNED TRAITOR AND THE PLAN STALLED.
ISSHIKI WAS FORCED TO LIVE AS A PARASITE INSIDE JIGEN'S BODY...
...AND GO ON WITH THE PLAN WITHOUT KAGUYA.
...
BY THAT YOU MEAN...
...THAT ISSHIKI WOULD HAVE TO FEED ***HIMSELF*** TO TEN TAILS TO MAKE THE DIVINE TREE GROW.
EX-ACTLY.
BECAUSE THERE WERE NO OTHER OHTSU-TSUKI.
!
OH!
?
WHAT IS IT, SUMIRE?
TELL US.

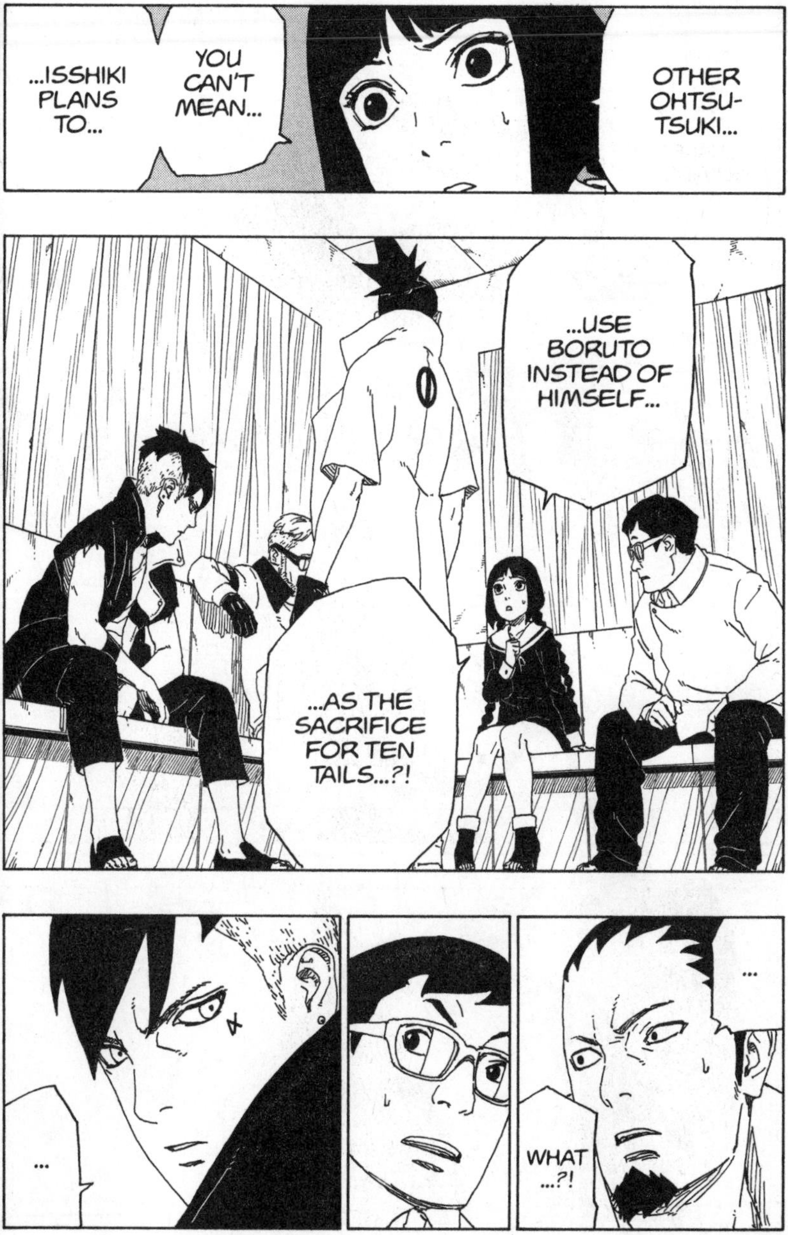
OTHER OHTSU-TSUKI...
YOU CAN'T MEAN...
...ISSHIKI PLANS TO...
...USE BORUTO INSTEAD OF HIMSELF...
...AS THE SACRIFICE FOR TEN TAILS...?!
...
WHAT...?!
...

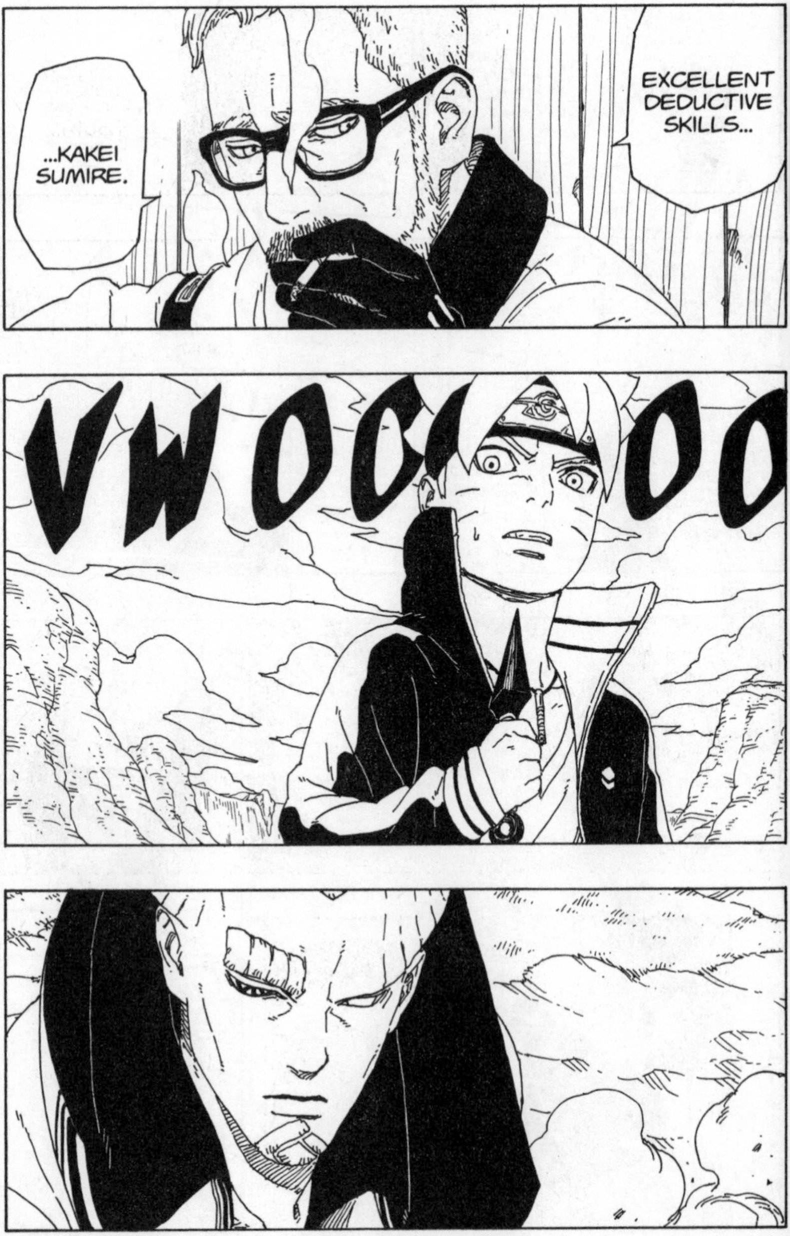
EXCELLENT DEDUCTIVE SKILLS...
...KAKEI SUMIRE.
VWOOO

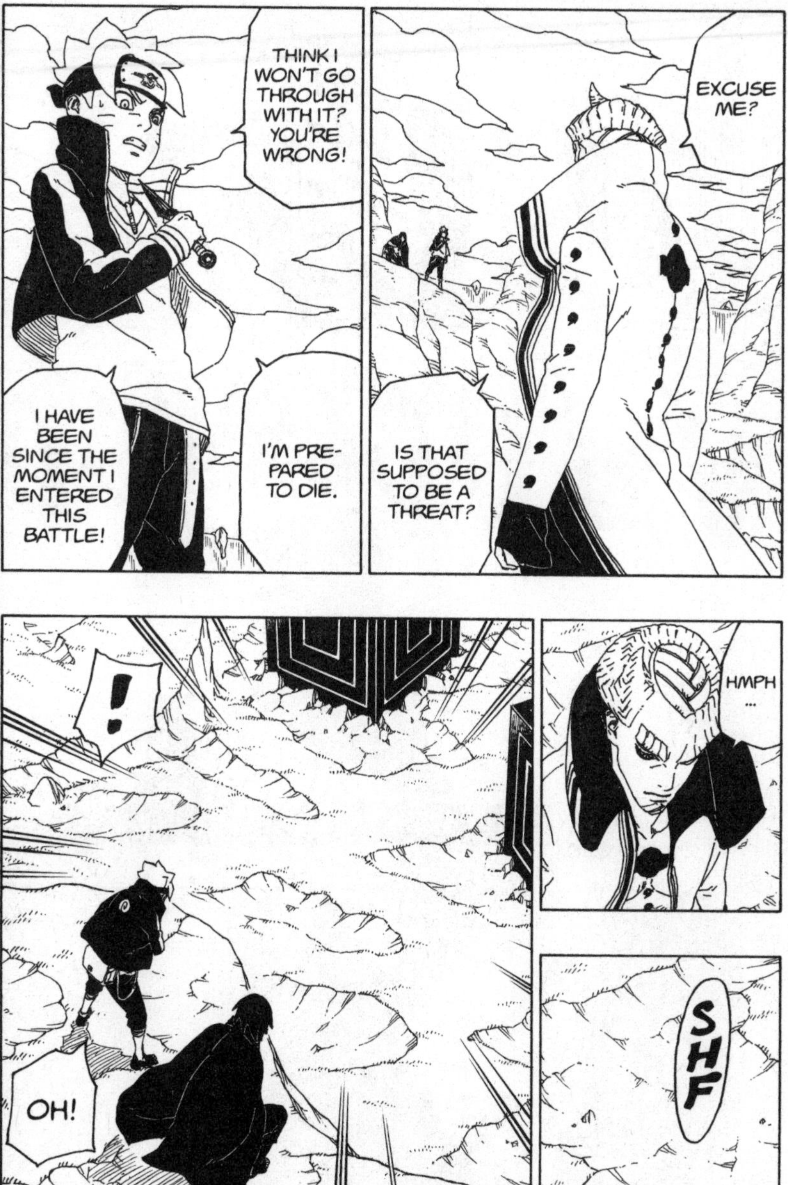

EXCUSE ME?
IS THAT SUPPOSED TO BE A THREAT?
THINK I WON'T GO THROUGH WITH IT? YOU'RE WRONG!
I'M PRE-PARED TO DIE.
I HAVE BEEN SINCE THE MOMENT I ENTERED THIS BATTLE!
HMPH ...
SHF
!
OH!

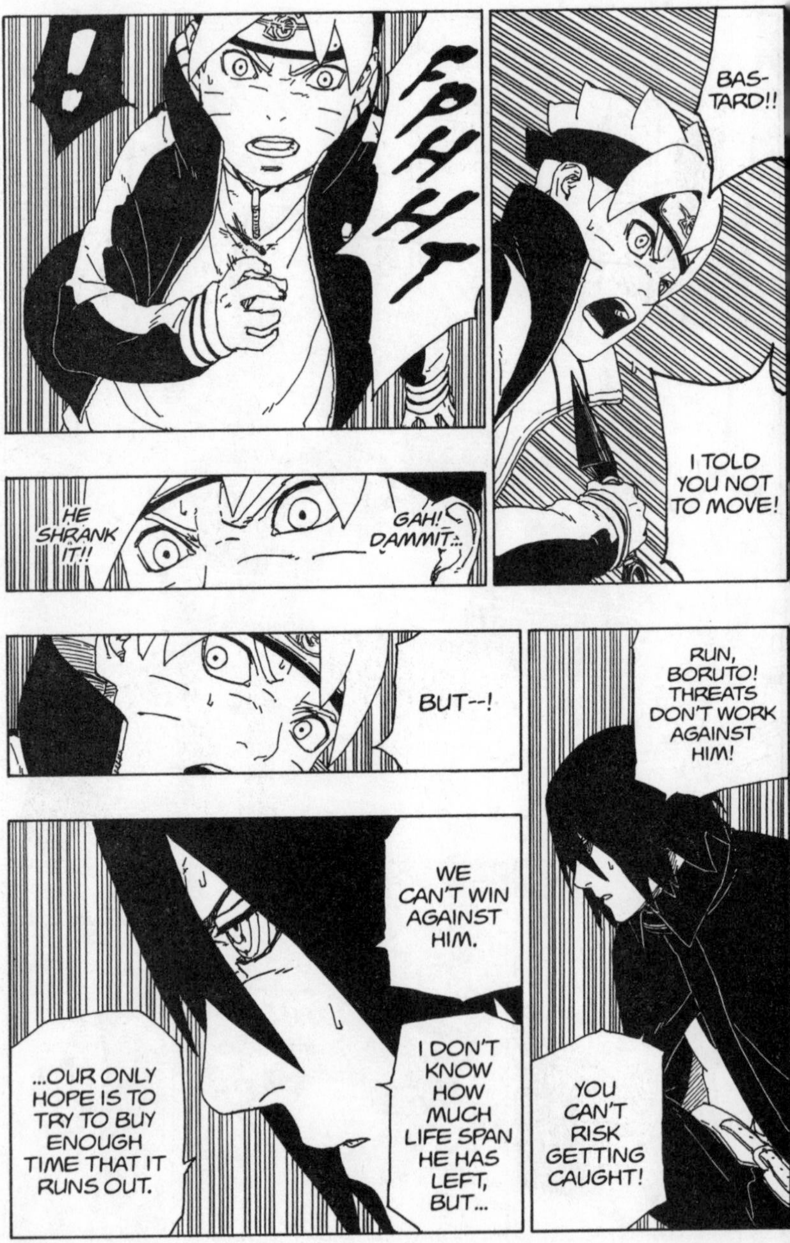
BAS-TARD!!
I TOLD YOU NOT TO MOVE!
!
FPHHT
GAH! DAMMIT...
HE SHRANK IT!!
RUN, BORUTO! THREATS DON'T WORK AGAINST HIM!
YOU CAN'T RISK GETTING CAUGHT!
BUT--!
WE CAN'T WIN AGAINST HIM.
I DON'T KNOW HOW MUCH LIFE SPAN HE HAS LEFT, BUT...
...OUR ONLY HOPE IS TO TRY TO BUY ENOUGH TIME THAT IT RUNS OUT.

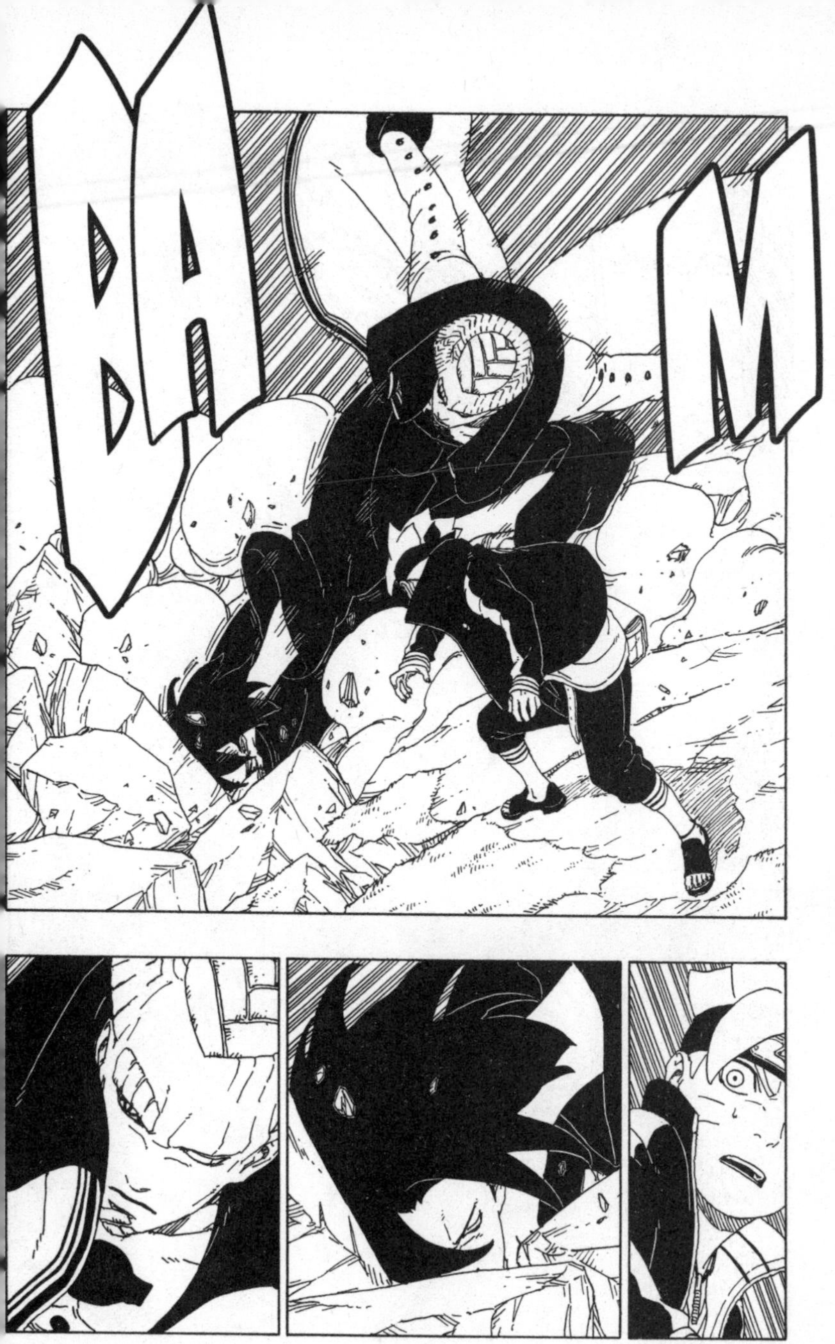
BAM

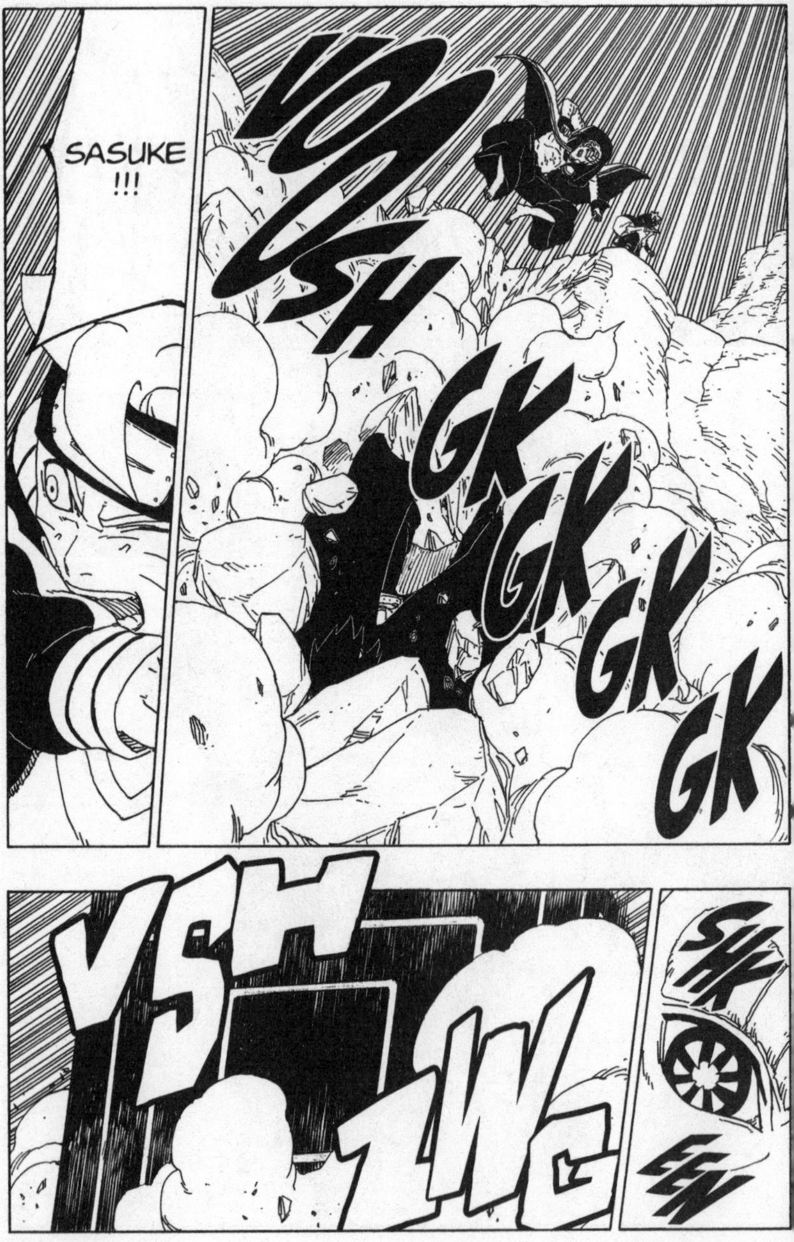

VOOSH
GK GK GK GK
SASUKE !!!
SHK EEN
VSH
ZWG

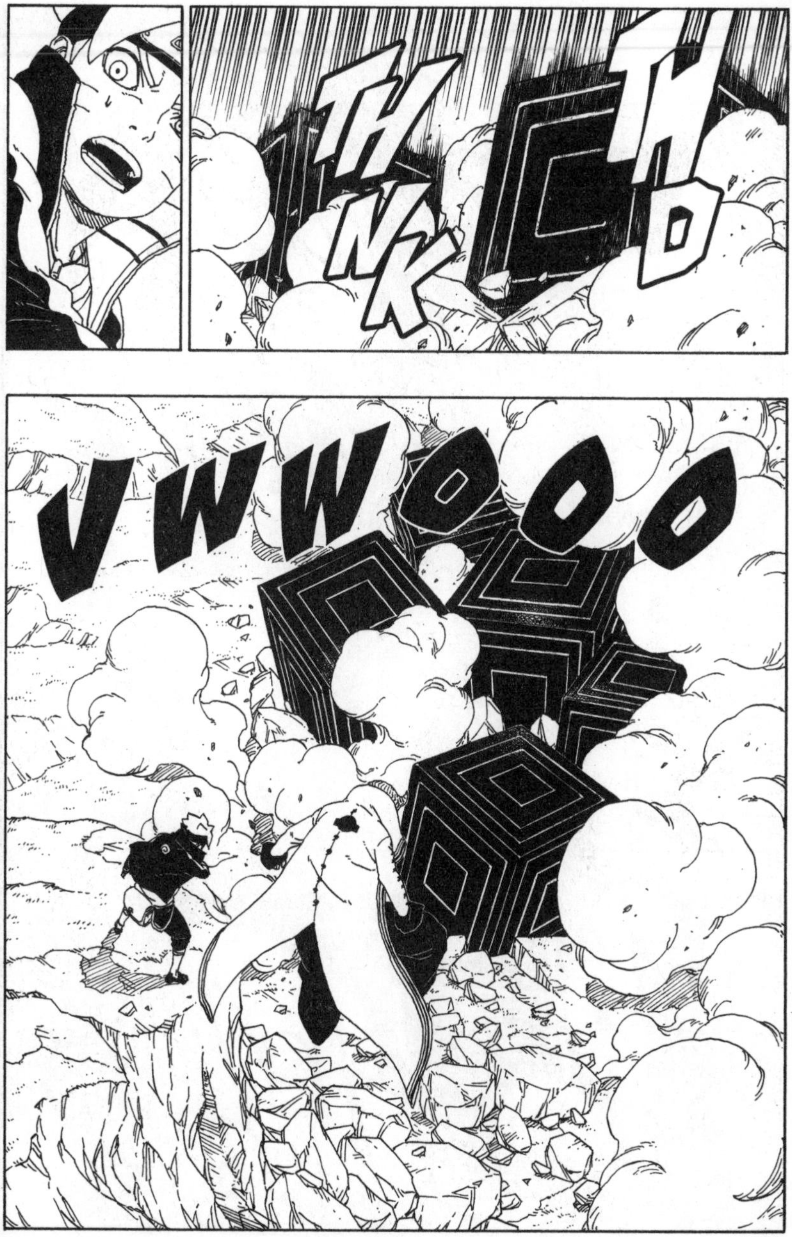
THD
THNK
VWWOOO

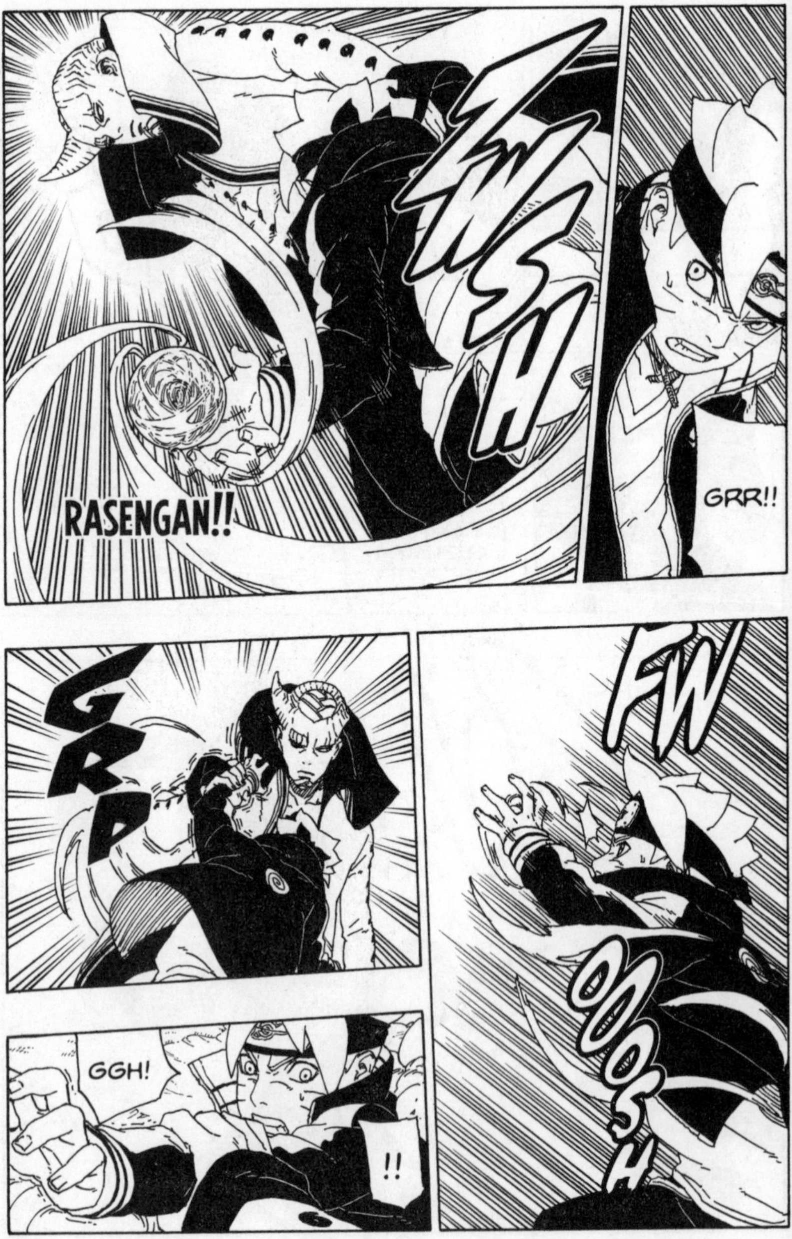
GRR!!
WHSH
RASENGAN!!
FW
OOOOSH
GRD
GGH!
!!

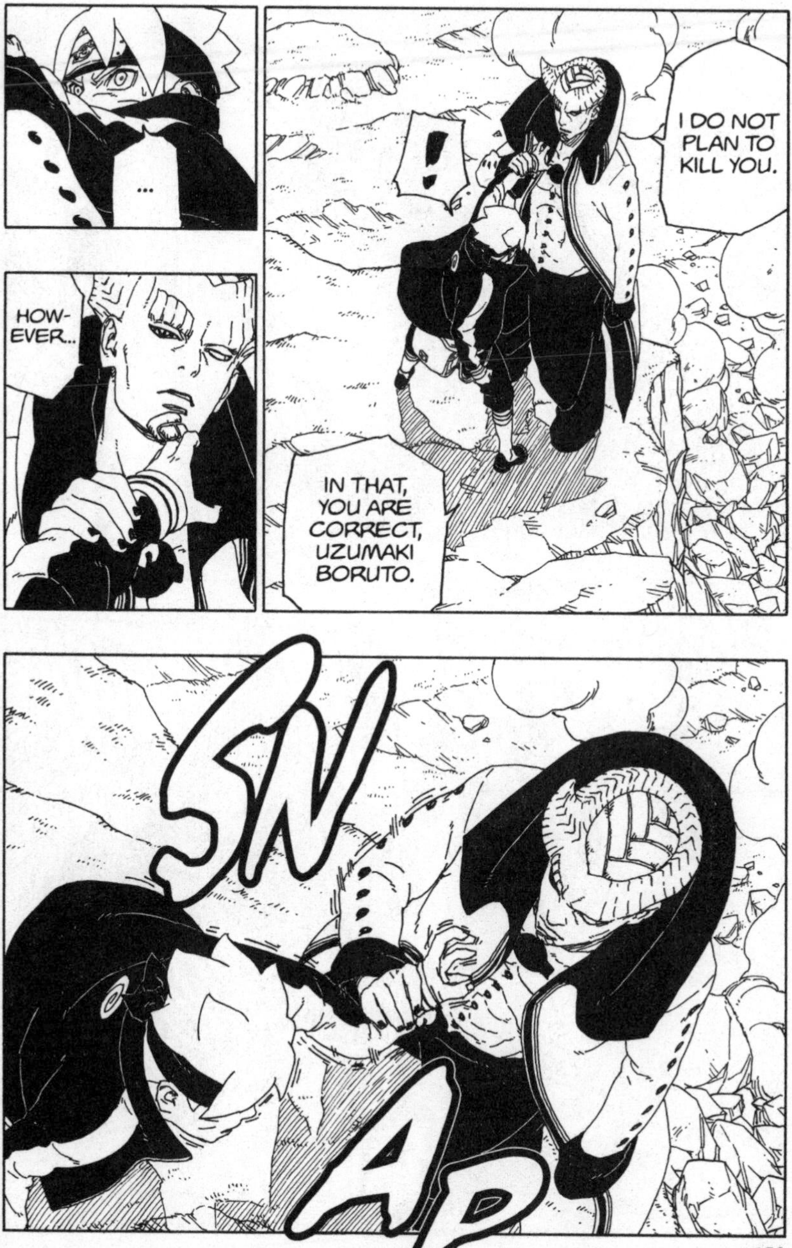
I DO NOT PLAN TO KILL YOU.
!
IN THAT, YOU ARE CORRECT, UZUMAKI BORUTO.
...
HOW-EVER...
SNAP

UNH...
AARG... GAH!!
...I HAVE NO QUALMS ABOUT HURTING YOU.
BAM
DMP
GOFF ...!
HACK ...
I APOLOGIZE FOR ANY MISUNDERSTANDING.

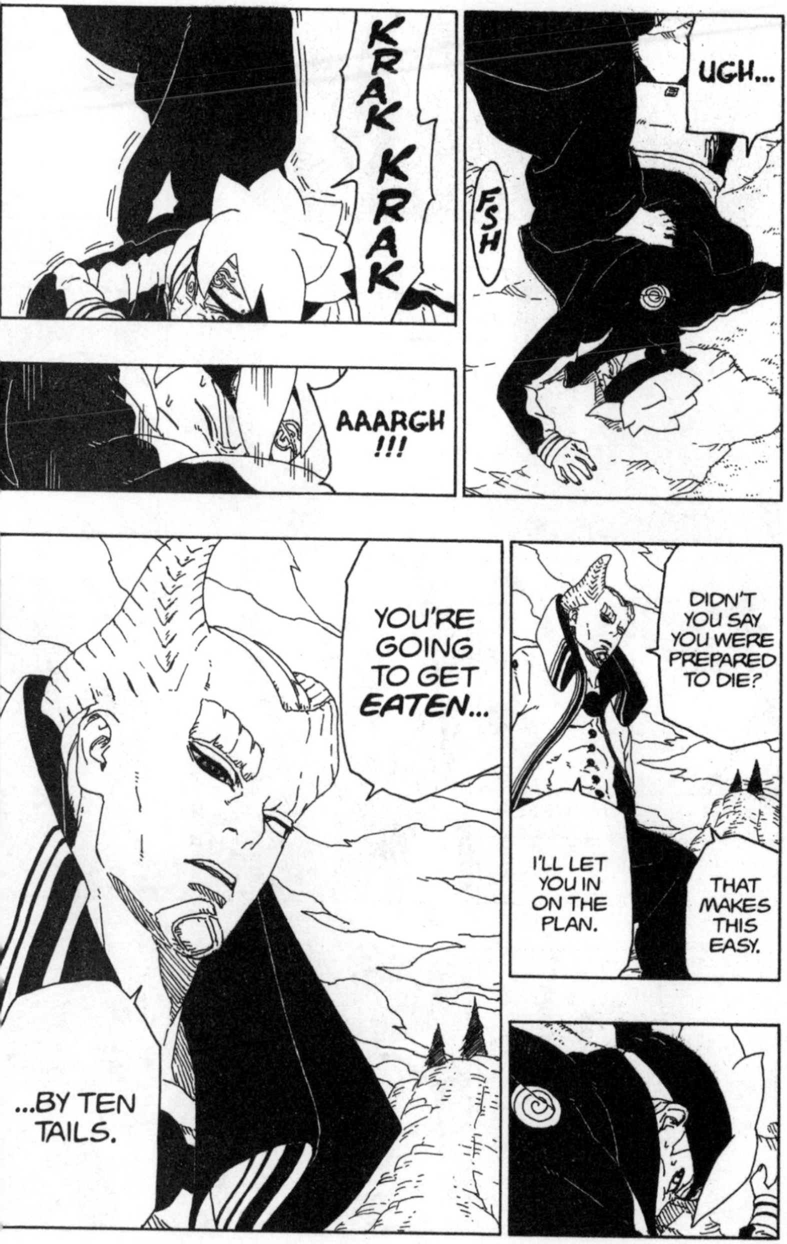
UGH...
FSH
KRAK KRAK
AAARGH!!!
DIDN'T YOU SAY YOU WERE PREPARED TO DIE?
THAT MAKES THIS EASY.
I'LL LET YOU IN ON THE PLAN.
YOU'RE GOING TO GET EATEN...
...BY TEN TAILS.

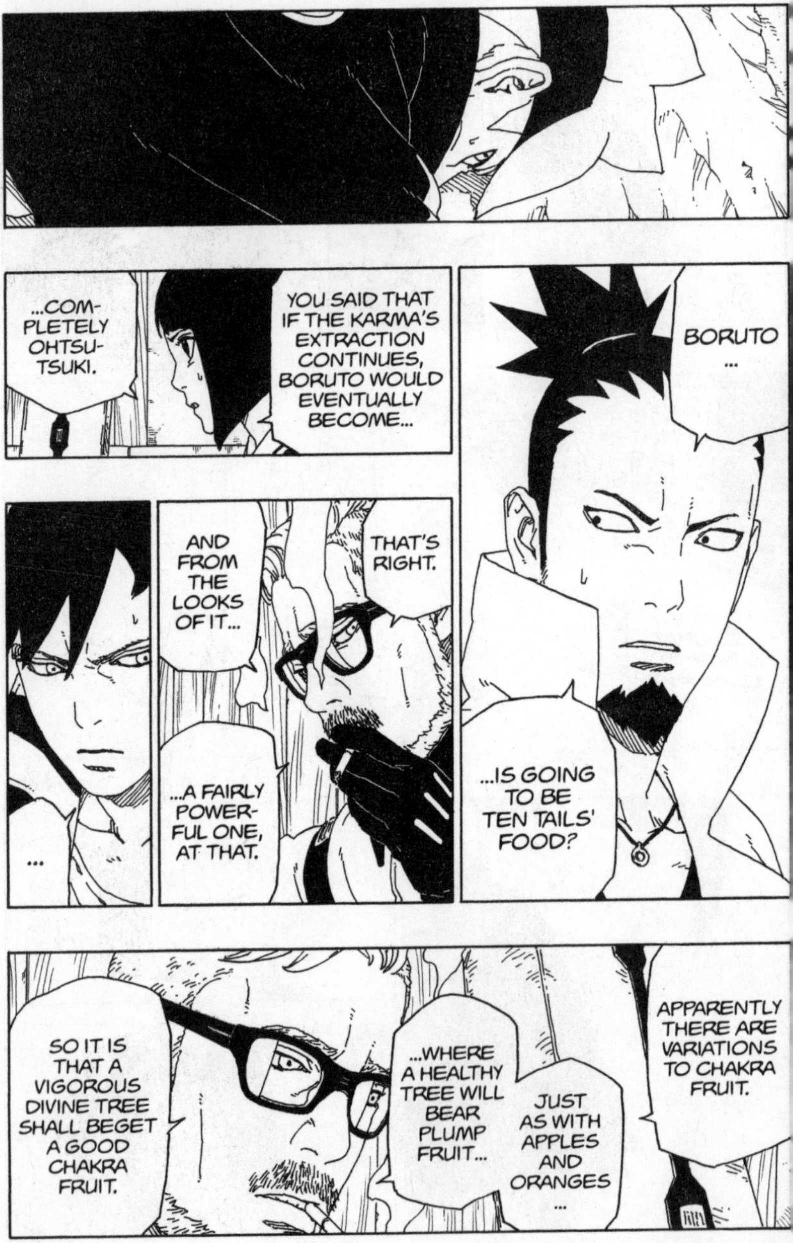
BORUTO ...
...IS GOING TO BE TEN TAILS' FOOD?
YOU SAID THAT IF THE KARMA'S EXTRACTION CONTINUES, BORUTO WOULD EVENTUALLY BECOME...
...COM-PLETELY OHTSU-TSUKI.
THAT'S RIGHT.
AND FROM THE LOOKS OF IT...
...A FAIRLY POWER-FUL ONE, AT THAT.
...
APPARENTLY THERE ARE VARIATIONS TO CHAKRA FRUIT.
JUST AS WITH APPLES AND ORANGES ...
...WHERE A HEALTHY TREE WILL BEAR PLUMP FRUIT...
SO IT IS THAT A VIGOROUS DIVINE TREE SHALL BEGET A GOOD CHAKRA FRUIT.

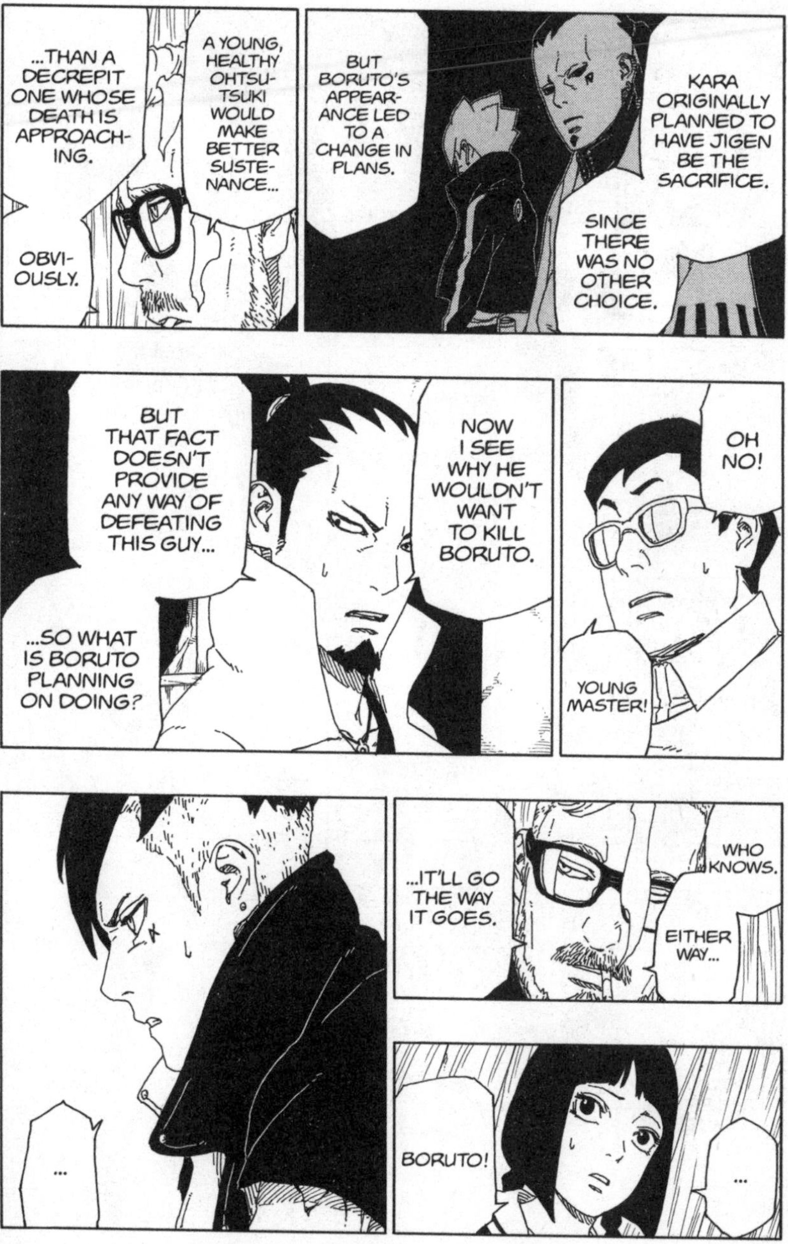
KARA ORIGINALLY PLANNED TO HAVE JIGEN BE THE SACRIFICE.
SINCE THERE WAS NO OTHER CHOICE.
BUT BORUTO'S APPEARANCE LED TO A CHANGE IN PLANS.
A YOUNG, HEALTHY OHTSUTSUKI WOULD MAKE BETTER SUSTENANCE...
...THAN A DECREPIT ONE WHOSE DEATH IS APPROACHING.
OBVIOUSLY.
OH NO!
YOUNG MASTER!
NOW I SEE WHY HE WOULDN'T WANT TO KILL BORUTO.
BUT THAT FACT DOESN'T PROVIDE ANY WAY OF DEFEATING THIS GUY...
...SO WHAT IS BORUTO PLANNING ON DOING?
WHO KNOWS.
EITHER WAY...
...IT'LL GO THE WAY IT GOES.
...
BORUTO!
...

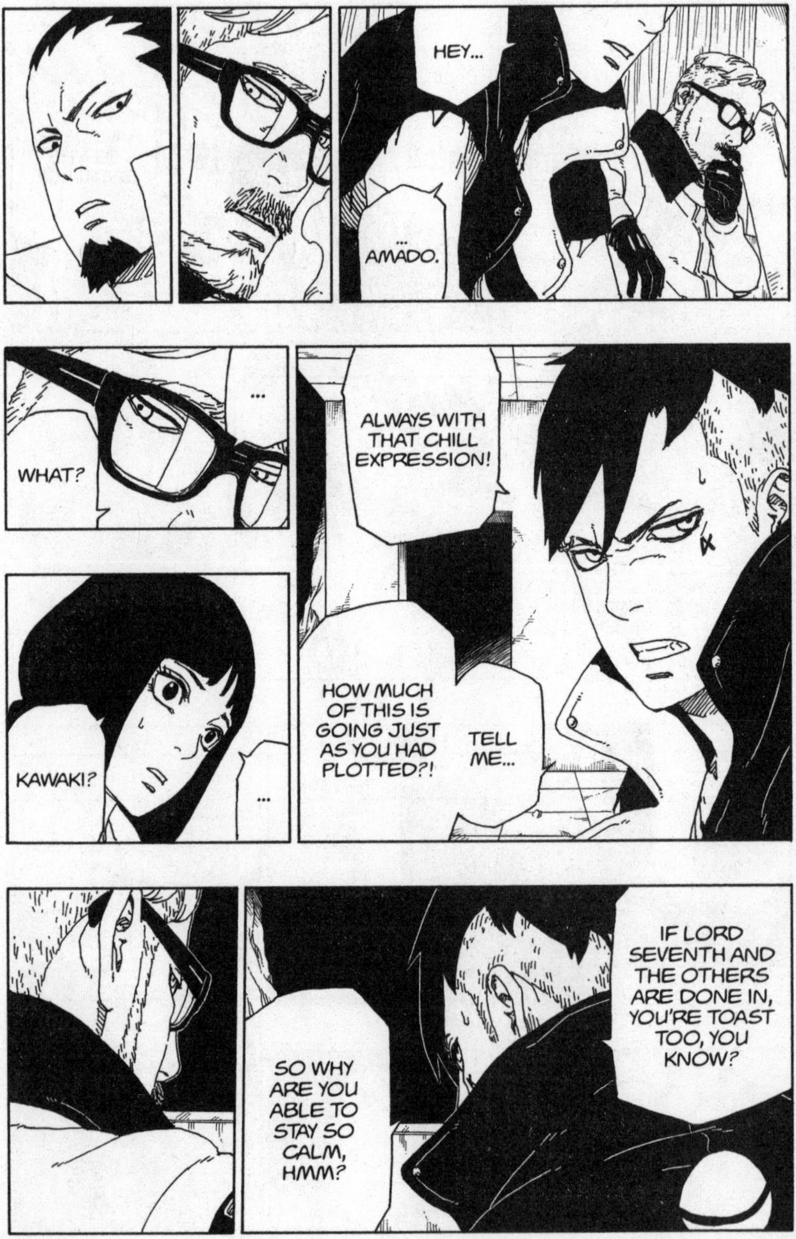
HEY...
... AMADO.
ALWAYS WITH THAT CHILL EXPRESSION!
TELL ME...
HOW MUCH OF THIS IS GOING JUST AS YOU HAD PLOTTED?!
...
WHAT?
KAWAKI?
...
IF LORD SEVENTH AND THE OTHERS ARE DONE IN, YOU'RE TOAST TOO, YOU KNOW?
SO WHY ARE YOU ABLE TO STAY SO CALM, HMM?

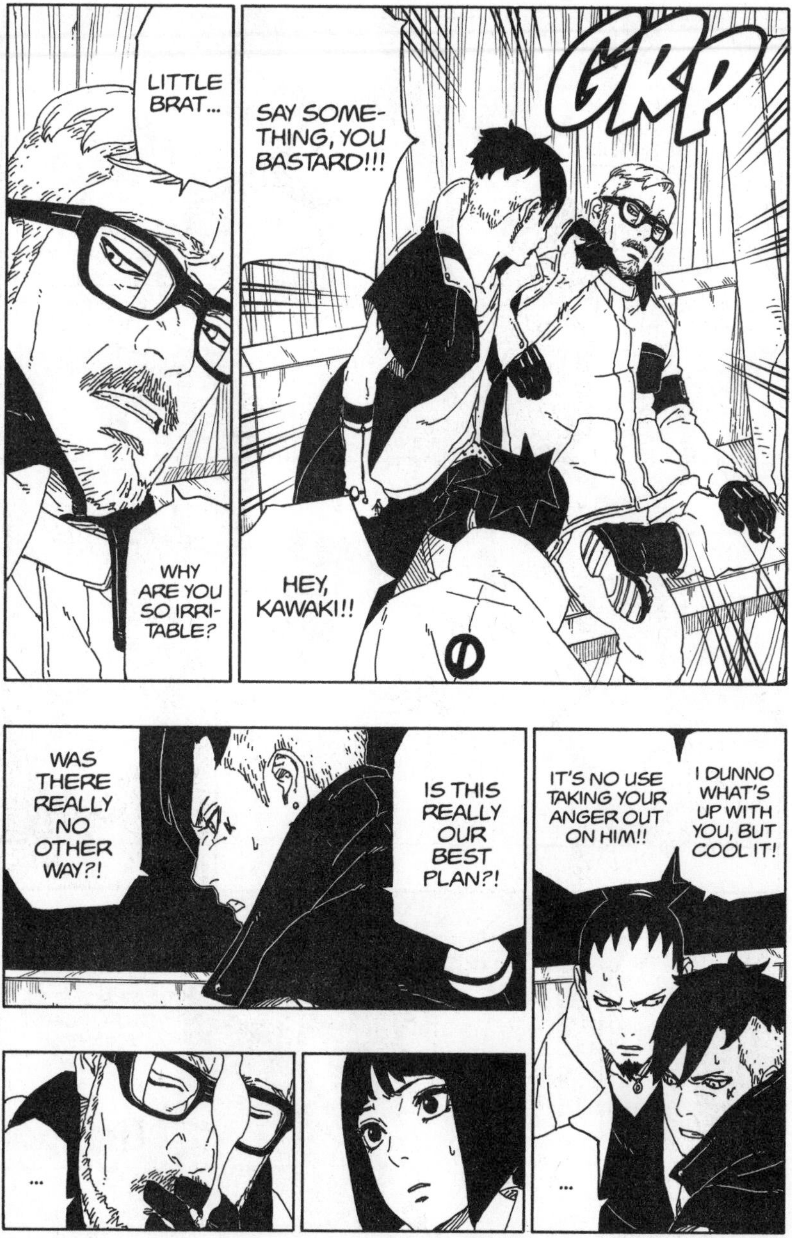
GRP
SAY SOME-THING, YOU BASTARD!!!
HEY, KAWAKI!!
LITTLE BRAT...
WHY ARE YOU SO IRRI-TABLE?
I DUNNO WHAT'S UP WITH YOU, BUT COOL IT!
IT'S NO USE TAKING YOUR ANGER OUT ON HIM!!
...
IS THIS REALLY OUR BEST PLAN?!
WAS THERE REALLY NO OTHER WAY?!
...

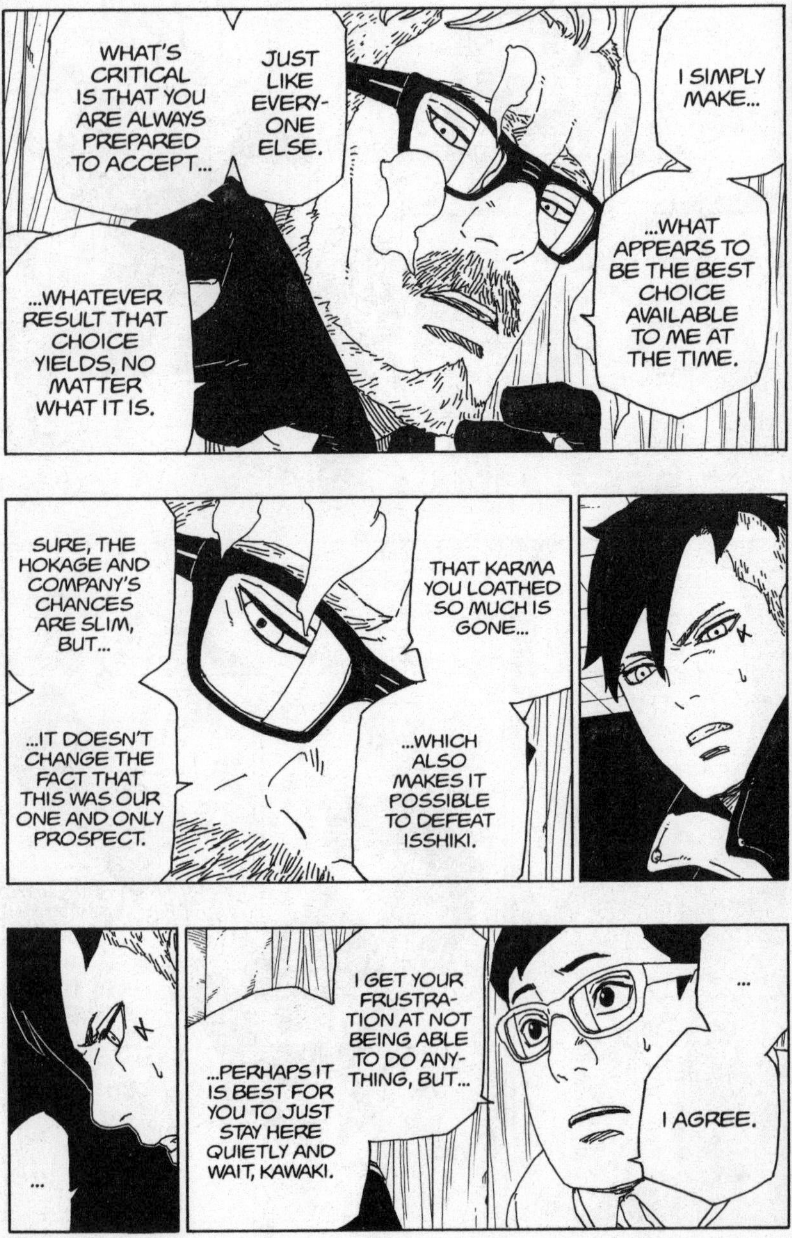
I SIMPLY MAKE...
...WHAT APPEARS TO BE THE BEST CHOICE AVAILABLE TO ME AT THE TIME.
JUST LIKE EVERY-ONE ELSE.
WHAT'S CRITICAL IS THAT YOU ARE ALWAYS PREPARED TO ACCEPT...
...WHATEVER RESULT THAT CHOICE YIELDS, NO MATTER WHAT IT IS.
THAT KARMA YOU LOATHED SO MUCH IS GONE...
...WHICH ALSO MAKES IT POSSIBLE TO DEFEAT ISSHIKI.
SURE, THE HOKAGE AND COMPANY'S CHANCES ARE SLIM, BUT...
...IT DOESN'T CHANGE THE FACT THAT THIS WAS OUR ONE AND ONLY PROSPECT.
...
I AGREE.
I GET YOUR FRUSTRA-TION AT NOT BEING ABLE TO DO ANY-THING, BUT...
...PERHAPS IT IS BEST FOR YOU TO JUST STAY HERE QUIETLY AND WAIT, KAWAKI.
...

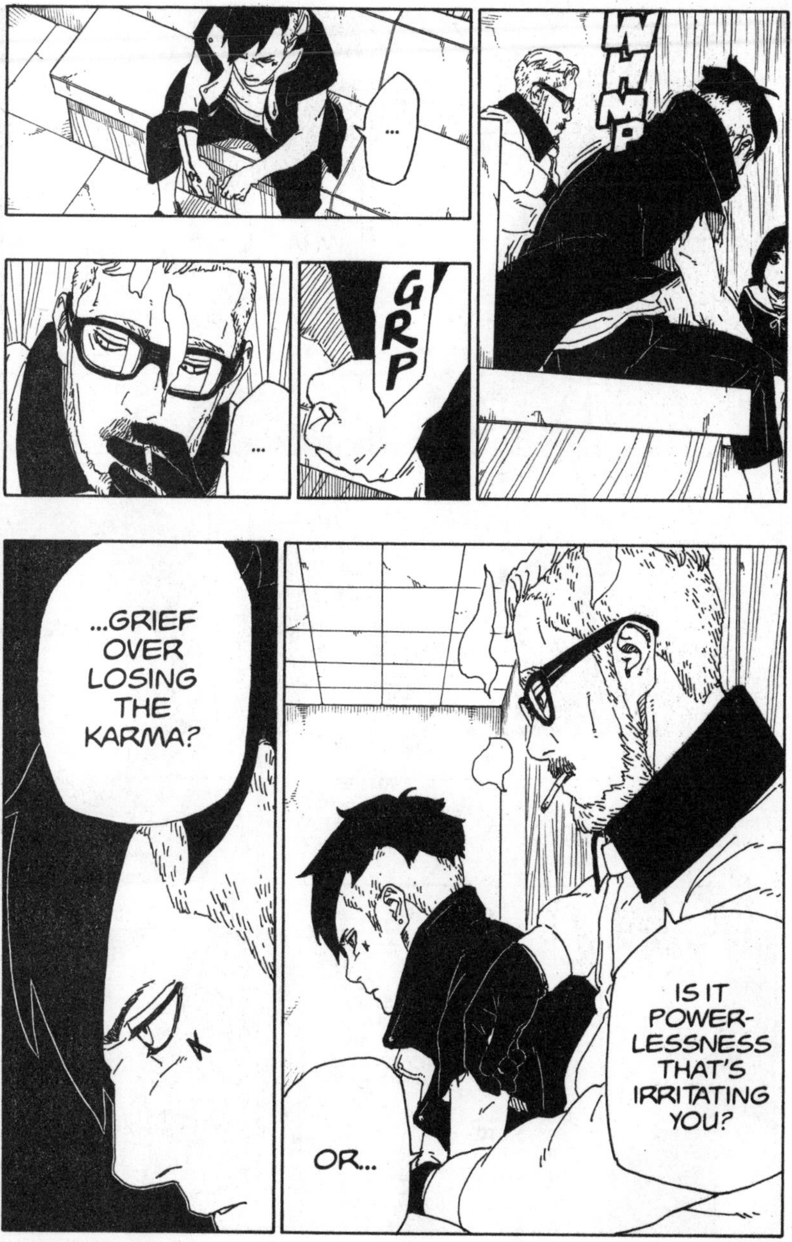
WHMP
...
GRP
...
IS IT POWER-LESSNESS THAT'S IRRITATING YOU?
OR...
...GRIEF OVER LOSING THE KARMA?

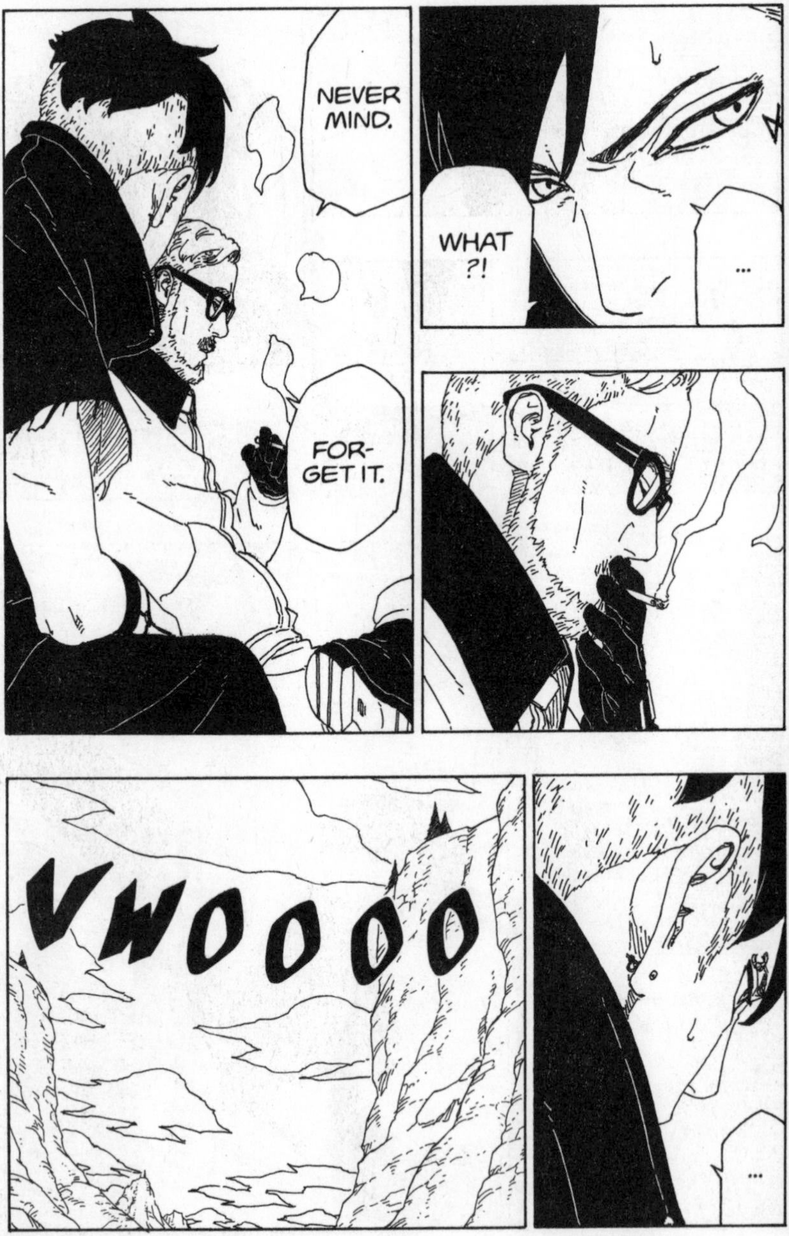
WHAT ?!
...
NEVER MIND.
FOR-GET IT.
...
VWOOOO

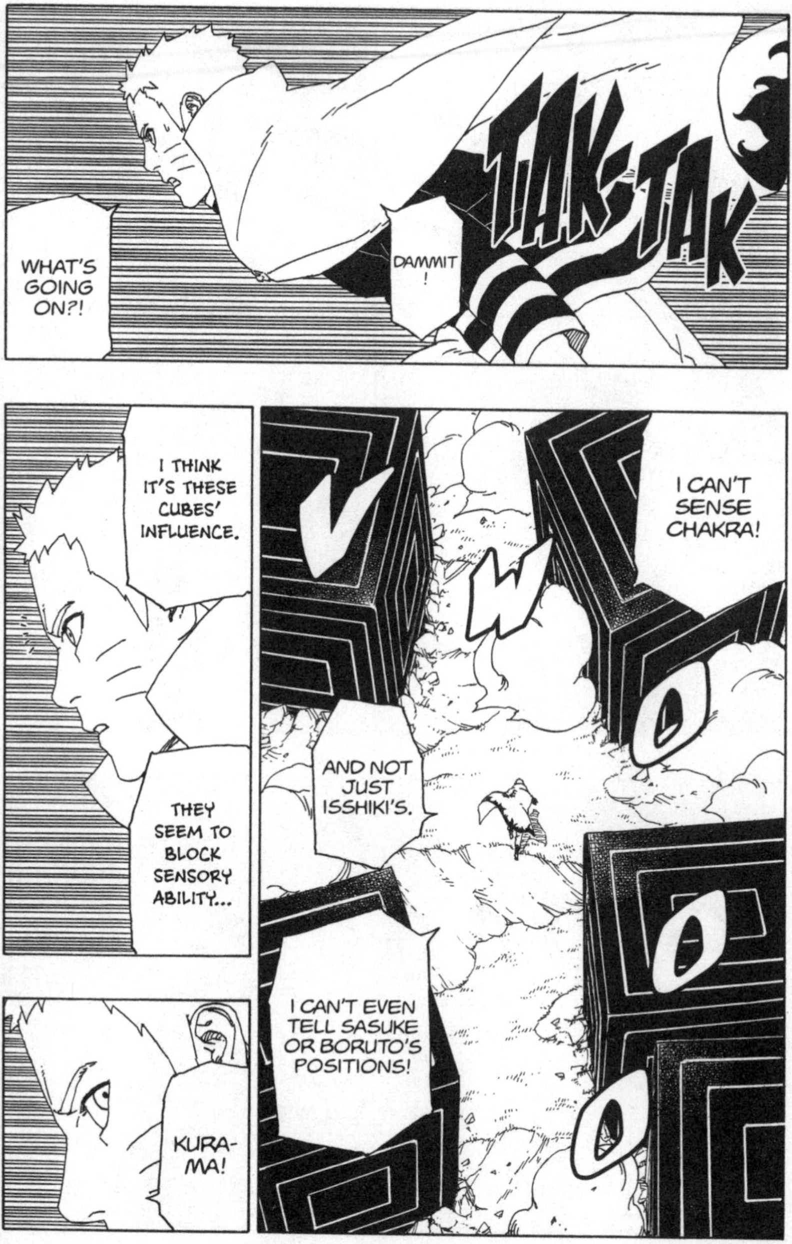
TAK-TAK
DAMMIT!
WHAT'S GOING ON?!
I CAN'T SENSE CHAKRA!
AND NOT JUST ISSHIKI'S.
I CAN'T EVEN TELL SASUKE OR BORUTO'S POSITIONS!
I THINK IT'S THESE CUBES' INFLUENCE.
THEY SEEM TO BLOCK SENSORY ABILITY...
KURA-MA!

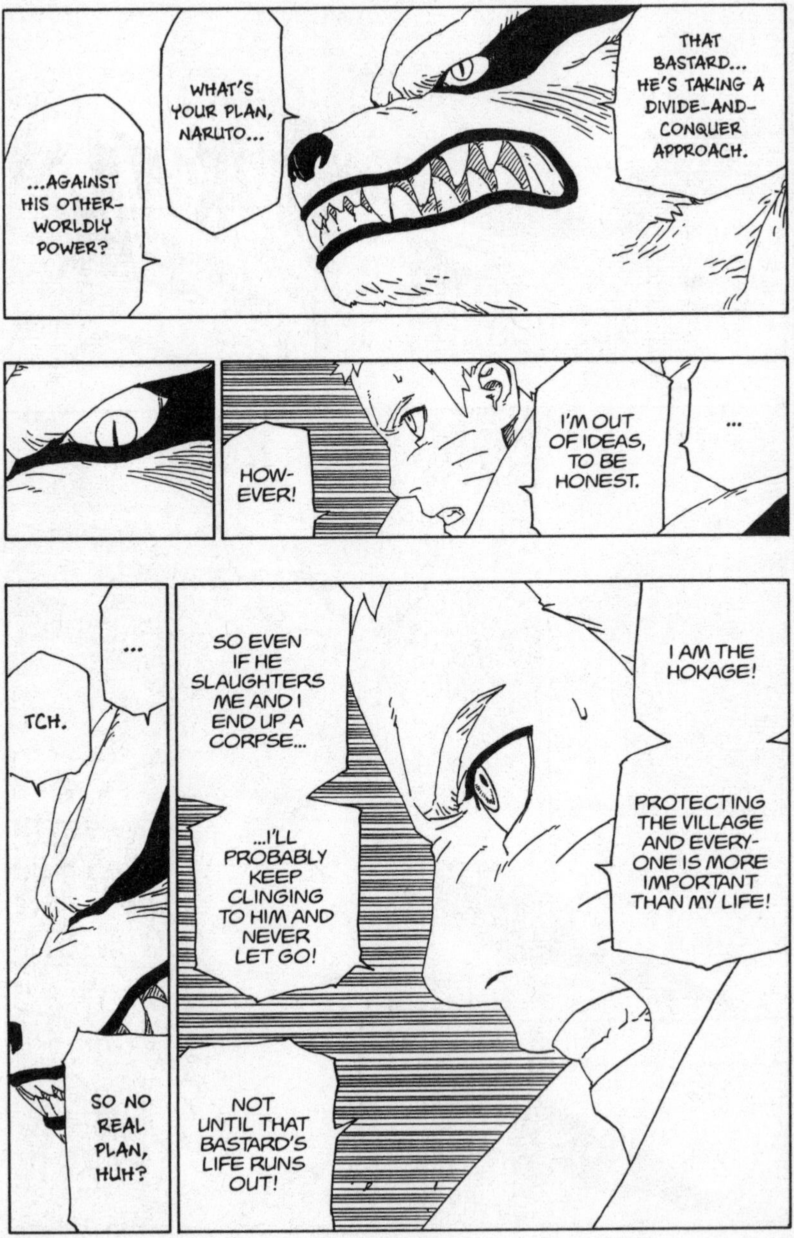

THAT BASTARD... HE'S TAKING A DIVIDE-AND-CONQUER APPROACH.
WHAT'S YOUR PLAN, NARUTO...
...AGAINST HIS OTHER-WORLDLY POWER?
...
I'M OUT OF IDEAS, TO BE HONEST.
HOW-EVER!
I AM THE HOKAGE!
PROTECTING THE VILLAGE AND EVERY-ONE IS MORE IMPORTANT THAN MY LIFE!
SO EVEN IF HE SLAUGHTERS ME AND I END UP A CORPSE...
...I'LL PROBABLY KEEP CLINGING TO HIM AND NEVER LET GO!
NOT UNTIL THAT BASTARD'S LIFE RUNS OUT!
...
TCH.
SO NO REAL PLAN, HUH?

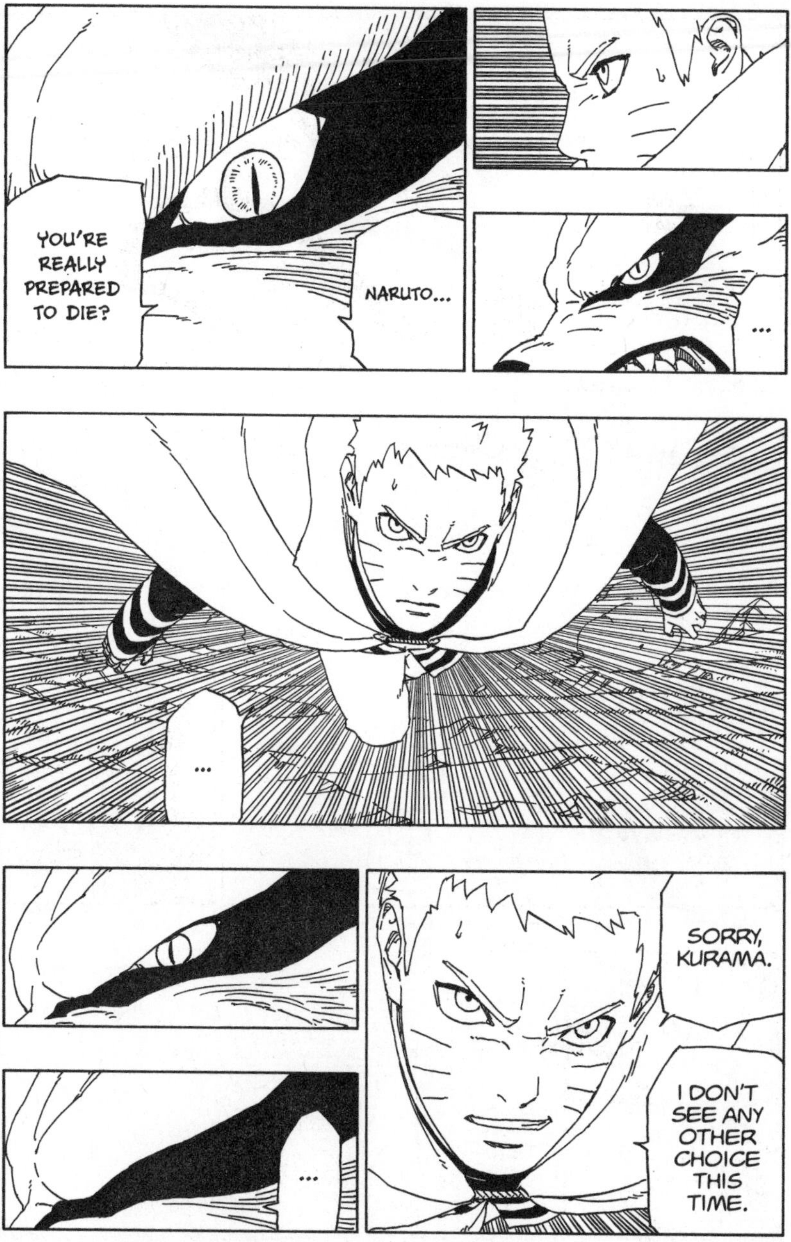
...
NARUTO...
YOU'RE REALLY PREPARED TO DIE?
...
SORRY, KURAMA.
I DON'T SEE ANY OTHER CHOICE THIS TIME.
...

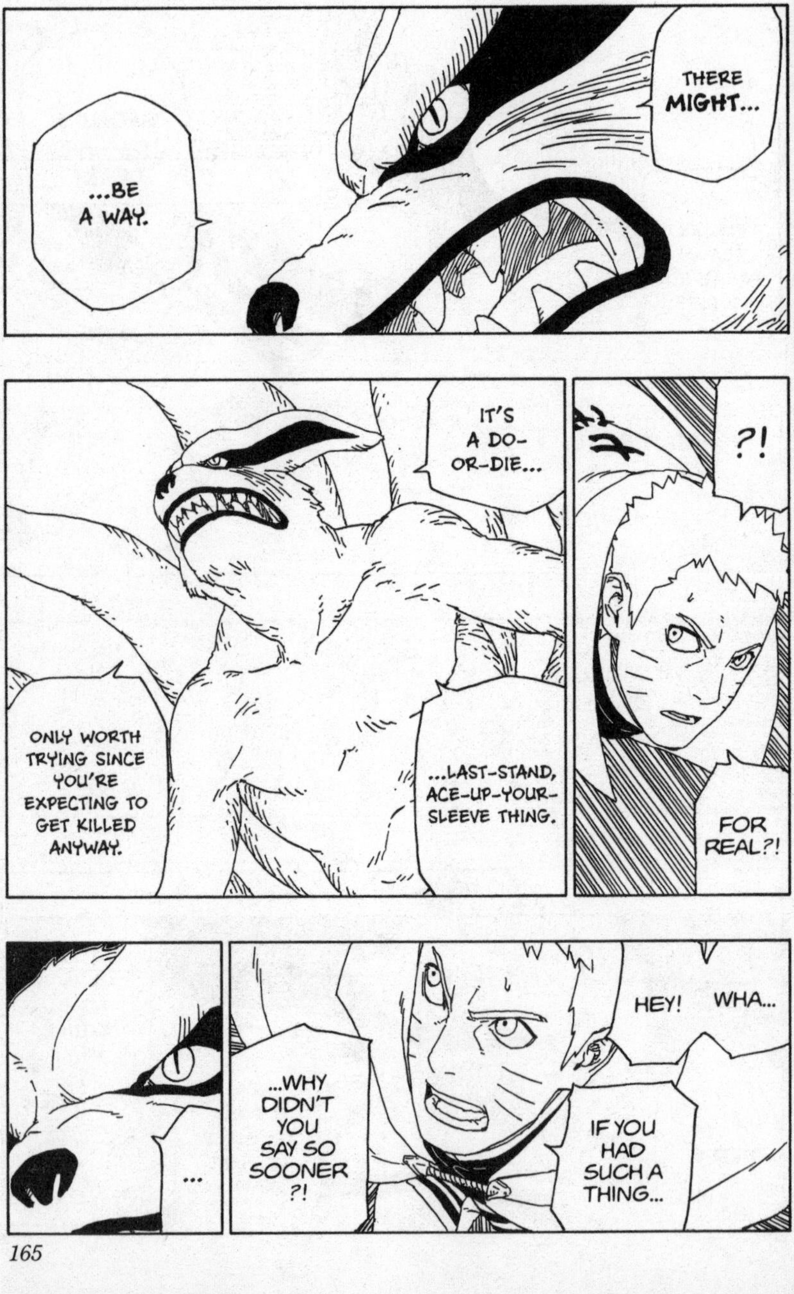
THERE MIGHT...
...BE A WAY.
?!
FOR REAL?!
IT'S A DO-OR-DIE...
...LAST-STAND, ACE-UP-YOUR-SLEEVE THING.
ONLY WORTH TRYING SINCE YOU'RE EXPECTING TO GET KILLED ANYWAY.
WHA...
HEY!
IF YOU HAD SUCH A THING...
...WHY DIDN'T YOU SAY SO SOONER?!
...

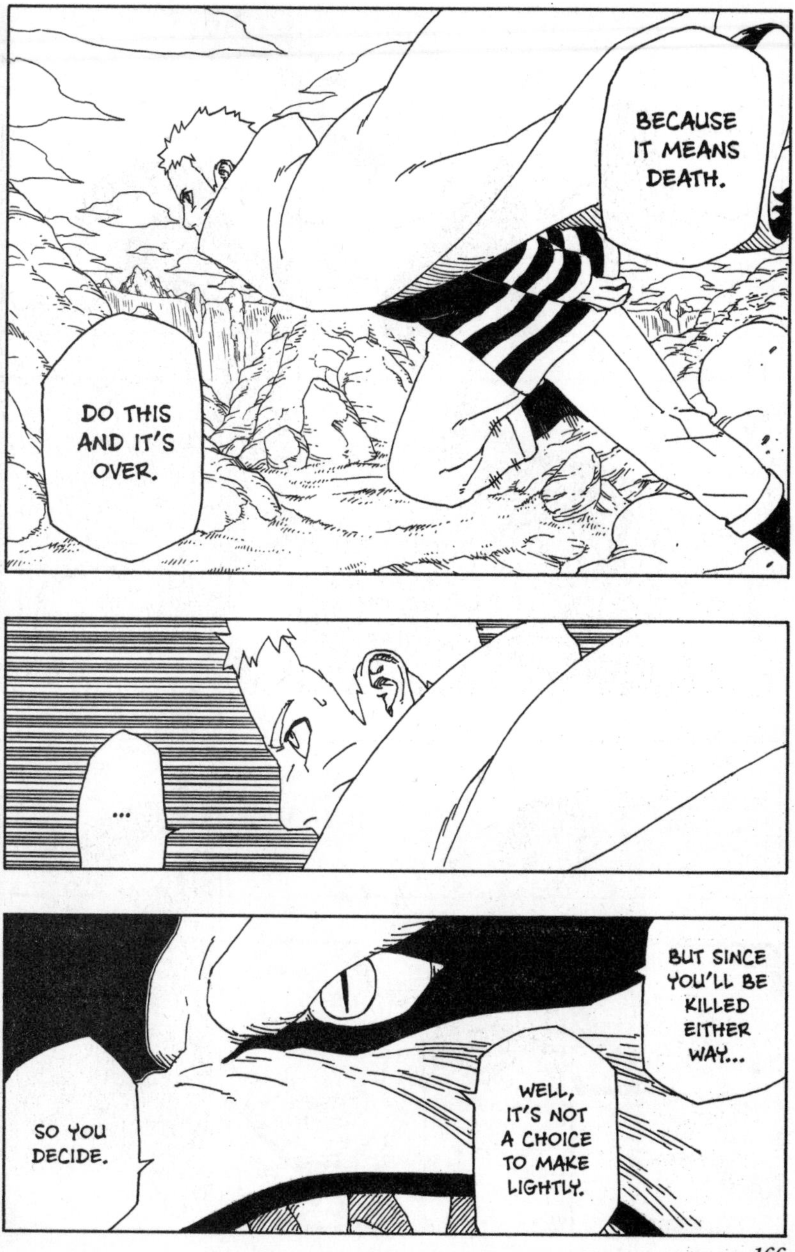
BECAUSE IT MEANS DEATH.
DO THIS AND IT'S OVER.
...
BUT SINCE YOU'LL BE KILLED EITHER WAY...
WELL, IT'S NOT A CHOICE TO MAKE LIGHTLY.
SO YOU DECIDE.

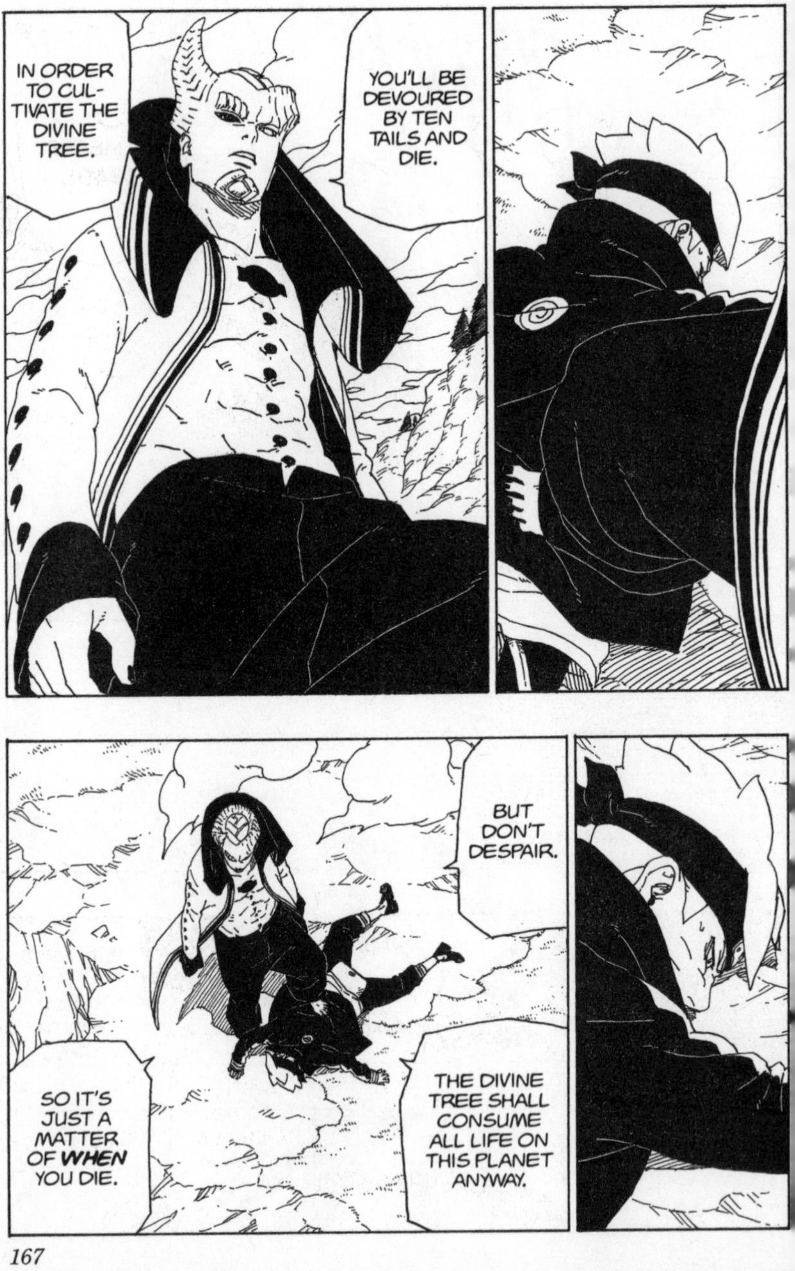
YOU'LL BE DEVOURED BY TEN TAILS AND DIE.
IN ORDER TO CUL-TIVATE THE DIVINE TREE.
BUT DON'T DESPAIR.
THE DIVINE TREE SHALL CONSUME ALL LIFE ON THIS PLANET ANYWAY.
SO IT'S JUST A MATTER OF **WHEN** YOU DIE.

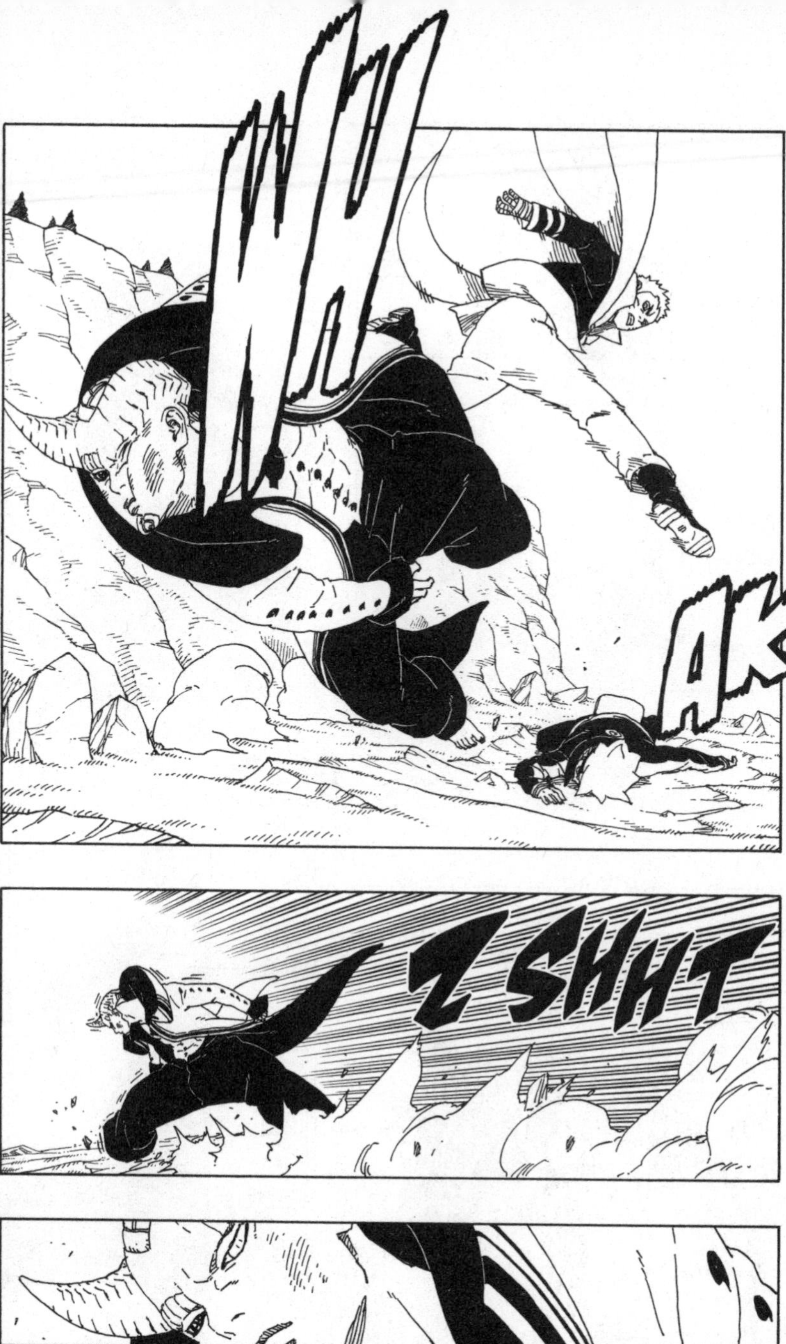
WHAK
Z SHHT

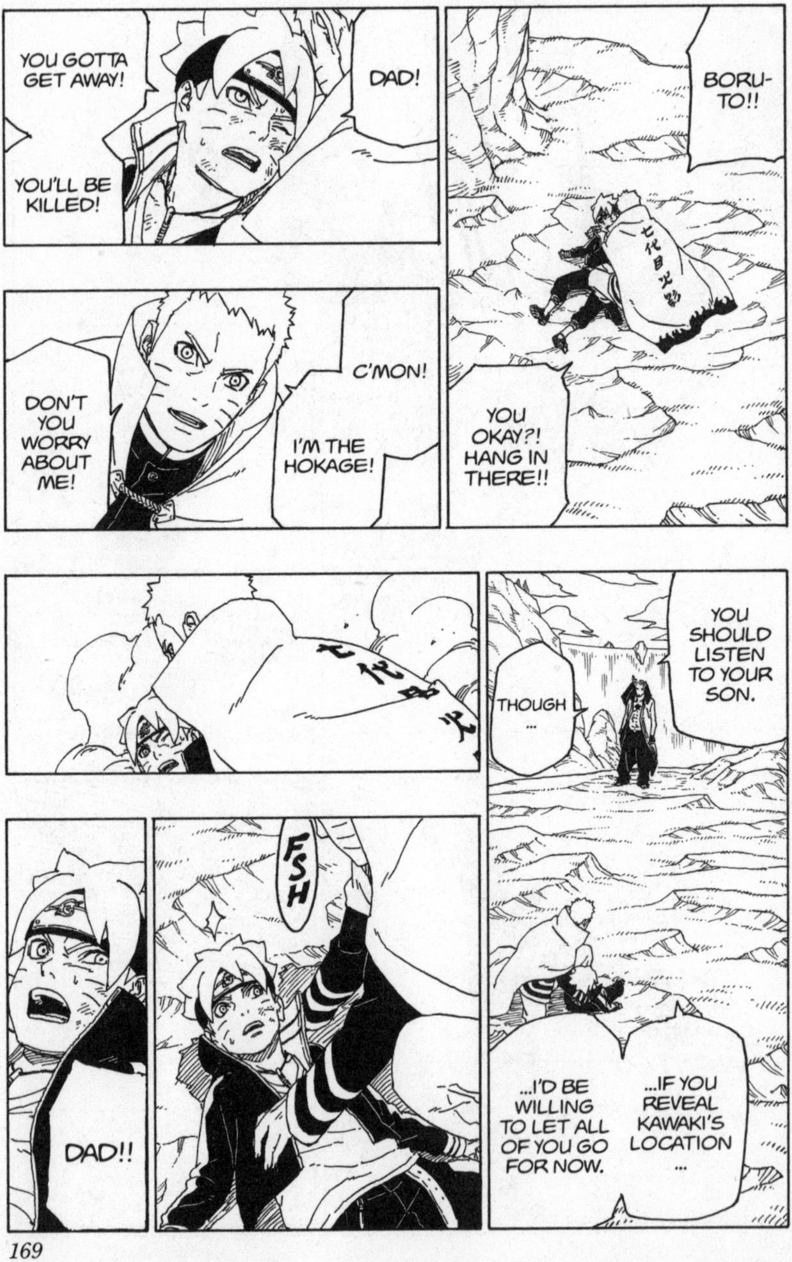
BORU-TO!!
YOU OKAY?! HANG IN THERE!!
DAD!
YOU GOTTA GET AWAY!
YOU'LL BE KILLED!
C'MON!
I'M THE HOKAGE!
DON'T YOU WORRY ABOUT ME!
YOU SHOULD LISTEN TO YOUR SON.
THOUGH...
...IF YOU REVEAL KAWAKI'S LOCATION...
...I'D BE WILLING TO LET ALL OF YOU GO FOR NOW.
FSH
DAD!!

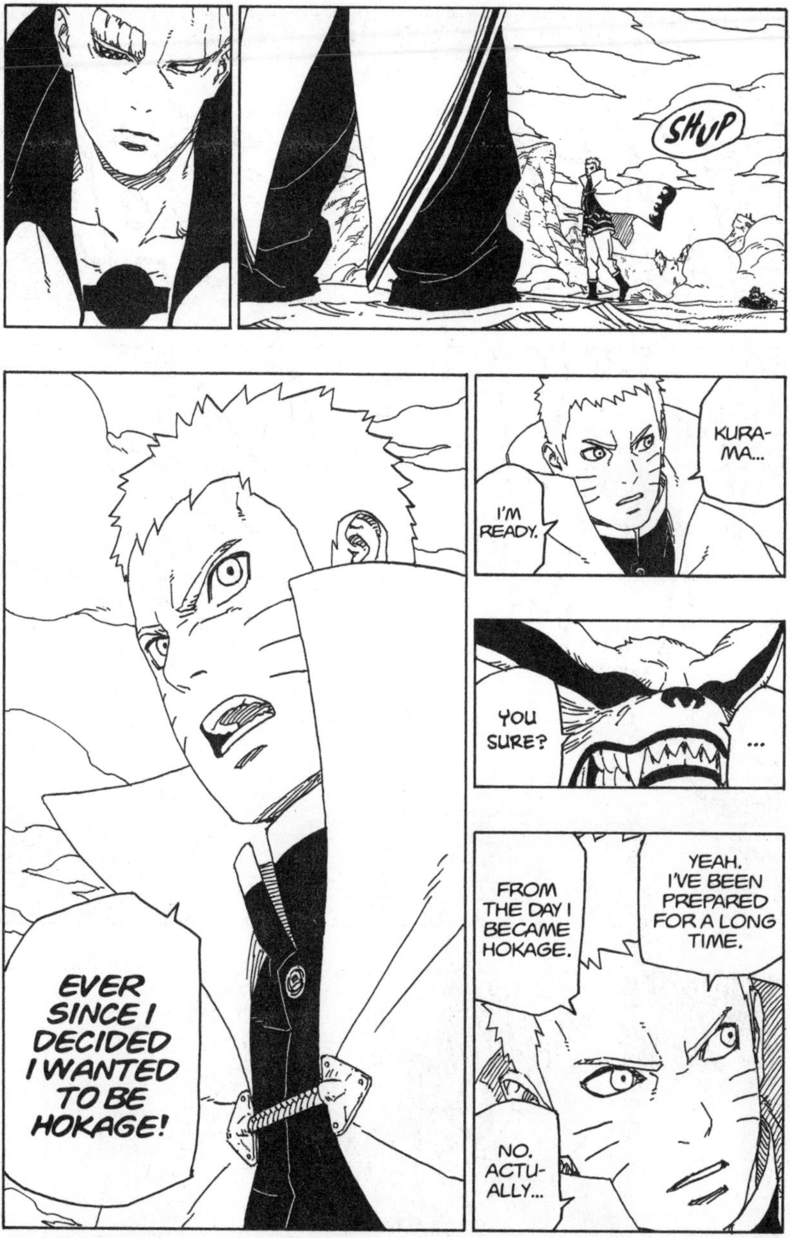
SHUP
KURA-MA...
I'M READY.
...
YOU SURE?
YEAH. I'VE BEEN PREPARED FOR A LONG TIME.
FROM THE DAY I BECAME HOKAGE.
NO. ACTU-ALLY...
EVER SINCE I DECIDED I WANTED TO BE HOKAGE!

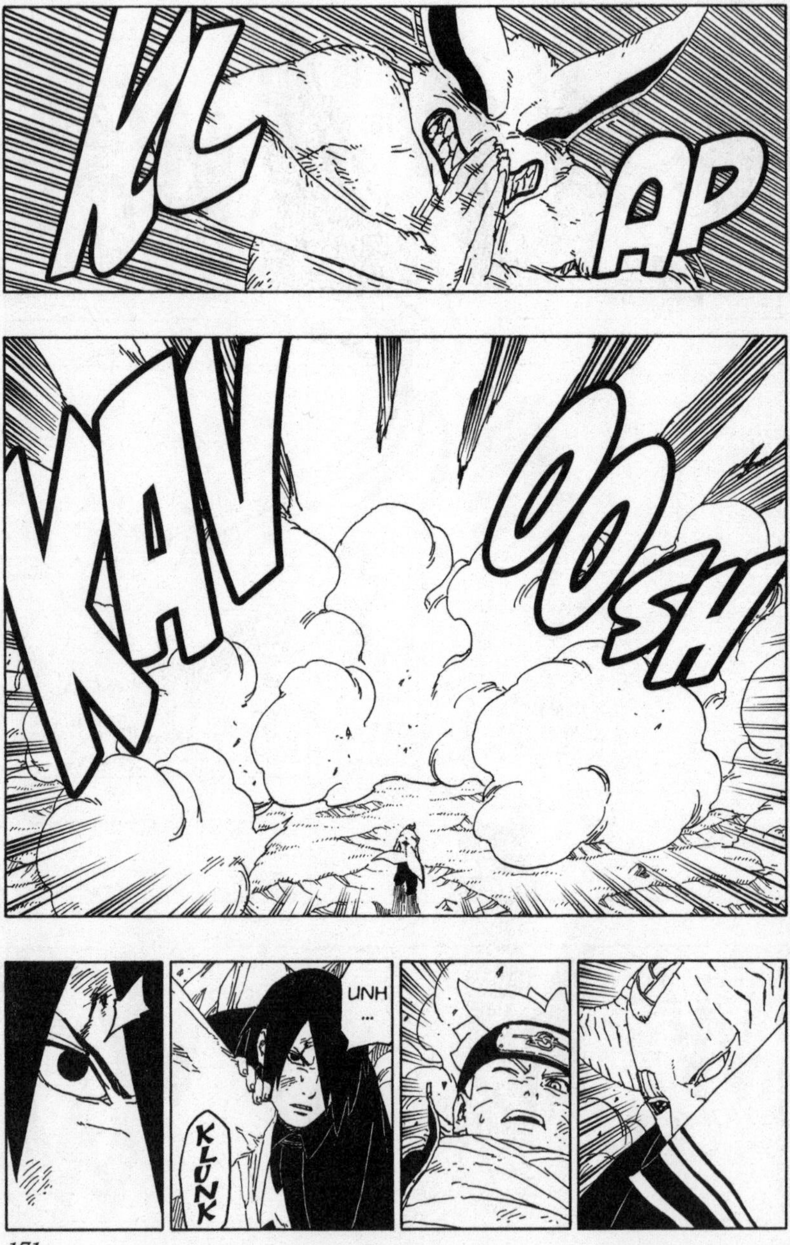
KL
AP
KAV
OOSH
UNH
...
KLUNK

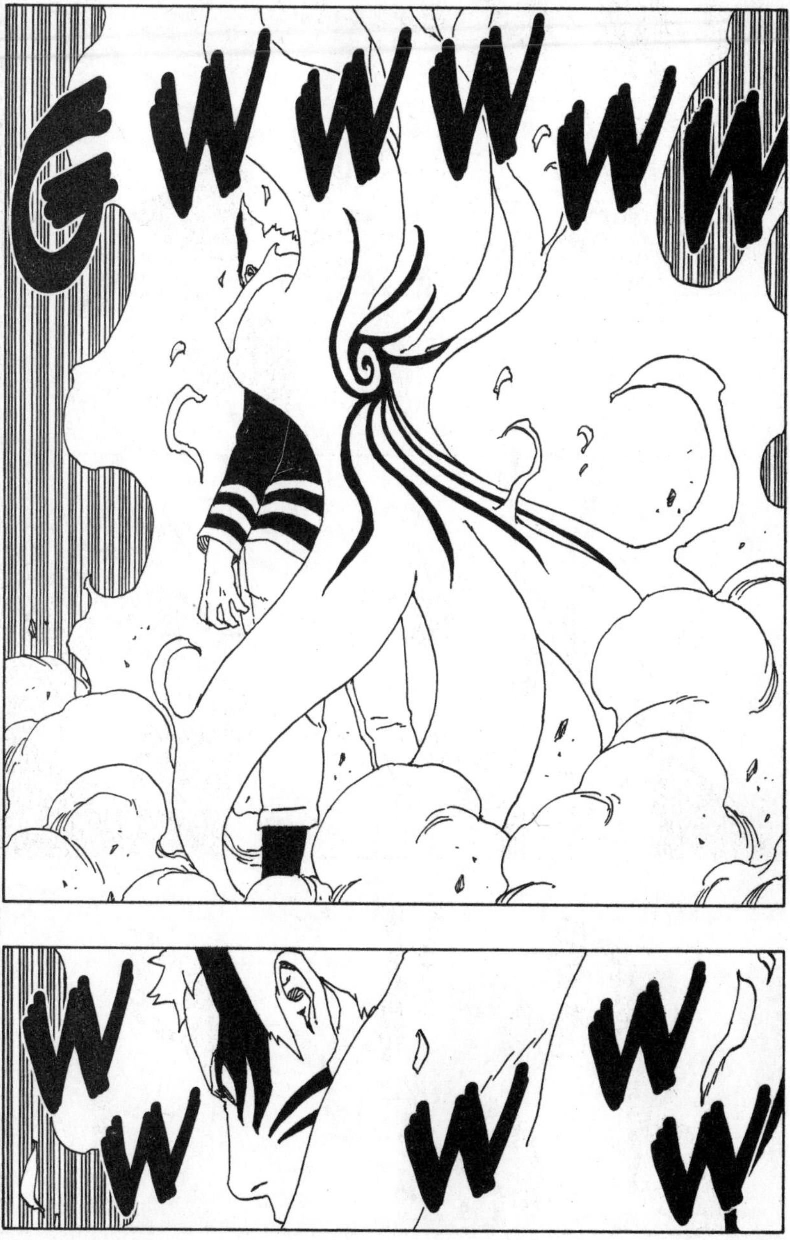
GWWWWW
WWWWW

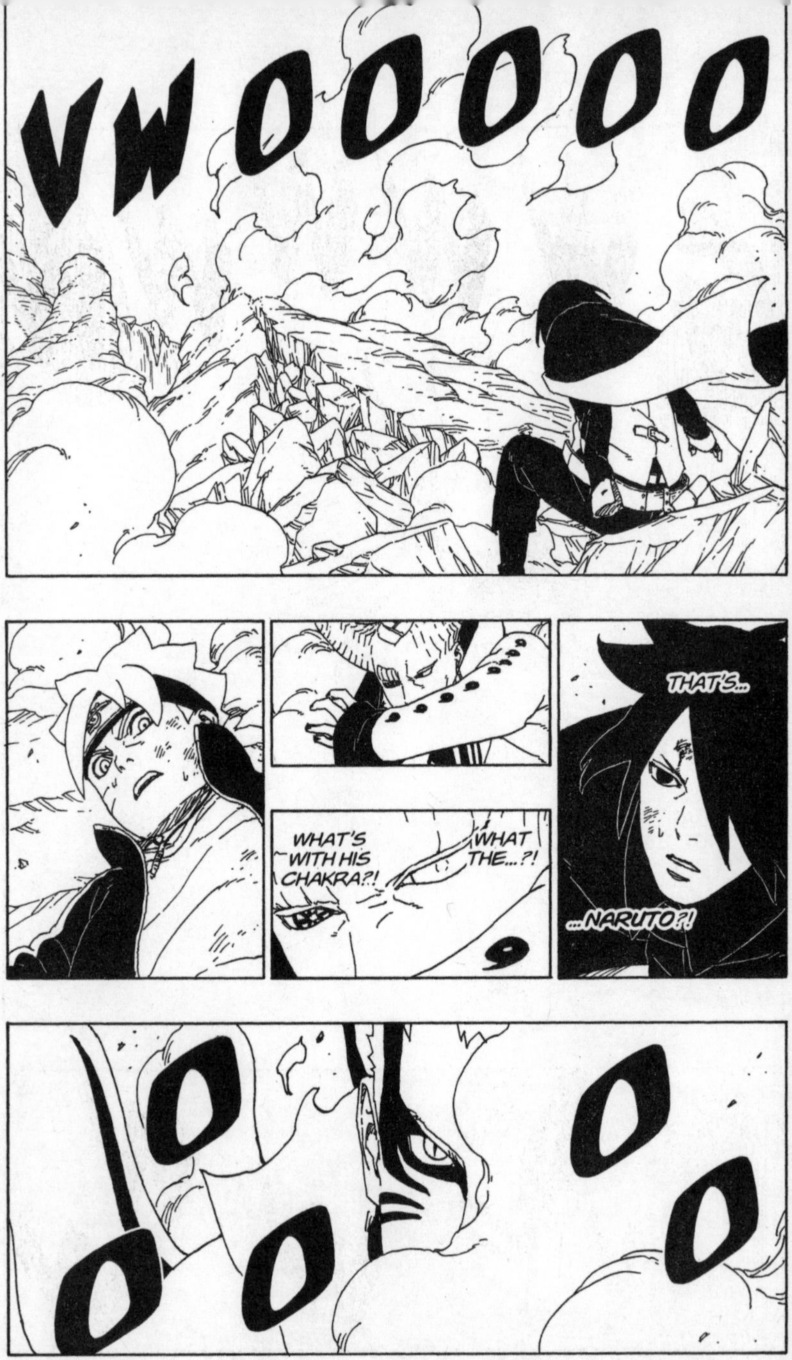
VWOOOOO
THAT'S...
...NARUTO?!
WHAT THE...?!
WHAT'S WITH HIS CHAKRA?!
OOOOO

Black * Clover

STORY & ART BY YŪKI TABATA

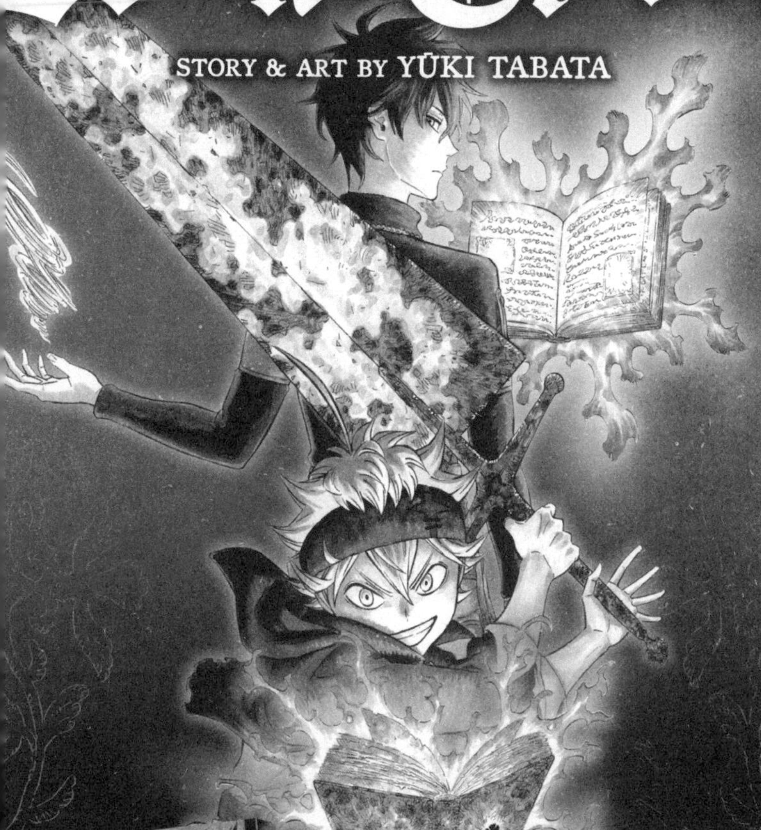

Asta is a young boy who dreams of becoming the greatest mage in the kingdom. Only one problem—he can't use any magic! Luckily for Asta, he receives the incredibly rare five-leaf clover grimoire that gives him the power of anti-magic. Can someone who can't use magic really become the Wizard King? One thing's for sure—Asta will never give up!

SHONEN JUMP   VIZ media
www.viz.com

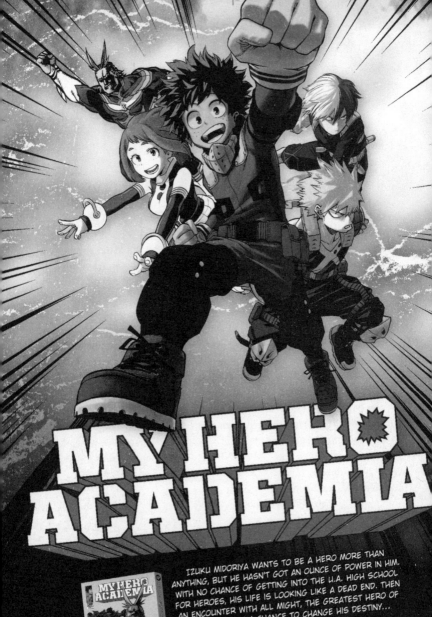

MY HERO ACADEMIA

IZUKU MIDORIYA WANTS TO BE A HERO MORE THAN ANYTHING, BUT HE HASN'T GOT AN OUNCE OF POWER IN HIM. WITH NO CHANCE OF GETTING INTO THE U.A. HIGH SCHOOL FOR HEROES, HIS LIFE IS LOOKING LIKE A DEAD END. THEN AN ENCOUNTER WITH ALL MIGHT, THE GREATEST HERO OF ALL, GIVES HIM A CHANCE TO CHANGE HIS DESTINY...

YOU'RE READING
IN THE
WRONG DIRECTION!!

WHOOPS! Guess what? You're starting at the wrong end of the comic!

...It's true! In keeping with the original Japanese format, **Boruto** is meant to be read from right to left, starting in the upper-right corner.

Unlike English, which is read from left to right, Japanese is read from right to left, meaning that action, sound effects, and word-balloon order are completely reversed... something which can make readers unfamiliar with Japanese feel pretty backwards themselves. For this reason, manga or Japanese comics published in the U.S. in English have sometimes been published "flopped"—that is, printed in exact reverse order, as though seen from the other side of a mirror.

By flopping pages, U.S. publishers can avoid confusing readers, but the compromise is not without its downside. For one thing, a character in a flopped manga series who once wore in the original Japanese version a T-shirt emblazoned with "M A Y" (as in "the merry month of") now wears one which reads "Y A M"! Additionally, many manga creators in Japan are themselves unhappy with the process, as some feel the mirror-imaging of their art alters their original intentions.

We are proud to bring you **Boruto** in the original unflopped format. Turn to the other side of the book and let the ninjutsu begin...!

—Editor

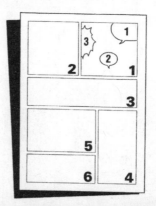